Colorado
Above Treeline

Scenic Drives, 4WD Trips, and Classic Hikes

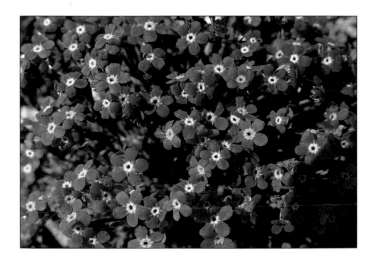

TEXT AND PHOTOGRAPHY BY

Jeremy Agnew

WESTCLIFFE PUBLISHERS
westcliffepublishers.com

INTERNATIONAL STANDARD BOOK NUMBERS:
ISBN-10: 1-56579-498-2
ISBN-13: 978-1-56579- 498-6

TEXT AND PHOTOGRAPHY COPYRIGHT:
Jeremy A. Agnew, 2005. All rights reserved.

EDITOR: Martha R. Gray
ASSOCIATE EDITOR: Elizabeth Train
DESIGNER: Rebecca Finkel, F + P Graphic Design, Inc.
PRODUCTION MANAGER: Craig Keyzer

PUBLISHED BY:
Westcliffe Publishers, Inc.
P.O. Box 1261
Englewood, CO 80150

Printed in China by Hing Yip Printing Co., Ltd.

LIBRARY OF CONGRESS CATALOGING-IN-PUBLICATION DATA:
Agnew, Jeremy (Jeremy A.)
    Colorado above treeline : scenic drives, 4WD adventures, and classic hikes / by Jeremy Agnew.
        p. cm.
    Includes index.
    ISBN-13: 978-1-56579-498-6
    ISBN-10: 1-56579-498-2
    1. Alpine regions--Colorado--guidebooks. 2. Tundras--Colorado--Guidebooks. 3. Colorado--Guidebooks. 4. Natural history--Colorado--Guidebooks. 5. Scenic byways--Colorado--Guidebooks. 6. Hiking--Colorado--Guidebooks. 7. Four-wheel drive vehicles--Colorado--Guidebooks. 8. Automobile travel--Colorado--Guidebooks. 9. Outdoor recreation--Colorado--Guidebooks. 10. Mountains--Colorado--Guidebooks. 11. Mountains--Colorado--Guidebooks. I. Title.
    F782.A16A345 2005
    917.8804'34--dc22   2004027901

To find more information about other fine books and calendars from Westcliffe Publishers, please contact your local bookstore, call us at 1-800-523-3692, write for our free color catalog, or visit us on the Web at westcliffepublishers.com.

PREVIOUS PAGE:
Small plants with colorful flowers, such as this alpine forget-me-not, are common above treeline.

OPPOSITE:
There are no trees on the tundra, but willow bushes grow in depressions where enough rain and snow accumulate to provide water for growth.

NEXT PAGE:
Meltwater collects in creeks that water the forests below.

PLEASE NOTE: Risk is always a factor in backcountry and high-mountain travel. Many of the activities described in this book can be dangerous, especially when weather is adverse or unpredictable, and when unforeseen events or conditions create a hazardous situation. The author has done his best to provide the reader with accurate information about backcountry travel, as well as to point out some of its potential hazards. It is the responsibility of the users of this guide to learn the necessary skills for safe backcountry travel, and to exercise caution in potentially hazardous areas, especially on glaciers and avalanche-prone terrain. The author and publisher disclaim any liability for injury or other damage caused by backcountry traveling or performing any other activity described in this book.

The author and publisher of this book have made every effort to ensure the accuracy and currency of its information. Nevertheless, a guidebook can often require revisions. Please let us know if you should find information in this book that needs to be updated, and we will be glad to correct it for the next printing. Your comments and suggestions are always welcome.

Dedication

For Thomas, Sylvia Brigham, Van Kirk, Sylvia, Christine and Tracy,
the five generations of our family who have seen Colorado change
into what it is today; and for Gage, the sixth generation,
who will see what it is to be tomorrow.

Contents

Preface

When I first moved to Colorado many years ago, I quickly developed a fascination for the scenic and isolated realm at the tops of the mountains. Over the years, as I hiked there, I wondered about the background of many of the things I saw. At that time, I could find no all-encompassing text to help satisfy my curiosity, so I gradually began to collect odds and ends of information about the biology and history of Colorado's world above the trees. Several years ago I realized that other people who journeyed to Colorado's mountaintops probably also wondered about what they were seeing, so I decided to put on paper some of the knowledge that I had accumulated over the years. This book, then, is the culmination of many trips and years of experience trudging up and down mountainsides, and is an attempt to share the beauty and grandeur of these unique and special places.

For help during the preparation of this book, I would like to thank Dr. Bob Davies of the Colorado Division of Wildlife for reviewing and commenting on the material on animals. Also, thanks to Tracy Predmore of the Colorado Division of Wildlife for helpful comments on the text. Thanks should also go to my longtime hiking buddy Pat Looney for providing good companionship and many bad puns while camping and hiking many miles over the tundra, over many years. Finally, thank you, John Fielder, for believing in this project.

Rugged high ridges are one of many habitats for plants and animals of the tundra.

Opposite: *Meltwater collects and forms small pools on the tundra that dry out by late summer.*

Overview Maps

White areas on these relief maps represent the state's highest-elevation terrain, which is generally above treeline. The red line on the map below illustrates the location of the Continental Divide.

Refer to the map legend for the symbols and designations found on the 30 trip maps in this book. The detail map on the opposite page shows major highways and locates each trip by number and category.

MAP LEGEND

70 Interstate Highway	▲ Campground	◉ Point of Interest
395 US Highway	**TH** Trailhead	● Water Feature
829 Colorado Highway	▬ ▬ Established Trail	Lake or Pond
▬ ▬ High-clearance or 4WD Road	▬ ▬ Undefined Trail	River or Creek
▬▬ Maintained Road/Main Route	▬ ▬ Other Trail	
▬▬ Other Road	▬▪▬ Continental Divide	

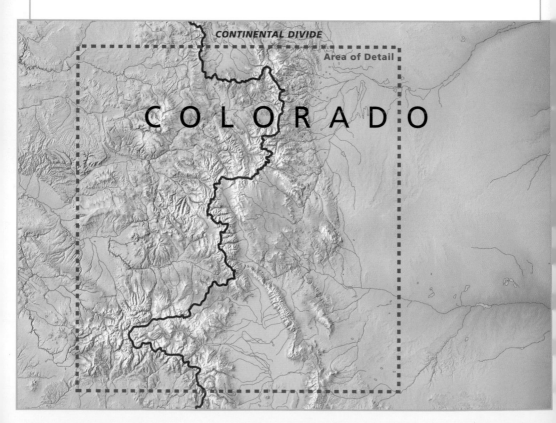

CONTINENTAL DIVIDE

Area of Detail

C O L O R A D O

SCENIC DRIVES

1. Trail Ridge Road
2. Berthoud Pass
3. Loveland Pass
4. Mount Evans
5. Guanella Pass
6. Boreas Pass
7. Independence Pass
8. Cottonwood Pass
9. Pikes Peak
10. Greenhorn Mountain

4WD TRIPS

1. Rollins Pass
2. Waldorf
3. Mosquito Pass
4. Hagerman Pass
5. Weston Pass
6. Mount Antero
7. The Alpine Tunnel
8. Hancock Pass–Tomichi Pass
9. The Alpine Loop
10. Imogene Pass

CLASSIC HIKES

1. Mohawk Lakes
2. Notch Mountain
3. Missouri Lakes & Fancy Lake Loop
4. Mount Elbert
5. Lake Ann
6. Snowmass Lake
7. Fravert Basin & Hasley Basin
8. Buffalo Peaks
9. Mount Princeton
10. Comanche-Venable Loop

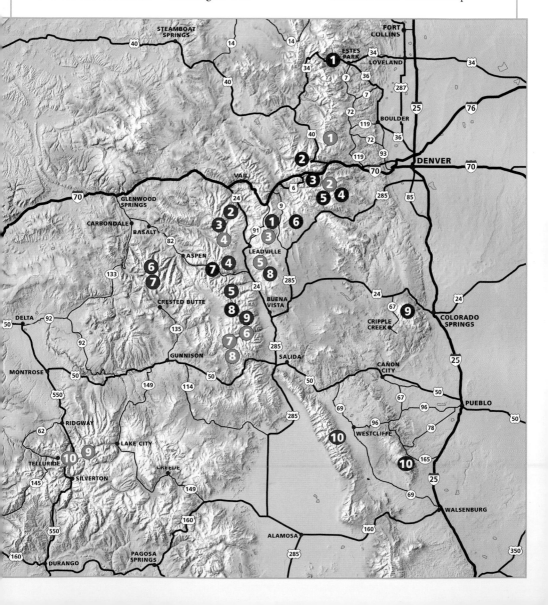

Introduction

THE LAND ABOVE TREELINE

For a traveler on the black ribbons of the interstate highways that stretch across the eastern plains of Colorado, the sight of the Rocky Mountains rising up in the distance is a majestic one. On a bright, sunny day in winter or spring, the lofty summits are particularly impressive, with their white covering of snow shimmering above the prairie against a cloudless blue sky. In summer the bald caps on top of the hazy, purplish peaks appear to have virtually erupted through the green belt of vegetation that mantles their lower slopes. Colorado's fascinating tundra environment lies there—the land above treeline.

Colorado's tundra occurs above 11,000 feet elevation, and these treeless expanses have a beauty all their own. Their unique, rugged landscapes are exposed to the harshest weather and extreme fluctuations in temperature, yet they host a variety of wildlife and flourish with grassy meadows and fields of low-growing flowering plants, many found nowhere else. This book introduces you to Colorado's alpine tundra and offers a variety of trips for exploring it firsthand.

The tundra environment seems hardy and tough, yet the alpine ecosystem is actually quite fragile. Increasing recreational use for camping, fishing, hiking, horseback riding, mountain climbing, mountain biking, and four-wheeling are impacting the tundra beyond the trails that access and cross it. Disturbed tundra soil and

plants take hundreds of years to recover because of the harsh weather, the amount of time required to create new soil, and the slow growth rate of new or existing plants above treeline. Problems result from trails that erode easily and irrecoverably, from the unfortunate tendency of some users to shortcut switchbacks, and from tracks that skirt wet areas of trail and leave a lasting impact. Trampled meadows, social trails that cut across the tundra, and an increased use of fire pits and camping sites have altered the vegetation in popular areas. The unfortunate result is that more and more regulations have been put in place in an effort to protect these fragile environments. Some designated wilderness areas, such as Indian Peaks, require permits for camping or even entering, and fires are prohibited in some areas. For special precautions to consider when hiking Colorado's tundra, please refer to Tundra Etiquette, p. 23.

    This guidebook presents a selection of trips, for both passenger car and four-wheel-drive vehicles, and dozens of hikes to showcase the tundra and allow visitors to appreciate this unique environment. For those who are less active, or who would prefer to leave the navigation to others,

Many colorful flowers, such as this yellow paintbrush, grow above treeline.

summer offers opportunities to ride trains in such mountain towns as Leadville, Durango, and Manitou Springs. Another option for seeing Colorado's tundra is to take a gondola ride above treeline; here are a couple of options.

The Gondola at Vail

This gondola ride is an easy and relaxing way to reach the tundra and enjoy wildflowers in summer. One can merely stroll in the meadows around the top, then ride back down. Longer walks from the gondola station are optional, as are hikes, mountain bike rides, and other activities, depending on your interests. From I-70 take Exit 176 into Vail, and follow the frontage road westbound to Lionshead, following signs to the Lionshead parking structure. From there, take the Eagle Bahn Gondola to Eagle's Nest at 10,350 feet. Inquire about hours and rates, which are subject to change.

The Gondola at Monarch Pass

The Monarch Crest Gondola ferries summer visitors from the top of 11,312-foot Monarch Pass, west of Salida, to the tundra 570 feet above. Perched atop the Continental Divide, the pass offers notable views of the high mountains to the east. From Salida, take US 50 about 18 miles west. Inquire at the base of the tramway about hours and rates, which are subject to change.

Opposite: *Much of the tundra consists of open meadows and gentle slopes.*

Monarch Pass also is the trailhead for two fine but strenuous hikes. From the summit parking area, FR 906 goes southeast, becoming TR 531, to the crest of the Continental Divide; 12,208-foot Mount Peck is some 2 miles away, with 1,000 feet of elevation gain. Alternatively, hardy hikers may arrange a shuttle and continue hiking south-southeast along the Divide to join the Colorado Trail and reach the summit of Marshall Pass, for a total of about 11 miles.

THE HUMAN HISTORY

Humans have ventured into Colorado's tundra environment as far back as 11,000 years ago. Early Indian hunters regularly crossed the Continental Divide and left stone walls and chipped stone points as evidence of their travels. Tribes such as the Ute and Arapaho followed migrating game in the warmer months up into the mountains and above treeline. Their paths and trails are still visible in some areas. White settlers began arriving en masse in the 1860s, and many followed these same

The ghost town of Sneffels with Stony Mountain in the background.

trails up into the mountains. These explorers, trappers, surveyors, and miners converted many of the Indian trails into dirt roads, often traversing mountain passes, to connect the new towns that began to dot the Colorado landscape. Railroads later followed some of these developed dirt roads to serve both towns and mines.

By the late 1800s more than 1,000 small towns dotted the landscape as gold and silver mining spread across the state. Most of these towns have vanished, destroyed by avalanches, decomposed by Colorado's climate, or stripped bare by souvenir hunters and scavengers. Cemeteries are often the only evidence left of their passing. However, many of these ghost towns and mines still exist in various stages of decay. Some have been restored, and others are in their natural state. This book takes you to many of these ghost towns, which are near or along the roads that access the tundra above treeline. Brief histories of the towns and mines are included with many of the trips in this guidebook.

When visiting ghost towns and mines, please use caution, as most structures are dilapidated and not sturdy. Do not climb on any of these historic structures. Sharp metal pieces, broken glass, and wooden splinters are also common, in addition to mining shafts and other dangers. These remaining structures are a valuable glimpse into Colorado's mining history, and any artifacts should be left where they are for the enjoyment of future visitors to these places. Recent studies estimate that there are about 22,000 open, abandoned mines in the state of Colorado. These mines vary from simple prospect holes only a few feet deep to large, deteriorating buildings and headframes, not to mention unexpected, deep shafts that may be hidden by trees and bushes. Tunnels and mine shafts can easily cave in, old buildings frequently collapse, and poisonous gases often collect in adits, tunnels, and shafts even a short distance from the surface. The Colorado Inactive Mine Reclamation Program was started in 1980 to seal off dangerous, abandoned mines, but only a relatively small amount of the work has been completed. Be aware also that these relics are protected from trespass under Colorado law and are thus best viewed at a distance.

A Brief History of Colorado Mining

In 1807, explorer Zebulon Pike ventured into what is now Colorado after being dispatched by President Thomas Jefferson to survey the American West. Rumors of small gold finds in the mountains of Colorado and made their way back East. The 1849 California Gold Rush bypassed Colorado, but mining finally arrived in 1858 after a nationwide depression caused some people to pull up stakes and head west. Prospectors first discovered gold at the confluence of Cherry Creek and Dry Creek near Denver. Then a big gold strike in Gregory Gulch, near Central City, and another in California Gulch near present-day Leadville, started a gold rush to Colorado. "Pikes Peak or Bust!" was a popular slogan as 40,000 newcomers arrived from the eastern United States. Of these, 25,000 people are estimated to have ventured into the mountains to establish mining camps. Most failed, and fewer than 5,000 made it through the winter.

The remnants of mining activity in the San Juan Mountains at the Virginius Mine in Governor Basin.

Gold and silver were used in the minting of coins, but by the late 1860s the supply of silver had become scarce. This provided the impetus for many rich silver strikes. Colorado towns named for the mineral include Silverton, Silver Plume, Silver Cliff, Silverthorne, and Silverdale. By 1870, gold had been discovered near Silverton, and waves of prospectors trespassed onto lands claimed by Indian tribes, sparking numerous conflicts. In 1874, a treaty with the Indians led to a gold rush to the San Juan Mountains. A big silver-ore strike in 1877 gave rise to the incorporation of Leadville in 1878, which then enjoyed a grand and storied heyday. More silver was found in 1878 near Aspen. Railroads sprang up in this booming mine economy, linking mines, towns, and mills and revolutionizing travel over the high mountains.

Silver mining made fortunes for some, but the market became flooded with silver and the price dropped, which jeopardized silver mining. Various agreements culminated in the Sherman Silver Purchase Act of 1890, which required the government to buy large amounts of silver for coinage each year. This action artificially inflated the price of silver, even as the real value of the bullion stored in the U.S. Treasury dropped. As a result of the ensuing financial panic, President Grover Cleveland asked Congress to repeal the Sherman Silver Purchase Act, which it did in 1893. This kicked the artificial props out from under Colorado's silver mining industry and caused most of the booming silver mines to shut down. Fortunes were lost, towns were abandoned, and the state's economy tumbled.

Rising costs, declining profits, and two World Wars finally caused the demise of most of the rest of Colorado's mines. Other minerals, like molybdenum found north of Leadville in 1915, sustained mining as an industry across the state. Towns with prosperous mining operations and larger populations were able to support schools, post offices, and other types of industry. Some of these towns, such as Telluride, Aspen, and Leadville, took root and remain today. Though prospecting and gold mining still continue in Colorado into the 21st century, very few miners live above treeline year-round anymore. Many of the trips in this guidebook will let you see firsthand some of the relics and ghost towns from Colorado's colorful mining history.

Hikers can still find miners' cabins high on the tundra.

How to Use This Guide

This guidebook is a compendium of information and an introduction to the world above treeline—an exotic, little-known world to many. It is intended for those who wish to explore Colorado's tundra. It is also for those interested in learning about the animals and plants that are found there and the area's geological and historical past. Vital safety precautions are also discussed for prospective visitors to this unique landscape.

ORGANIZATION

The book is divided into six sections. The first three sections describe the environment, plant communities, and types of wildlife found in Colorado's tundra. The last three sections—Scenic Drives, Four-Wheel-Drive Trips, and Classic Hikes—describe specific trips and hikes you can take to visit and explore this alpine wonderland. The Scenic Drives section is devoted to trips by passenger car, another is for four-wheel-drive vehicles, and the last section is just for hikers. Each section begins with a contents list showing ten trips included in that section and hikes described within each of the ten trips. The ten trips in each section illustrate different aspects of

View into Yankee Boy Basin from the Governor Basin road.

Colorado's alpine lands. They were selected because they contain outstanding examples of tundra features. The trips were also chosen because of their relative accessibility to major Front Range communities between Pueblo and Fort Collins. Each trip provides descriptions of hikes that lie along the way, other nearby hikes, scenic stops, and descriptions of historic relics, such as ghost towns, mining operations, and railroads, that you may explore.

Each trip description delineates highlights, hiking difficulty, type of access, what National Forest map to use, location, directions to get there, and length of featured drives and hikes. You will also find a brief summary of the trip, local history, and hiking directions where applicable. Bear in mind that all the distances listed should be considered to be approximate, given differences in odometers, pedometers, driving styles, and exact starting points. Also note that some areas have a rich history, while others have relatively little.

In the back of the book is a glossary of tundra terms (Appendix A, p. 228) for easy reference. A second appendix lists all the hikes and the difficulty rating for each (Appendix B, p. 230), and a third appendix offers recommended reading for those wanting more information about various aspects of Colorado's tundra (Appendix C, p. 232).

Roads

All the trip destinations were visited by the author during the preparation of this book, and the road descriptions and directions were accurate at that time. Ratings were based on the conditions of these roads and a consideration of the types of vehicles that were driving on them as well as those parked at trailheads. Please be aware, however, that conditions on these roads change constantly with weather and wear, and specific vehicle capability, individual driving ability, and a driver's

The view to the east from the summit of Independence Pass with La Plata Peak in the distance.

confidence are inconsistent variables. If you do not feel comfortable with road conditions as you find them, it is important either to turn back or to park and hike the questionable terrain.

Hiking the Mount Princeton Trail.

Hikes

The three sections in this book devoted to visiting Colorado's tundra (Scenic Drives, 4WD Trips, and Classic Hikes) all profile hikes available along the way or located nearby. The hikes are indexed at the beginning of each section for easy reference. Individual hiking ability and capability depends on many factors. I have tried to ensure that all readers—from families and older hikers to backpackers and young, energetic mountaineers—can find activities suitable to their respective fitness level. The hikes in this book, generally speaking, are suited to people in reasonable physical shape who can participate in moderate hiking at high altitude. All hikes are rated as Easy, Moderate, or Strenuous. Though there are a few strenuous hikes for those who enjoy physical exertion and the solitude of the Colorado backcountry, most hikes are fairly easy, and none are technical climbs. Most can be done as day hikes, though to gain the experience of the solitude of the tundra, even the shorter hikes may be better enjoyed by backpacking to see the sun set and then rise again from high altitude.

   Note: *All hikers in the tundra should refer to the important precautions listed under Traveling Above Treeline, opposite.*

Maps

National Forest maps are available from U.S. Forest Service offices and also in many bookstores and outdoor-oriented stores across the state. You can also order them directly from the U.S. Geological Survey in Lakewood, during business hours, by phoning 303-202-4700. An invaluable tool for mountain travel is DeLorme's *Colorado Atlas & Gazetteer;* check for the latest edition wherever maps are sold.

Traveling Above Treeline

WHEN TO GO

Because the snow lics deep on the Colorado mountains for much of the year, the time span for most tundra visits is limited to a few months during the summer. Some roads and trails may not be clear of snow until late June and may close again by late September. The best flower displays tend to be in July, though blooms start appearing in the middle of June and last until about the middle of August.

Morning is the best time to explore the tundra, when the day is usually clearest and the sun is bright for photography. In the afternoon, dark clouds tend to gather on summer days, and lightning storms are not uncommon. It is also preferable to be off of high peaks and ridges by early afternoon, particularly when climbing a four-teener, in order to avoid these electrical storms. September and early October are

The historic townsite of Independence on the west side of Independence Pass.

often good times to hike on the tundra and to climb fourteeners, as summer storms are over and winter snows have not yet closed the trails. In early autumn, the clear blue skies last for most of the day.

ROADS AND PASSES

Some of the roads discussed in this book, and particularly those over backcountry mountain passes, include sections that should only be attempted by experienced drivers with suitable vehicles. Four-wheel drive (4WD) specifically refers to vehicles such as Jeeps that have high clearance, off-road tires, a transfer case, and a low gear range; it does not refer to generic SUVs or all-wheel drives.

When driving, be mindful that road and weather conditions can change quickly, some roads close seasonally, road signs may be missing or inaccurate, and backcountry road numbers and access can change. Current maps do not always accurately reflect trail and forest road numbers. Also, dirt roads can be slippery or impassable because of snow or heavy rains, so it's always smart to check with the appropriate land-management agency for road conditions before you set out. The following is a list of major passes that cross Colorado's tundra, many of which appear in this book.

Jeeping up the Mount Antero road.

USE CAUTION AT HIGH ALTITUDE

Traveling and hiking at high altitude involve special precautions, some of which are common sense, others of which are not so obvious.

• **Drink plenty of fluids**

Increased exertion in the dry, thin air can lead to dehydration, so it is important to drink lots of water, whether you feel thirsty or not.

• **Avoid drinking alcohol**

Its effect is enhanced at high altitude and may lead to errors in judgment. Alcohol also aggravates dehydration.

• **Always bring adequate clothing and gear**

A warm jacket, hat and gloves, and long pants are necessities year-round. The weather on the tundra is unpredictable and can change from warm and sunny to hail or a snowstorm within a few minutes. Hypothermia may happen faster

MAJOR MOUNTAIN PASSES

Passenger Car

NAME	ELEVATION
Berthoud Pass	11,315 feet
Boreas Pass	11,481
Cottonwood Pass	12,126
Cumberland Pass	12,000
Fall River Pass	11,796
Guanella Pass	11,669
Hoosier Pass	11,539
Iceberg Pass	11,827
Independence Pass	12,095
Loveland Pass	11,992
Monarch Pass	11,312
Rollins Pass	11,671
Weston Pass	11,900

4WD/Jeep

NAME	ELEVATION
Black Bear Pass	12,830 feet
Cinnamon Pass	12,620
Engineer Pass	12,800
Georgia Pass	11,585
Hagerman Pass	11,925
Hancock Pass	12,120
Imogene Pass	13,114

Jones Pass	12,451
Mosquito Pass	13,186
Pearl Pass	12,705
Schofield Pass	10,707
Stony Pass	12,588
Tomichi Pass	11,979
Webster Pass	12,096

Hiking/Biking

NAME	ELEVATION
Altman Pass	11,940 feet
Arapaho Pass	11,905
Argentine Pass	13,207
Browns Pass	12,010
Buckskin Pass	12,461
Chalk Creek Pass	12,150
Devils Thumb Pass	11,747
Fancy Pass	12,380
Missouri Pass	11,986
Rogers Pass	11,860
Timberline Pass	11,484
Trail Rider Pass	12,410
Vasquez Pass	12,521
Virginius Pass	13,100
Williams Pass	11,762

Backpacking up a tundra trail.

at altitude than at lower elevations, and frostbite can occur more readily because of reduced blood flow to the extremities. Always wear sunglasses, as the high intensity of sunlight, especially on snowbanks, can literally be blinding. Wear a wide-brimmed hat and use plenty of sunscreen. The strength of solar radiation can quickly lead to painful burns on face, ears, and neck. The hat should preferably cover your ears on cold, windy days.

• **Take a map and compass**
Sudden storms at high altitude can cause a loss of visibility and orientation.

• **Avoid ridges and open areas during storms**
Seek shelter below treeline immediately to avoid becoming a lightning rod.

• **Don't drink the water**
Even though streams and lakes on the tundra appear to be pristine, they may be contaminated by *Giardia lamblia* and *Cryptosporidium parvum,* which can cause severe intestinal distress. Always filter and treat stream water before drinking it. Streams below mines may also contain lead, mercury, and other toxic heavy metals, the presence of which is often evident from slimy-looking, yellow or orange beds and banks.

• **Stay out of abandoned mines**
Old tunnels, shafts, headframes, and structures should always be observed from a distance. Shafts (vertical holes) can collapse. Adits (horizontal mines) or tunnels can cave in or contain toxic atmospheres or tailings, not to mention rattlesnakes. Mine tailings (pulverized waste rock from processed ore) may be toxic. Old dynamite, blasting caps, and other explosives can be very dangerous. Abandoned mine buildings may also be sources of hantavirus, a deadly lung infection spread by deer mice.

TUNDRA ETIQUETTE

The alpine ecosystem above treeline is a fragile one. Increasing numbers of visitors are impacting the tundra and the trails that access and cross it. Disturbances and damage to this environment can remain visible for many years. Please do your part to protect these unique and beautiful areas by following these simple guidelines when hiking on the tundra.

Tread lightly and minimize your impact

• Use established roads and trails, and avoid creating new routes. Never shortcut switchbacks; this leads to rapid soil erosion.
• Hike through fragile areas in small groups of four to six to minimize impacts on trails, picnic stops, and campsites.
• Avoid bogs and marshy areas, as footprints and tire tracks are not easily erased.
• Don't set up your own rock cairns, use marking paint, or tie surveyor's tape to bushes and rocks to mark routes. This visual pollution is a form of graffiti and is offensive to many seeking a pristine wilderness experience.
• Mountain bikes ridden off-trail and onto tundra meadows exert approximately 6 to 7 times the pressure per square inch of a typical hiking boot.
• When driving, dirt biking, or using other motorized vehicles, stay on established roads. Resist the temptation to drive across the tundra; it will not recover from such activity in your lifetime.

Comanche Lakes from the trail to Comanche Pass.

- Don't build fire rings. They are unsightly and sterilize delicate tundra soil for hundreds of years.
- Don't break dead branches or twigs from treeline trees or use them for firewood. They may be acting as protection for branches or plants growing downwind.
- Pack out all trash and litter—don't bury it.
- Use biodegradable soap and carry water to a wash site. Never wash in tundra streams and lakes.

The alpine sunflower has the largest blooms on the tundra.

Respect Colorado's Environment and History

- Leave plants, animals, and historic artifacts for the next visitor to enjoy.
- For your own safety and an animal's protection, don't approach wildlife closely.
- Control dogs and other pets to avoid harassing wildlife or others seeking to enjoy the backcountry. Wilderness areas and national parks may have restrictions on dogs.
- For more information, visit the Leave No Trace website, lnt.org.

THE EFFECTS OF ALTITUDE

Whether a visitor above treeline chooses to take the train up Pikes Peak, drive over a high pass road, or hike Colorado's tundra, he or she will find that the high-altitude environment on the top of a mountain is different from that at sea level and takes some getting used to.

The first and most obvious difference is that the air is much thinner on the top of a mountain, and consequently less oxygen is available. At sea level, the atmospheric pressure, or force exerted by the weight of the earth's atmosphere, is 14.7 pounds per square inch (psi). This relatively high pressure forces the oxygen-rich air of sea level through the membranes of the lungs and into the bloodstream with ease. Though the amount of oxygen in the air stays constant at 20.1% at all elevations, the atmospheric pressure drops as the elevation rises. At an elevation of 12,500 feet, the atmospheric pressure has dropped to 9.1 psi, or 62% of that at sea level. This reduction of atmospheric pressure with increasing elevation means that oxygen cannot pass as easily through the lining of the lungs as it does at sea level.

To compensate for this, people who live permanently at high altitudes, such as the Indians of the Andes and the Tibetans of the Himalayas, both of whom live above 15,000 feet in elevation, have developed larger lung capacities and larger red

Camping using minimal-impact techniques is a great way to enjoy the solitude and beauty of the tundra.

blood cells in order to function efficiently. This adaptation also occurs, though to a lesser extent, in mountain residents of Colorado, such as those living in Leadville, at 10,152 feet above sea level.

Over time, the body compensates for high altitude by increasing the depth of breathing and the number of red blood cells. Most of the increase in blood cells occurs within the first 10 days after reaching the higher elevation and is complete after about 6 weeks. Collectively, these adaptations are called acclimatization. Unfortunately, acclimatization is lost at about the same rate that it is gained, so a Colorado resident who is at sea level for a month will go through a period of re-acclimatization upon returning back home to Colorado.

For the infrequent visitor to high altitudes, the lowered level of oxygen carried by the blood is immediately noticeable and may result in headaches, fatigue, and shortness of breath. Exertion leads to an increase in the depth and rate of breathing as the body tries to obtain as much oxygen as it is used to getting at lower elevations. Skiers on vacation, summer tourists, and new arrivals in Colorado may feel tired upon exertion and notice an increased heart rate. Permanent Colorado residents might feel the same effect when going from Denver or Colorado Springs to the top of a fourteener because of a similar relative increase in elevation.

One of three alternative methods may be employed to lessen the initial stress of high altitude if going to the tundra for a multi-day trip. One is to ascend to high altitude in one step, but only perform light activities for the first few days. The second is to ascend to an intermediate altitude and stay there for a day or two before going on to a higher altitude. The third is to ascend gradually to high altitude, gaining a few thousand feet in elevation per day over a period of several days. This third method is the one used most often by mountain climbers going to extreme elevations for extended trips.

Until acclimatization is achieved, symptoms generically referred to as altitude sickness may occur, including mild headache, fatigue, shortness of breath, nausea, dizziness, and mild disorientation. High altitude can cause a number of other physiological effects. For example, nosebleeds may occur more readily, and alcohol will act faster and have a greater inebriating effect than it does at sea level. For some individuals (such as myself), it should be noted, exposure to the grandeur of high altitude brings on a sense of euphoria, even without the use of alcohol!

Dehydration is also common at high altitudes. The faster and deeper breathing patterns necessary to provide adequate oxygen to the lungs leads to a loss of body fluids in the dry tundra air. Aggravating these effects is increased sweating from the physical exertion of hiking, skiing, or mountain climbing. Cold temperatures and the lowered oxygen content of high-altitude air also increase urination, further aggravating water loss. To compound this, the sense of thirst is often dulled. For these reasons, it is wise to drink plenty of water, even if you are not thirsty. It has been suggested that severe dehydration at high altitude can lead to impaired judgment and potential accident situations.

The sunlight on the tundra is more intense than at lower elevations as well. Without the shielding effect of the denser air at sea level, greater amounts of ultraviolet radiation penetrate the rarefied atmosphere. The level of ultraviolet radiation at 12,000 feet is approximately double that at sea level. This intense radiation is reflected very efficiently by snowbanks on the tundra and can rapidly lead to severe sunburns, as well as snow blindness and other damage to eyes that do not have adequate protection.

ALTITUDE-RELATED ILLNESS

Acute Mountain Sickness

Acute mountain sickness, also called altitude sickness, typically occurs at elevations higher than 10,000 feet, but is also common in people who ascend rapidly to altitudes above 7,000 feet. Approximately 20% of those who ascend from sea level to above 9,000 feet in one day will develop some degree of altitude sickness. Typical onset is anywhere from 6 to 96 hours after arrival at high altitude. Common symptoms include headache, nausea, muscular weakness, light-headedness, loss of appetite,

Rain, snow, and hail help to fill high-altitude lakes during early summer.

and sluggishness. Drowsiness is also common, but insomnia may occur in older people. Severe cases may result in mental confusion. Symptoms usually disappear after 24 to 48 hours at altitude. A diet that is high in carbohydrates is thought to reduce the effects of altitude sickness; fatty meals may aggravate it.

The onset of altitude sickness does not occur at a specific elevation, but varies from person to person and even from trip to trip, though it is uncommon for it to occur below 9,000 feet. Part of the reason for this variation is that the earth is not a perfect sphere, and it tilts on its axis as it rotates. Atmospheric pressure, therefore, varies with location and time of year. Seasonal weather patterns also affect barometric pressure in an erratic way, as storms and weather fronts move through a given area.

High-Altitude Pulmonary Edema (HAPE)

A more serious illness occurs when decreased oxygen in the air at high altitude leads to an accumulation of fluid in the lungs. This usually occurs at altitudes above 12,000 feet, but can occur at as low as 9,000 feet. This problem is particularly prevalent in unacclimatized individuals who ascend rapidly to high altitude and then participate in strenuous activity. Typical onset is 36 to 72 hours after arrival at altitude. The primary symptom is an incessant, dry cough, but other symptoms include nausea, vomiting, and headache. Occurrence of HAPE depends on the individual, the rate of ascent, and the degree of exertion, but it is more common in young males in their late teens to early twenties.

It is vital that anyone with symptoms of HAPE move or be moved immediately to a lower elevation (at least 2,000 to 3,000 feet lower) and seek medical attention.

High-Altitude Cerebral Edema (HACE)

Another serious illness, HACE is caused by hormonal changes from lowered oxygen content in the air, typically above 12,000 feet, that can produce an accumulation of fluid in brain tissue. The primary symptom is severe headache, but others include loss of muscle coordination, disorientation, hallucination, stupor, paralysis, and coma. Lips and fingernails may turn blue.

It is vital that anyone with symptoms of HACE move or be moved immediately to a lower elevation (at least 2,000 to 3,000 feet lower) and seek medical attention.

FOURTEENERS

The continental United States has 68 fourteeners, or peaks whose summits are above 14,000 feet in elevation. Colorado, dubbed The Highest State before Alaska was annexed, has 54 of those fourteeners. One of the popular forms of recreation in the Colorado mountains is climbing them. A complete list of Colorado's fourteeners is included on page 30. Hikers who wish to "bag" all 54 may want to consult one of the specialized guidebooks that give detailed information on trailheads and routes. Refer to Appendix C, p. 232, for some recommended books on the subject.

The climbing difficulty of Colorado fourteeners ranges from relatively easy walk-ups to challenging technical climbs. Be advised, however, that fourteeners are seeing increased pressure from hikers. In summer, the parking lots at trailheads for popular fourteeners are often overflowing, and some mountains, such as Grays Peak and Torreys Peak, have a constant stream of hikers following multiple social trails to their summits.

A vintage photo of the author from the top of Mount Democrat, one of Colorado's fourteeners.

COLORADO'S FOURTEENERS

PEAK NAME	ELEVATION	PEAK NAME	ELEVATION
Mount Elbert	14,433 feet	Mount Democrat	14,148 feet
Mount Massive	14,421	Capitol Peak	14,130
Mount Harvard	14,420	Pikes Peak	14,110
Blanca Peak	14,345	Snowmass Mountain	14,092
La Plata Peak	14,336	Mount Eolus	14,083
Uncompahgre Peak	14,309	Windom Peak	14,082
Crestone Peak	14,294	Mount Columbia	14,073
Mount Lincoln	14,286	Culebra Peak	14,069
Grays Peak	14,270	Missouri Mountain	14,067
Mount Antero	14,269	Humbolt Peak	14,064
Torreys Peak	14,267	Mount Bierstadt	14,060
Castle Peak	14,265	Sunlight Peak	14,059
Quandary Peak	14,265	Handies Peak	14,048
Mount Evans	14,264	Ellingwood Point	14,042
Longs Peak	14,259	Mount Lindsey	14,042
Mount Wilson	14,246	Little Bear Peak	14,037
Mount Shavano	14,229	Mount Sherman	14,036
Mount Belford	14,197	Redcloud Peak	14,034
Mount Princeton	14,197	Pyramid Peak	14,018
Mount Yale	14,196	Wetterhorn Peak	14,017
Crestone Needle	14,191	Wilson Peak	14,017
Mount Bross	14,172	North Maroon Peak	14,014
Kit Carson Mountain	14,165	San Luis Peak	14,014
El Diente Peak	14,159	Huron Peak	14,005
Maroon Peak	14,156	Mount of the	
Tabeguache Peak	14,155	Holy Cross	14,005
Mount Oxford	14,153	Sunshine Peak	14,001
Mount Sneffels	14,150		

NOTE: These are traditional figures. More recent measurements by the U.S. Geological Survey have resulted in slight adjustments.

Debate continues as to whether Colorado has 53 or 54 fourteeners. Some authorities deem Ellingwood Point to be a separate fourteener; others argue that it is part of Blanca Peak. To be considered a separate peak, the Colorado Mountain Club (CMC) has declared that summits must be at least one-third of a mile apart and the ridge between them must drop at least 300 feet. This definition actually eliminates some existing U.S. Geological Survey fourteeners, hence the controversy. According to these CMC criteria, Mount Cameron (14,239 feet) is part of Mount Lincoln. This list follows the guidelines of the CMC.

The land above treeline varies from jagged peaks, such as the aptly named Pyramid Peak near Aspen, shown here, to flat, grassy meadows.

The Tundra Environment

The word *tundra* comes from a Russian variation of a Lapp word referring to the open plains of the Arctic regions beyond the northern limit of tree growth in Scandinavia. The word is also used to describe mountaintop ridges and meadows, because of the similarity in environment and appearance between the two. Colorado's tundra typically occurs at an elevation of between 11,000 feet and 12,000 feet, depending on the environmental conditions of a particular location, and rises from the forested lower slopes to the highest reaches of jagged peaks. The popular image of a mountain above treeline is one of jagged rocks, boulders, and towering peaks—a landscape of utter desolation. This is only partially true. The wide, treeless expanses of Colorado's peaks also host a variety of unique wildlife and low-growing flowering plants. This is the land of Colorado's alpine tundra.

The primitive Rocky Mountains consisted of sharp peaks that eroded into the mountains of today.

A Land of Extremes

Winter snows usually start to dust the high peaks in mid-September. Since the temperatures at this time of year are still relatively warm, the snow melts quickly under the daytime sun. By late September, snow starts to linger and soon envelops the dormant tundra. Much of this snowfall is then redistributed by powerful winter winds. Howling blizzards can lash Colorado's tundra with snow and hail, gusts of 60 to 100 miles per hour are common , and temperatures can drop below −70°F. One winter, instruments at the Alpine Visitor Center on Trail Ridge Road in Rocky Mountain National Park recorded a wind speed of 173 miles per hour! One of the most beautiful winter sights is the sun shining out of a brilliant blue sky on long plumes of **snow banners**, snow that is blown from ridges by the wind. The gales that sweep over the peaks and ridges keep these areas free from snow accumulation, while valleys and areas just below treeline drift deep with snowbanks that do not melt until the following summer. The average annual amount of snow that falls on the Colorado tundra is somewhere between 40 and 60 inches. However, the effective localized precipitation may be much less or far more. Wildlife above treeline in the harsh winter season either migrates to lower elevations, hibernates, or uses the snow for protection from the cold.

Summer temperatures above treeline can vary widely. Average temperatures may reach 50°F, or even the mid-60s on a sunny July day, but they can rapidly plunge below freezing. The temperature close to the ground, out of the wind, is usually higher. Tundra soil is a poor conductor of the sun's heat and helps keep the surface of the ground warm. During most summer days the intense rays of the sun beat down through the thin mountain air and warm the rocks and meadows. Since dark-colored surfaces absorb heat more easily than

Old miner's cabin on the Mountain Boy Gulch hike.

Late afternoon in winter on Loveland Pass.

light-colored surfaces, animals and plants above treeline tend to be dark in color. This helps them stay warmer than the surrounding air. Summer winds on the tundra can vary from a light breeze or to a gust of up to 90 mph, sweeping away the thin alpine soil and sucking valuable moisture from earth and plants.

Thin Air

Many facets of the extremes of climate on the tundra are a result of the thin, clear air of high elevations. The thin air at high altitudes has an extremely low moisture and particulate content, allowing solar radiation to easily penetrate to the tops of the mountains and the tundra. The intense solar radiation that travels through thin air during daylight hours rapidly heats objects above treeline, and at night the reverse occurs. The air of the mountains cannot hold the day's heat on the ground as efficiently as the thick, moisture-filled air at sea level, so the heat of the day radiates back into space again, and rocks cool rapidly. Temperatures on the tundra at night may be 30°F lower than in the daytime.

Because they receive higher levels of solar radiation than those at lower elevations, plants benefit from thin air. The level of ultraviolet radiation at treeline is about twice that at sea level. This abundance of sunlight also means that shade-loving plants are often not able to grow in the alpine environment.

The air on the tundra is thinner because atmospheric pressure drops with increasing altitude. At sea level, the barometric pressure is 14.7 pounds per square inch (psi). At 15,000 feet, the pressure decreases to 8.2 psi, or almost half that at sea level. This reduction of pressure means that water boils at a lower temperature at high altitude. For example, a backpacker wishing a morning cup of tea atop a ridge on Mount Massive at 12,500 feet will find that the water boils at 162°F instead of the normal 212°F at sea level. The atmosphere at sea level is also more dense, has a higher water-vapor content, and contains more particulate matter, such as dust and pollen. This allows it to absorb heat at the earth's surface, creating a greenhouse effect that keeps the ambient temperature relatively constant versus that of the tundra environment.

The thin air at high altitudes contributes to the intense blue of the sky above the tundra. Blue light becomes more pronounced at higher elevations because it is unobstructed by particulates in the air. The shorter wavelengths of light—blue and violet—are more scattered by air particles than the longer wavelengths—red and orange—at the other end of the visible spectrum, giving our sky the appearance of a diffuse blue color. Space explorers heading toward outer space see the sky darken to a deep violet color and then eventually turn to black above the layer of atmospheric scattering.

Constant Wind

Large changes in temperature between day and night help to create the wind that blows constantly on the tundra. During the day, sunlight falling on the mountains warms the air in the lower valleys. As the heated air rises, it creates an updraft onto the tundra during the afternoon. At night the process reverses: When the sun goes down, the thin air of high altitudes allows the soil and rocks to lose heat faster than the better-insulated forests of the lower elevations. As the air cools, it flows down the sides of the mountains into the low valleys. This creates a down-flowing wind during the night and early morning from the tundra into the valleys below.

Updraft winds during the day are partially responsible for weather conditions on the tundra. If the rising air from the lower elevations contains moisture, it will condense and form clouds as it rises and cools. This creates the typical mountain weather pattern of sunny mornings followed by cloudy afternoons. The clouds cooled by the effect of the air rising may not be able to hold all of this moisture and may release it onto the mountains as a storm with hail, snow, rain—or even all three!

Lightning

Open tundra meadows are generally flat, and the tallest objects on them are the most likely to be hit by lightning. High-altitude lightning storms are also often accompanied by marble-sized chunks of hail that pound the tundra—and unlucky hikers—with savage intensity. Hikers caught above treeline may feel the hair on the back of their necks and arms rise and their skin tingle with a creeping sensation. Should you be caught on the tundra when a storm is approaching, move below treeline as soon as possible. If you see a storm nearby, you can approximate how far away it is in miles by counting the number of seconds between a lightning flash and the sound of the thunder, and then dividing the total by five. Light travels almost instantaneously, so you see a lightning flash at essentially the same time that it occurs. Sound, however, is slower: traveling through air at about 1,000 feet per second, it takes about 5 seconds to travel a mile.

Electrical storms occur when charges of opposite electrical polarity build, either between two clouds or between a cloud and the ground. The air that separates them initially prevents these electrical charges from neutralizing each other by acting as an insulator, or nonconductor, of electricity. However, if the charges build to a magnitude that exceeds the air's insulating capabilities, an electrical pathway is forged through the air itself and a giant spark—lightning—leaps through the air to neutralize the charges, exploding in a thunderous boom. A static electrical charge can build between a mountaintop and clouds. As the static charge builds, rocks may start to develop an eerie purplish glow as the air surrounding them ionizes. St. Elmo's fire—blue-colored balls of fire created by electrical discharge—may roll along the ground. Rocks with sharp points start to make audible buzzing and clicking sounds, and metal objects hum or click as miniature electrical discharges take place. At the breaking point, a bolt of lightning relieves the electrical tension by flashing down to hit a rock, followed almost immediately by resounding clap of thunder. Fortunately, electrical storms usually rage for only a short time before the energy expends itself, the clouds blow away, and the sun emerges into clear, blue sky to warm the tundra again.

Hail

Hail forms when the appropriate combination of moisture, temperature, and wind patterns occur. When warm, moisture-laden air is blown up against the side of a mountain, it rises under the influence of the prevailing wind and attempts to pass over the obstructing peak. As the air rises, it cools, and the moisture it contains condenses to form clouds. If the air is sufficiently cooled, it cannot hold all its moisture and releases some of it as precipitation.

Hailstones form when vertical updrafts are strong and carry the air upward rapidly, freezing the precipitation. The size of the resulting hailstone is determined largely by wind patterns. If hail falls straight to the ground, it will be relatively small in size. What often happens, however, is that the falling hailstones are caught in the original updraft and are propelled to the top of the cloud again, sometimes more than once. These pellets of ice moving up

Snow covers up trees and protects the branches from the wind in winter.

through the clouds attract more moisture, increasing their size each time. Finally, the weight of the hailstones becomes more than the updraft can support, and the balls of ice break free from the cloud and fall to the ground. Half-inch hailstones are not uncommon on the tundra, where they often fall with a savage intensity.

Snow

A good thermal insulator, deep accumulations of snow help to protect trees and other tundra plants during the winter. Though it sounds contradictory, it is the cold, not the snow, that kills tree limbs. A snowdrift consists of a matrix of ice crystals with pockets of trapped air. The air gives the snowdrift excellent insulating properties. Even if the air temperature above the snowbank plummets considerably, the temperature several inches under the surface does not drop below 26° F.

The amount of air trapped in a snowdrift varies with the type of snow. In the southern Rocky Mountains, newly fallen snow that is light, dry, and fluffy typically has a moisture content of only about 4%. The remainder is trapped air. A wet snow contains about 10% moisture and 90% air. Old snow, compacted throughout the winter by its own weight, has an even higher moisture content.

The heavy winter snow that accumulates on the peaks and in the high valleys of the Rocky Mountains has become the lifeblood of farmers, ranchers, the ski industry—and the cities below on the plains. People in Kansas, Nebraska, Arizona, California, and even Mexico depend on the water that flows from the mountains when the tundra snowpack melts in spring and summer.

The big rivers of the Colorado plains and deserts—the Colorado, the South Platte, the Rio Grande, and the Arkansas—originate as drips of melting snow high on the tundra. The Arkansas River's headwaters originate on the east side of 10,424-foot Tennessee Pass north of Leadville; the Colorado River begins on the west side of 10,192-foot La Poudre Pass in Rocky Mountain National Park; the headwaters of the Rio Grande River are east of Silverton on the east side of 12,588-foot Stony Pass; and the South Platte River begins on the east side of 11,539-foot Hoosier Pass, north of Alma. The east-side rivers eventually flow into the Atlantic, while the west-side Colorado flows into the Gulf of California and from there into the Pacific Ocean.

The warmth of the sun soon draws moisture from the ocean into the sky as water vapor; this vapor will be pushed by prevailing winds back over land and, eventually, up against the Rocky Mountains. Here, moisture-laden warm air will try to rise up over the peaks and as it rises, it cools, and the moisture condenses to form clouds. The clouds are pushed even higher over the mountain slopes and, once they become saturated, moisture will fall as rain, snow, or hail. So a drop of water from snowmelt on the tundra eventually returns back to the mountains in a never-ending cycle. This cycle also erodes the mountains and shapes the alpine environment over time, creating a variety of geographical features that help define the land above treeline.

Weathering and Erosion

Early-to-mid-summer sees the greatest snowmelt and runoff on the tundra. Warmth from the sun starts to overcome the bitter cold of winter, and snow crystals turn to meltwater. Tiny rills and rivulets trickle and bubble their way across the greening tundra, turning some alpine meadows into bogs. Rushing streams and torrents foam and swell as they travel down the mountainsides.

As a stream rushes downhill, it lifts dirt, sand, and gravel from its banks and bed, depositing the debris farther downstream. In this manner, runoff assists in the process of erosion. A stream carrying a few particles of sand may not seem like a major factor in changing the landscape, but this action has formed many of the spectacular canyons in Colorado. The Gunnison River's Black Canyon was formed as the river cut a narrow, V-shaped valley, now as much as 53 miles long and 2,689 feet deep, through volcanic and metamorphic rock. Nature took about 2 million years to produce this spectacular gorge. This same erosive force weathers mountaintops and alters their features.

Snowmelt gathers into small streams on the tundra, such this one in the San Juan Mountains, which is watering magenta Parry's primrose and yellow marsh marigold.

THE TUNDRA ENVIRONMENT 39

Rain

Water in the form of rain is an example of more subtle weathering and works in two ways. The physical impact of raindrops on rocks wears mountains away a grain at a time through mechanical action. The softer the rock, the faster it will weather, so sandstone weathers faster than granite. Rain also moves soil, sand, gravel, and small pieces of rock by washing them into streams and flushing them off the mountaintops. Physical weathering can be dramatic: Cloudbursts cause colossal washouts and mudslides, and streams and rivers, swollen in the spring by snowmelt, carve V-shaped valleys.

Rain also weathers rock chemically: As it falls through the air, rain absorbs carbon dioxide and forms carbonic acid, which dissolves rocks in infinitesimal amounts. Rainwater also

leaches minerals from the soil, which can combine with rotting organic material to form chemically erosive compounds. Year after year, century after century, and millennium after millennium, snow, rain and groundwater steadily gnaw at the mountains, dissolving them, with streams carrying them away piece by piece. Rain plays less of a role in weathering the high peaks than hail, snow, and ice do, however. The temperatures of the exposed high-mountain peaks are usually too cold for precipitation to fall as rain, so the water is converted into hail or snow.

The split between the two halves of this rock on Independence Pass has widened 7 inches over a period of 21 years.

The Role of Ice

Ice plays another important role in weathering and can literally break rocks apart. The sequence starts when water seeps into cracks or crevices in a rock. When the temperature drops, the water turns to ice, expanding its volume by about 9%. Pressure builds inside the crack, gradually widening it in a process called **frost wedging.** As the crack widens, more water seeps in and freezes, and the cycle continues. The power of ice can be seen when household plumbing freezes in winter: Ice formed inside a metal pipe is often powerful enough to split it. Similarly, mica crystals in granite absorb moisture, which freezes and expands, resulting in pressure that loosens and breaks other components of the rock.

In winter, moisture in the ground freezes the tundra soil to a depth of several inches to several feet, depending on the intensity and duration of the cold weather. Deep soil may remain permanently frozen except for its top 10 to 40 inches, which thaw in

The bowl-shaped cavity hollowed out at the head of a glacier is called a cirque, such as this one on Horseshoe Mountain, west of Fairplay.

summer. **Permafrost** is common in the Arctic but rare on Colorado's tundra. This freezing and thawing of subsurface water also weathers the soil.

Soil sometimes slumps downhill over permafrost or buried rock when the ground thaws in the summer in a process known as **solifluction.** This results in solifluction terraces, which give a shelflike appearance to some hillsides. The annual cycle of freezing and thawing also causes other subsurface stresses and movements. Wide temperature swings create differing rates of expansion and contraction between rocks and soil, termed **frost heaving,** which causes the rocks under the surface of the ground to shift. Buried rocks are slowly pushed to the surface, sometimes forming stripes, circles, or curious polygons of rock known as **patterned ground,** which may be several yards across. Broken rock may even form riverlike configurations that move under the influence of gravity, water, and ice. These rock glaciers creep downhill at a much slower rate than ice glaciers.

Glaciers

Most of the alpine lakes, or **tarns,** that are scattered like brilliant jewels among the high mountain peaks today are evidence of Colorado's glacial past. They occupy the scoured-out basins and cirques where glaciers had their beginnings. Some lakes, such as Lake Ann in San Isabel National Forest, often exhibit lingering traces of glacial action in their cloudy, bluish green color, due to traces of "rock flour" held in suspension in the water. The sun's rays refract and reflect off these particles, causing the lake to appear bright blue—almost turquoise.

Lake Ann from above.

Anderson Lake, above Lincoln Creek in White River National Forest, usually has a greenish tinge, and the aptly named series of Blue Lakes in the Mount Sneffels Wilderness glisten like jewels in the sunlight.

A few remnants of glaciers still exist in Colorado today, most of them in Rocky Mountain National Park. They are so small that experts are divided on whether or not they should be classified as active glaciers. These include Taylor Glacier, at 12,700 feet, at the head of Loch Vale gorge; Tyndall Glacier, below Hallett Peak at 12,300 feet, which drains into Emerald Lake and Dream Lake, then flows down Glacier Creek; and Sprague Glacier, at 12,000 feet, which drains into Spruce Canyon.

St. Mary's Glacier, about 2 miles west of Idaho Springs at the end of the Fall River Road, is the most accessible glacier in Colorado. It flows from a cirque south of Kingston Peak. The largest active glacier in Colorado is Arapaho Glacier, which starts at an altitude of 13,300 feet, near the tops of North and South Arapaho Peaks, just to the east of the Indian Peaks Wilderness. Much of this 70-acre glacier is on restricted land, because its meltwater is used to supply drinking water to the city of Boulder. Evidence of glaciers past can also be seen from the Forest Canyon Overlook on Trail Ridge Road in Rocky Mountain National Park. Across the valley, the Gorge Lakes stair-step down a succession of glacial basins which are also called hanging valleys.

Freezing and thawing of tundra soil forces rocks to the surface and forms strange patterns.

Merriam Life Zones

In this book, we look at the upper limits of the subalpine zone, or treeline, where the trees disappear and lush meadows blend into the tundra, and with the alpine zone itself: the land of the tundra and the high mountain peaks. The alpine zone is not continuous in Colorado but instead comprises islands of tundra and rock that jut up out of the forested slopes of the mountains. The tundra is estimated to make up only approximately 5% of the state. But first let's consider the genesis of such life-zone designations.

In 1889, the American naturalist C. Hart Merriam and a team of scientists started an extensive study of the forms of life on the San Francisco Peaks of Arizona. This research produced a system of classification for mountain ecosystems that Merriam linked to existing life zones determined by latitude. He concluded that if environmental conditions such as soil quality, sunlight, and seasonal temperatures were the same in different locations, the plants and animals in these locations would also be the same.

Merriam proposed that someone who started in the Sonoran Desert of the Southwest and traveled northward to the North Pole would pass through analogous life zones to those experienced when climbing a mountain. One journey would end in the cold expanses of the Arctic; the other would finish at the top of a peak. He noted that each zone was measurable by a drop in average summer temperature of 7°F and characterized by different plants and animals.

The **Lower Sonoran Zone** and the **Upper Sonoran Zone,** named for the Sonoran Desert of southwest Arizona and northwest Mexico, is characterized by arid desert features such as cactus and snakes. Life forms of the Lower Sonoran Zone are not found in Colorado,

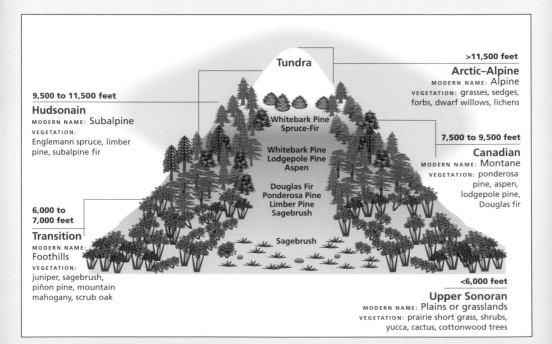

Tundra

>11,500 feet
Arctic–Alpine
MODERN NAME: Alpine
VEGETATION: grasses, sedges, forbs, dwarf willows, lichens

9,500 to 11,500 feet
Hudsonain
MODERN NAME: Subalpine
VEGETATION:
Englemann spruce, limber pine, subalpine fir

Whitebark Pine
Spruce-Fir

Whitebark Pine
Lodgepole Pine
Aspen

7,500 to 9,500 feet
Canadian
MODERN NAME: Montane
VEGETATION: ponderosa pine, aspen, lodgepole pine, Douglas fir

Douglas Fir
Ponderosa Pine
Limber Pine
Sagebrush

6,000 to 7,000 feet
Transition
MODERN NAME: Foothills
VEGETATION: juniper, sagebrush, piñon pine, mountain mahogany, scrub oak

Sagebrush

<6,000 feet
Upper Sonoran
MODERN NAME: Plains or grasslands
VEGETATION: prairie short grass, shrubs, yucca, cactus, cottonwood trees

but plants characteristic of the Upper Sonoran Zone, such as shortgrass prairie, do exist on the Eastern Plains and in the foothills at elevations of less than 6,000 feet.

The **Transition Zone** is the meeting of desert and forest at the mountain foothills, such as those west of Denver or Colorado Springs. This life zone is typified by sandy soil, grasses, and sparse, dry forests of scrub oak, juniper, and mountain mahogany.

The **Canadian Zone** is marked by wooded slopes, typically consisting of white fir, lodgepole pine, Douglas fir, and aspen. The predominant tree here is the Ponderosa pine, also called yellow pine.

The **Hudsonian Zone** is named for the Hudson Bay region in northern Canada. Here, the forests thin out as their northernmost limit is reached. At the zone's upper limit, the forests consist of twisted and gnarled dwarf trees. Limber pine, subalpine fir, Engelmann spruce, and bristlecone pine live here, mostly in islands amid stretches of grassland.

Farther north, rolling plains replace the trees—the mark of Merriam's **Arctic-Alpine Zone.** This is the tundra: the flat countryside that stretches to the permanent snow and ice fields of the North Pole. The highest features of the landscape are rocks and boulders splashed with colorful lichen. A few small, stunted shrubs appear in well-watered locations, and clumps of dwarf willows and birches grow in some of the rolling depressions. The ground is mostly covered by sedges, grasses, and, during the brief summer season, fields of dwarf flowers that hug the ground.

Because the Colorado mountains more closely resemble the European Alps than the Arctic, **alpine** is the more precise name for the state's tundra than Merriam's Arctic-Alpine designation. When climbing a tall mountain in Colorado—let's say, Pikes Peak—a hiker starts at the base in semidesert conditions and passes through the foothills of the Transition Zone, the forested slopes of the Canadian Zone, and the sparse forests of the Hudsonian Zone before arriving at the summit in an environment almost identical to that found in the Arctic.

During this hypothetical journey, our hiker experienced a drop in the average ambient temperature with upward travel similar to the change felt when traveling between the desert and the North Pole. This drop is about 3.5°F for every 1,000-foot rise in elevation. Thus, when Manitou Springs at the foot of Pikes Peak is basking in a mild 70°F, the temperature at the summit, 8,000 feet higher, will be approximately 28°F lower, or a chilly 42°F. By correlating the temperature drop of northward travel with a climb up the side of a mountain, scientists have calculated that a 1,000-foot rise in altitude is roughly equivalent to traveling 300 miles north in latitude (estimates vary from 200 to 600 miles per 1,000-foot rise).

Though Merriam set the groundwork for classifying life zones in the mountains, subsequent research has refined and expanded his system. The chart on p. 42 compares Merriam's life-zone nomenclature to modern terminology, lists the typical elevations at which each zone occurs in Colorado, and notes the characteristic vegetation of each. Today, various classification schemes are employed to describe ecological communities, some of which entail minute subdivisions to delineate specific environments in a general landscape; the example, opposite, is only one of them.

Plant Communities At and Above Treeline

Plants above treeline are hardy and resilient and have adapted to Colorado's tough alpine climate in a number of ways. Many are unique to this high-altitude environment and found nowhere else in the state. Several types of plant communities occur in the tundra and are defined by such factors as moisture availability and sunlight. A variety of colorful and interesting plants await those who venture up into these highest of plant communities.

Wildflowers on the trail to Hasley Basin.

Opposite: *Snowmelt can cause bogs to form at the base of talus slopes.*

Limitations and Adaptations

Tundra plants face many challenging and limiting factors that they would not have to contend with at lower elevations: a short growing season, poor-quality soil, moisture-stripping winds, and year-round cold weather. Tough as these conditions are, all tundra plants have adapted and cope successfully with this harsh environment.

Growing Season

There are essentially two seasons on the tundra: winter, which dominates for about nine to ten months of the year, and summer, lingering for only two to three months. The transition from winter to summer and back is so abrupt that spring and fall cannot really be considered distinct seasons. The average annual temperature on the tundra is around 26.5°F— about 5°F below freezing. Frost is possible above 9,000 feet on any night of the year. In some areas of the tundra, the growing season—the period between spring and fall frosts—is less than 60 days. Compare this to the plains of Colorado, with a typical growing season of 150 days, or to New York City, at sea level, which normally has about 210 frost-free days. Spring comes roughly one day later and fall comes one day earlier for every 100-foot rise in elevation in the mountains. The growing season does come earlier to the tundra than to treeline, because the shade of the trees tends to hold snowbanks longer than do alpine meadows fully exposed to the sun.

Because winter lasts so long on the tundra, summer—when it finally comes—arrives with a rush. Plants don't have time to leisurely turn green as do their counterparts at lower elevations. Alpine plants must grow, bloom, and spread seeds in a few short weeks. The fast growth of early summer is very demanding for a plant, requiring large amounts of nutrients in the form of sugar—a plant's primary source of energy. Most tundra plants have adapted by storing nutrients for fast growth or for use during periods of harsh weather.

Islands of timberline trees often grow out over ridges, shaped by the wind.

Fields of colorful wildflowers, including rosy paintbrush, grow above and below treeline.

During late summer, when water and sunlight are plentiful, plants like the alpine avens manufacture and store starches in their large roots. The following spring, when the plants revive from their dormant winter state and new growth starts, starch in these subterranean roots is converted to sugar to supply nutrients for rapid cell growth. Later in the summer, when new growth is complete and food requirements drop, the plants deposit starch in their roots again to prepare for the following spring's growth. Plants such as the glacier lily and the alpine buttercup illustrate this cycle; both emerge in a burst of fast growth from bulbs and flower early in the spring. Another, pygmy bitterroot, is also called Bread of the Mountains, because American Indians dug up its large root for food.

Some tundra plants prepare for rapid growth by forming new shoots and buds at the end of the summer or in early fall. This new growth remains dormant during the winter but is ready to spring forth as soon as the snow melts and temperatures warm. Other plants begin growing underneath the snow in late spring. Their roots and buds form under the protective, insulating blanket, so by the time the snow finally melts, plant growth is already well under way. Some flowers, such as the snow buttercup, even bloom underneath the snow. This little plant generates enough heat during its growth process to melt some of the snow around it, creating a small space for its bloom to unfold. As soon as the snow is sufficiently melted, showy, yellow flowers burst forth.

Though most tundra plants have adapted to the short summer season by growing rapidly, some species thrive by growing very slowly. It may take as long as seven years— and sometimes up to thirty—for these plants to store enough energy to flower. The alpine sunflower stores energy for ten years or more, until it has enough to produce its flamboyant flowers. Then it blooms, produces seeds, and dies.

By mid-August most of the colorful blossoms have gone, and the green grasses and flowering plants begin to turn russet, red, or gold. Frost glistens on plants in the early morning, particularly alongside small streams. Though this frost melts as soon as it is touched by the sun, it brings an early chill to the tundra. Soon ice forms on standing pools and water trapped in pockets among rocks.

By late August the high ridges have turned brown with dead grass, and tiny, slender, white flowers stand like speckled goblets close to the ground. This is the Arctic gentian; its blooming season signals an end to the fleeting tundra summer and marks the start of another prolonged, frigid winter.

Reproduction

Even at best, reproduction for tundra plants is a chancy business. Given the odds against them, plants of the tundra use several methods to reproduce. Still, most require insects to pollinate them, and tundra flowers tend to be showy and vividly colored to attract bees, flies, and butterflies. As it moves around, an insect will pick up pollen from a flower and transfer it to another plant, thereby fertilizing it.

Many of the insects that live above treeline have evolved protective mechanisms in order to survive the rigors of the alpine environment. The bees and flies up here have dark, hairy bodies to better absorb and trap heat. Like all insects, however, they are cold-blooded. If there is a prolonged cold spell, insects are immobilized and cannot perform pollination. Consequently, plants that require insects to pollinate them may not be able to reproduce during a particularly harsh growing season. Some plants escape this problem through wind-blown pollination. However, given the nature of the winds on the tundra, this can be a haphazard system as well.

The big-rooted springbeauty has a long taproot to seek water in rocky soil.

Even if it has been pollinated successfully, a plant faces other hazards that can prevent it from propagating. Pollinated seeds may fall on rock or on soil unsuitable for germination. To compensate for this, some plants reproduce by vegetative, or asexual, reproduction rather than seed bearing. Extensive underground stems called **rhizomes** spread from the original plant and then creep to the surface, eventually producing new plants. Plants such as the whiplash saxifrage spread runners called **stolons** that look like little whips. Runners from the parent plant grow along the top of the soil and root themselves into the ground at intervals to produce new plants. The viviparous bistort produces little bulbs on its lower flowers. These eventually drop off the main stem of the parent and grow into new plants.

Vegetative methods such as these are effective for immediate plant reproduction; however, they have one drawback for long-term survival. The new plants produced by these methods are exact genetic copies, or clones, of the parent plant. Without genetic mutations, the plant has no chance to alter itself subtly—nature's way of adapting plants to new or evolving environments. And such fine adjustments in a species can become necessary for long-term survival in an ever-changing world.

Conservation of Moisture

Moisture conservation is as crucial for all the plants above treeline as it is for those in the American desert. A tundra plant's worst enemy is the wind. It blows constantly—relentlessly—up here, varying between a breeze and a howling gale, but averaging 20 to 25 miles per hour. (Winter wind can drive snow and hail at speeds of well over 100 miles per hour, but plants are unaffected by these wild displays of nature's power, as they are dormant during this period.)

Like their cousins in the desert, alpine plants evolved several ways to combat the moisture loss inherent in their environment. Plants on the tundra typically

A perennial favorite, a Colorado blue columbine blooms in the San Juan Mountains.

have small leaves with tough, leathery skins to reduce evaporation and avoid desiccation. Hairy coverings on leaves, flowers, and stems help many plants retain moisture. Long taproots allow the plants to seek out subterranean water deep in sandy soil, while anchoring them firmly to the ground to prevent being blown away by the wind. And alpine flora rise on short stems or, in the case of cushion plants, no stems at all. Low-growing plants offer less resistance to the wind, and so are less affected by it.

Plants such as the big-rooted springbeauty, sky pilot, and black-headed daisy have waxy coatings on their leaves, similar to pine needles, to hold in moisture and reduce abrasion from material blown by the wind. The thick leaves of king's crown, a plant from the stonecrop family, enable it to thrive in dry alpine areas. Black-headed daisy, which grows only a few inches tall, has a ring of black or purplish woolly hairs at the base of its flower cluster to capture warmth. The alpine sunflower has a short, stiff stem covered with shaggy, white hairs that help retain moisture. Alpine forget-me-nots also grow fine, silky hairs, as do the catkins on dwarf willow bushes. Some tundra plants, such as the yellow stonecrop and some of the saxifrages, store excess water in their stems and leaves.

The grasses and sedges that make up the primary vegetation on the low-moisture tundra thrive despite harsh conditions by combining these methods. They have thick, deep roots to trap and gather available moisture; they grow low to the ground to stay out of the wind; and their narrow leaves help reduce moisture loss due to evaporation.

The moss campion is a good example of a tundra cushion plant.

Keeping Warm

Plants need warmth to survive and perform photosynthesis. The vegetation at sea level requires minimum temperatures in the 40s in order to produce nutrients and grow. On the tundra, however, a "warm" temperature can be surprisingly frigid, and many plants can continue to produce nutrients and grow as long as the temperature is above freezing. Many tundra plants contain a chemical, similar in effect to vehicle antifreeze, which allows them to perform photosynthesis at very low temperatures. Plant *seeds,* however, require warmth for germination—often the same temperatures of about 68°F or higher as their lowland cousins.

Like the dwarf trees at treeline, tundra plant species are generally shorter than their counterparts at lower elevations. These low-growing plants live in a microclimate at ground level that is warmer than the ambient air temperature. Intense solar radiation beating down on the tundra warms up the top of the ground. Since soil, like rock, is a poor thermal con-

ductor, heat stays at the surface and raises the temperature of the top layer of soil above the air temperature. At ground level, below most of the wind, the temperature may be 10°F or 15°F higher than the air temperature 4 feet above it.

Many alpine plants have developed ways to raise their internal temperature. Adaptations such as leaf shape, leaf color, height above the ground, and specific biochemistry help them to carry out photosynthesis and reproduction more effectively. Tundra plants have adapted their shapes to absorb as much solar radiation as they can. The big-rooted springbeauty, to name one, is a low, round plant with rosette-shaped leaves, promoting the greatest exposure to sunlight and warmth while maintaining the least exposure to the wind.

The leaves of the big-rooted springbeauty are red with anthocyanin in spring and fall, but green in the summer.

Because dark colors absorb more of the sun's heat than do light colors, most tundra plants have dark green leaves and, in many cases, dark flowers. This coloring helps to raise the internal temperature of the plant above that of the surrounding air by several degrees. Dark colors are not necessarily the rule, however. The flowers of the pygmy bitterroot may be red, pink, or white. Similarly, the common form of the alpine forget-me-not has deep blue flowers, but the less-common white version thrives on the tundra as well.

Many plants of the tundra contain a reddish pigment called **anthocyanin,** which is visible at the extremes of the growing season— immediately after snowmelt and again at the end of the summer. Anthocyanin absorbs ultraviolet radiation from the sun, converting it

The blooms of the alpine sunflower almost always face to the east.

to heat to warm the plant. Scientists also theorize that it reduces damage to the leaves from the high levels of ultraviolet radiation. In addition, it assists in the production of sugar in the plant during cool, bright weather. Present all the time in the leaves, the pigment is masked in summer by the bright green color of chlorophyll, which the plant uses in photo-synthesis. The leaves of the big-rooted springbeauty are a traditional green color throughout most of the summer, but are reddish from anthocyanin in the early and late seasons.

The fuzzy leaves, stems, and other hairy extensions on tundra plants do more than retain moisture. They also help to keep the plants warm. Hairs increase the surface area of a plant that is exposed to the sun's rays, and thus provide a greater area to absorb heat. These silky or fuzzy surfaces also trap air around the plant, creating dead air space that acts as an insulating blanket. These pockets of air are quickly warmed by the sun and help to keep the plant's temperature above that of its surroundings.

The alpine sunflower exemplifies many of the methods of survival used by tundra plants to keep warm. It has fine, silky hairs on its stem and leaves that keep it warm and retard moisture loss. The internal space in the plant's hollow stem absorbs and holds heat like a miniature greenhouse, helping to raise the temperature of the plant. Additionally, the alpine sunflower's blooms face east, toward the rising sun, in order to take advantage of

Cushion plants grow like mats to trap heat and offer low resistance to the wind.

the strongest light and absorb the maximum amount of solar energy. (Incidentally, this is one way hikers on the tundra can quickly determine which direction is east, even on cloudy days. Simply look at the direction in which the blooms of the alpine sunflowers are pointing. A majority of blooms will be facing east, with only a few stragglers facing other directions.)

The alpine sunflower is a short plant with bright yellow flowers that are 2 to 4 inches in diameter—by far the largest blooms on the tundra. The woolly actinea looks similar, and the two plants are often confused. The actinea has smaller and differently proportioned flower heads, and it grows much closer to the ground. Its blooms typically face upward, whereas those of the alpine sunflower face to the east.

Cup-shaped flowers with light-colored, glossy petals also help tundra plants trap warmth. The yellow flowers of the snow buttercup act as reflectors that concentrate the sun's heat inside the blooms, raising the temperature and creating a warm microclimate for the plant's seed-producing organs. This warm, sheltered area also attracts insects, which increases the plant's chances of pollination.

Cushion plants trap heat from the sun by growing in thick, low, matlike forms. The amount of heat absorbed may vary in different parts of the plant depending on its orientation to the sun. This leads to different rates of development from one area of the plant to the next, so that warmer parts of a cushion plant may be in bloom while cooler areas are still preparing buds.

A sampling of some of the common and scientific names of alpine plants is listed at the end of this section (pp. 65–66). This list isn't meant to be comprehensive. Readers specifically interested in plant identification may wish to consult Appendix C, p. 232, Recommended Reading, which offers several comprehensive guides to alpine flower identification.

Ecosystems At and Above Treeline

Subalpine Valleys

Warmth, soil type, and moisture dictate what kinds of plant communities will grow in different parts of the mountains, and the relatively sheltered and perpetually moist environment of the subalpine valleys at and around treeline enables colorful plants to thrive. These valleys are typically flat-bottomed basins with steep sides that protect them against the harsh wind of the tundra above. A plentiful supply of water, from both melting snowbanks on the ridges and the permanent snowfields above, feeds treeline lakes and streams along the valley bottoms throughout the summer. Spectacular flower displays grace the valleys during late June and July. Reds, blues, yellows, and purples lie like a patchwork quilt over the bright green of the lush grass. Tall, green plants with brilliant blooms, such as chiming bells and rosy paintbrush, grow here.

Alpine valley carpeted with yellow alpine avens and rosy paintbrush.

The Colorado blue columbine is the state flower of Colorado.

By far the most famous of these subalpine flowers, however, is the Colorado blue columbine. It was chosen as the state flower in 1899 and the official state song, "Where the Columbines Grow," was adopted by the Colorado legislature in 1915. The blue in the bloom is said to represent the Colorado sky; the creamy white, the snow-capped peaks; and the yellow center, the mineral that caused the 1859 gold rush in the Rockies. The plant's genus name, *Aquilegia,* means eagle, after the supposed resemblance of the flower's spurs to raptor's talons; the species name, *coerulea,* means blue. At high elevations, the blue of the bloom becomes paler, and above treeline some specimens are almost white. Formerly, tourists would pick these flowers by the armful, stripping them from mountain meadows at will. Today it is against the law to pick columbine—indeed, any wildflowers—on public lands.

A species with which Colorado blue columbine is often confused, Rocky Mountain columbine is a less common plant that grows only above treeline. In spite of their common names, Colorado blue columbine grows widely in the Western high country, but Rocky Mountain columbine is endemic to Colorado. Reaching only 4 inches tall, with miniature, lavender-blue flowers about an inch across, this tiny species grows in the meager patches of soil among the broken rock of fellfields and other rocky areas.

Treeline (Timberline)

The term "treeline," which is used here instead of the traditional life-zone designation "timberline," denotes the upper limit of tree growth and the start of the alpine tundra. This transition zone, where forests fade into alpine tundra, hosts dwarf spruce, pine, and fir trees that have been twisted into gnarled shapes by the elements. Rare and ancient bristlecone pines, which commonly live hundreds of years and may survive thousands of years, are also found in this ecosystem. The transition between two ecosystems is called an **ecotone** and the change in environment below and above tree-line is so drastic and unmistakable that it is impossible to overlook. Forests cover the slopes of the mountains below, and windswept rocks and tundra tower above.

As the ecotone between the subalpine zone and the tundra, treeline contains a rich representation of the flora and fauna of both. The ecotone at treeline also supports luxuriant wild-flower gardens sheltered by dwindling tree cover and watered by melting snowbanks. Localized conditions of soil, wind, and snow cover prevent the growth of trees in some areas, resulting in islands of small, densely clustered

The branches of the trees at treeline often stream downwind like flags.

Greenhorn trail to the summit.

trees intermingled within open grassland dotted with rocks. In other areas, trees grow in ribbonlike stands with bands of meadow between them. With an increase in elevation, the flowers and long grasses of the subalpine zone fade away, making way for the short grasses, sedges, and showy alpine flowers of the tundra. Because subalpine and alpine species mix in the area where trees dissolve into the wide reaches of the mountaintops, treeline is richer in plant life than either one individually.

Factors like soil conditions, prevailing winds, snow accumulation, average summer and winter temperatures, and sunlight exposure determine the elevation at which treeline occurs in a particular location. These factors do not create an abrupt change in environment, but rather they progressively affect and stunt growth patterns as trees try to creep up the slopes. Just as the starting and ending points of other life zones are not exact, the elevation of treeline varies somewhat from one location to another. Though treeline generally drops in elevation with northward travel, its specific location may vary over a range of several hundred feet at any particular latitude.

Snowbanks linger as summer comes late to tundra lakes.

Though treeline is not entirely contingent on latitude, it is an important factor in the equation. Even within the approximately 275 north–south miles of Colorado, treeline drops with northward travel. On Pikes Peak it is about 12,000 feet, and on Longs Peak in Rocky Mountain National Park, 125 miles or so farther north, it drops to about 11,000 feet. In Wyoming it drops to about 9,500 feet; in the Northern Rockies of Glacier National Park it occurs at about 6,000 feet; in the mountains of Alaska's Denali National Park it falls to 3,000 feet; and in the flat, treeless plains of the Arctic, treeline is at sea level.

Alpine Meadows

Rolling meadows and windswept ridges represent the most common ecosystem of the tundra. The combination of high winds and thin, porous soil in alpine meadows creates dry conditions for the plants that grow here. However, of all the tundra ecosystems, the meadows are free from snow for the longest period, which lengthens the growing season. Here, ground-hugging grasses and sedges create a turf landscape accented in summer by

colorful, dwarf plants, such as alpine forget-me-not, alpine sunflower, yellow paintbrush, bistort, and blue gentian. Each of these latter plants is an example of a **forb,** a general term for any broad-leaved, nonwoody flowering plant that is not a grass or sedge.

Sedges and grasses form a type of sod, holding the soil together in high meadows. Alpine sedges can grow from 12 to 16 inches tall and form dense tussocks. There are more than 100 species of sedge in the Rocky Mountains, all belonging to the genus *Carex. Kobresia* looks similar to sedge and grows in the same environment. Various species of these two plant genera create a dense turf in alpine meadows. Although sedge looks like grass, you can distinguish between the two by rolling them between your fingers: Grasses have flat leaves and round stems, whereas the stems of sedges are triangular in shape (just remember "sedges have edges").

American bistort is also known as knotweed due to its knotty reddish stems.

Alpine thistle also thrives in the tundra. One of the taller plants in the meadows and on ridges, it stands out against its surroundings. This plant has a heavy, dense, nodding head and contains small yellow flowers that are often almost hidden by white hairs that resemble a mass of cobwebs.

American bistort, which has a dense cluster of white flowers on top of a thin stalk, is common in the high alpine meadows as well. American Indians used its starchy roots in soups and stews. The plant is also known as knotweed, due to its bamboolike stalk, and miner's socks, because the flower's odor is slightly unpleasant. Perhaps this is why flies like the bistort!

The alpine avens is probably the most abundant flowering plant on the tundra.

The most abundant plant on the tundra is the bright yellow alpine avens, which is sometimes

Well-watered slopes above treeline are covered with dwarf willow bushes.

mistaken for a type of dwarf buttercup. When the plant is in bloom in the summer, the tundra meadows appear to be covered by a yellow and green carpet. In the fall, the alpine avens' dark green leaves change color, often turning large patches of the tundra into a dramatic, deep red. The plant has root nodules that "fix" nitrogen, a process by which living organisms draw nitrogen from the air via specialized bacteria and combine it with other chemical elements to form nutrients vital for plant existence. The ability of an alpine plant to extract nitrogen directly from the air helps it to establish itself in nitrogen-deficient soil. Parry clover, an alpine plant and member of the legume family, has the ability to do this, as do common domestic legumes like garden peas and beans.

The Arctic gentian is the last flower to appear each year on the tundra. In late August and September, these low-growing, greenish white flowers, shaped like delicate goblets, signal the end of the tundra summer and the approach of another cold winter.

Several types of willow (genus *Salix*) commonly grow on the tundra and provide the alpine equivalent of shrubbery. The Arctic willow, also known as the rock willow, creeping willow, or alpine willow, is primarily found along streambanks in alpine meadows. This dwarf shrub grows in mats that are typically 2 to 8 inches high, though their trunks can be up to a half-inch in diameter. The plant has dark leaves with long, white hairs on the underside. The Arctic willow is a favorite food of elk, and increasing herds—the result of a loss of natural predators—have decimated the plant in some areas.

The Nelson willow, a low-growing plant with shiny twigs and bright green leaves, and the snow willow, which has strongly veined leaves and dark red, pollen-producing organs, are also common on the tundra. The snow willow, a dwarf shrub similar to the Arctic willow, reaches about 6 inches tall. This plant tends to grow in drier places than its cousin, and can be found in the well-drained areas of alpine meadows and on talus slopes. Though these plants are often small, they serve an important role in tundra ecology by providing food and shelter for ptarmigan and snowshoe hares.

The appearance of arctic gentian signals the end of summer on the tundra.

Queen's crown grows near streams and other wet areas.

A riot of colorful flowers flourishes in a gopher garden, an area where gophers have disturbed the soil.

On the tundra, willows often grow in depressions, allowing snow to accumulate on and protect them in winter, and providing the plants with a meltwater reservoir in the early summer. If the snow is too deep, however, it will take more time to melt and so shortens the growing season for the willows.

Gopher Gardens

Many of the tundra's most showy flowers grow in areas where the soil has been disturbed by gophers. The animals' digging and burrowing kills off grasses and alters vegetation patterns, allowing colorful tundra plants such as alpine avens, alpine sunflower, sky pilot, purple fringe, bistort, mountain harebell, and snowball saxifrage to move in and flourish.

Gophers don't like to eat these plants and so eventually move to new territory in search of food. After the gophers leave, the colorful flowers die out, grasses and sedges move back in, and the area eventually returns to its previous state.

Meltwater Bogs

Snowmelt in early summer produces a constant trickle of water, which often accumulates faster than it can evaporate or be absorbed into the soil. In fact, the solid bedrock beneath this very thin layer of soil limits the amount of water the earth can absorb, and in marshy areas, water collected in depressions forms

Boggy areas provide good growing conditions for Parry's primrose and marsh marigold.

shallow, ice-cold ponds. In many places the soil is so well watered that one wrong step can leave hikers up to their ankles in rich, boggy earth. Water may pool all summer long in areas fed by large snowbanks, but the bogs beneath smaller snowbanks dry out by late summer.

The margins of these snowmelt wetlands are frequently lined by white marsh marigold and pale yellow globeflower, both members of the buttercup family. These two plants bloom early in wet, cold areas and may grow in standing water and at the edges of melting snow. They are sometimes mistaken for each other; however, the two can be differentiated by the colors of their blooms and by their leaves. The marsh marigold has inverted heart-shaped leaves that look somewhat like lips, hence its other name, elk's lip. The globeflower, by contrast, has leaves with serrated edges arranged in a double sawtooth pattern. Marsh marigold often grows up through the melting snowbanks. It contains poisonous compounds, though it is a favorite food of elk.

Blue gentian, also called bog gentian, flourishes around alpine and subalpine meltwater bogs, wet meadows, and streambanks. This plant has a deep blue, cup-shaped flower that grows on a stem about 4 inches tall. Early settlers made a bitter tonic from this plant. Many of its cousins, such as Parry gentian and Arctic gentian, close up tightly during the cold of

The blue gentian is commonly found around alpine bogs.

night or whenever the sun goes under a cloud. Another species, the moss gentian, is one of the smallest tundra flowers, its blooms often measuring barely three-eighths of an inch.

Queen's crown is another plant whose roots take hold near water. The aptly named snowlover, a white member of the figwort family, often leans to one side as it grows. It blooms in July and August in areas where winter snow was deep and slow to melt. Subalpine valerian looks like a white pincushion and grows in wet meadows near melting snowbanks.

Reaching about a foot tall and topped by brilliant magenta flowers, Parry primrose is also common in meltwater areas. The high level of the pigment anthocyanin in its petals accounts for the primrose's vivid color, which often intensifies with rising elevation and solar-radiation levels. This plant grows commonly along streambanks and seldom occurs below 10,000 feet in elevation. Like some other tundra plants, Parry primrose has an unpleasant odor, which seems to be part of the attraction for the insects that pollinate the flowers. This and several other plant species are named for Dr. Charles Parry, an Englishman who first visited Colorado in 1861. One of his passions was botany, and he spent more than 40 years collecting plants in the western states.

Elephantella, or elephant head, is a favorite of hikers—and small children. Favoring wet meadows and marshy areas close to melting snowbanks, this plant blooms from mid-June

Some tundra basins and meadows are a dry combination of rocks, scant grass and coarse soil.

into July. Numerous purplish flowers are concentrated up and down a single 6- to 12-inch stem, and each flower looks like the head of a tiny elephant, complete with large ears and a long, upraised trunk. This unusual shape is perfect for pollination, as bees are easily covered with pollen while they gather nectar. The Latin name for the plant, *Pedicularis,* means louse, which comes from the belief that animals would develop lice if they ate this plant. Elk commonly eat them, with no such ill effects!

Snow-Accumulation Areas

Snow accumulates in places on the tundra where the sun's rays can't provide sufficient warmth for rapid melting. The deep winter snows in these sheltered places often linger late into the spring and shorten the already brief tundra summer.

Elephantella blooms look like elephant heads.

Nevertheless, some plants, such as snowlover, snow lily, and snow buttercup, have adapted to this frozen environment and thrive in this ecological niche.

Pink snow is a colorful, if not startling, sight on the tundra snowbanks in early summer. This coloration is caused by *Chlamydomonas nivalis,* a one-celled alga that covers itself with a pink, jellylike casing when it is on snow. The alga requires water to flourish, and its optimum temperature for growth is around 32°F. Thus, it usually appears in depressions on the surface of the snow after a snowbank starts to melt in May or June. The same alga also occurs at lower altitudes, but it is usually greenish in color there. This phenomenon is also called watermelon snow, because its scent resembles that of watermelons.

Colorful cushion plants, like moss campion, are pioneer plants that stabilize the soil.

Fellfields

Fellfields, or fields of stone, host the most hardy tundra plants. Windy slopes covered with masses of broken rock, fellfields offer only sparse amounts of coarse soil for plants to take root and grow. Nevertheless, groups of tiny, compact plants cling to pockets of soil in the fellfields and create their own microclimates.

Cushion Plants are tightly knit mats of greenery that hug the ground. The leaves and flowers of a cushion plant trap pockets of air that act as thermal insulators. As the intense sunlight of high altitude beats down on the plant, it warms quickly and the air pockets hold the heat. The interior of a cushion plant can rise to 20°F—even 30°F—higher than the temperature of the surrounding air. This encourages plant growth and serves to lengthen the plant's growing season. The compact, streamlined cushion shape also affords it low aerodynamic resistance to the alpine wind.

Cushion plants, such as moss campion (not actually a moss but mosslike in appearance), are pioneers. They are some of the first plants to colonize the barren areas of ground that make up the sparse soil of the fellfields. Along with lichens and mosses, they help to break up rock and create soil, then stabilize it, leading the way for more complex plants to follow. If a seed from a different plant falls on a cushion plant, the seed may take root and grow up through the cushion.

Because they grow in poor soil and lack plentiful supplies of water, cushion plants grow at an extremely slow rate and delay blooming for many years in order to conserve energy. A moss campion plant of 1 foot in diameter may be 25 years old and have grown for 10 or 15 years before it flowered for the first time. This delay allows the plant to establish itself well in the soil and grow a good root system for water collection, thereby attending to the basic needs of survival before tackling the additional burdens of bearing blooms and reproducing. Consequently, cushion plants often live long, some reaching several hundred years old.

In order to gather enough moisture to survive in their arid environment, cushion plants typically have long taproots that enable them to seek water deep in sandy soil. These taproots also anchor the plant firmly to the ground, preventing them from being blown away by the wind. Big-rooted springbeauty, a plant common on the highest peaks and talus slopes, can have a taproot as large as 3 inches in diameter that may reach 6 to 9 feet into the ground. Roots on the moss campion may be up to 3 feet long, even though the surface parts of both of the plants may be only a few inches in diameter. The alpine forget-me-not, the Rocky Mountain nailwort, and the alpine phlox also have long taproots.

Rocky Peaks

The pinnacles of the mountains, towering above the tundra, are composed of solid rock. Very little grows here, but lichens, mosses, and cushion plants cling to crevices and small ledges among the rock faces. The plants that survive here have adapted to their environment by developing ways to live with very little water and soil.

Moss campion attaches itself to a rock with roots no bigger than a human hair and then grows a taproot that seeks water in tiny cracks and crevices. The alpine primrose hugs the

ground in the protection of grasses or rocks. The five petals of this flower are a bright rose color with a yellow throat that encircles a tube in the middle. The Latin genus name, *Primula*, meaning first, is one of the first plants to flower on the high peaks in the spring.

Snowball saxifrage takes hold in cracks in rocks, eventually helping to widen them as

High, vertical rock faces, such as this one in the Sangre de Cristo Mountains, are popular with rock climbers.

the roots grow. The Latin name *saxifrage* literally means "rock-breaker." With its white cluster of flowers in a ball at the top of a single stem, snowball saxifrage is one of the most noticeable plants of alpine meadows. The diamond shape of its leaves has earned it the alternate name of diamondleaf saxifrage.

Purple fringe, or purple pincushion, is also found on windy alpine ridges. This short plant has deep purple blooms that bristle with extended pollen-bearing stamens, making the flower look like it has been stuck full of pins.

The weakstem stonecrop grows on rocky ledges and in scree and talus slopes, sometimes projecting from cracks in the rocks. The stonecrop family received its name because it can grow on rocks with very little soil.

Jacob's ladder, also called skunkweed or skunkleaf because of its strong odor when crushed, is common in rocky areas as well. Ironically, the flowers have a sweet, pleasant smell.

Lichen

Because its leaves and stems are covered with a smelly, sticky substance, the plant is sometimes also called sticky polemonium.

Lichens add splashes of green, orange, gray, brown, yellow, black, and tan to the rocks above treeline. Most of these lichens are dark in color in order to absorb the maximum amount of solar radiation. This absorbed warmth raises the internal temperature of the plant, creating a microclimate several degrees higher than the ambient temperature and allowing the plant to sustain itself. Crustose lichens, which adhere firmly to rocks in a thin crust, are the most common species to be found above treeline.

Common Plants At and Above Treeline

Flowering Plants

The plants of the tundra, with one exception, are **perennials:** They go dormant each fall in order to survive the winter and then revive in the spring to bloom and reproduce again. Perennials use the same roots year after year, which may make up 90% of the plant's structure. Because of their longer life and seasonal growth cycle, perennials have time to stabilize in the cold tundra environment without the stress of seed bearing during the first growing season; in fact, some tundra plants grow for years before they bloom or bear seeds. The hardy seeds of tundra plants are often encased in tough, protective material to prevent desiccation, and producing these seeds requires plants to manufacture and use sugar, their primary source of energy. In particularly cold years, when extra energy is required to simply survive, some tundra plants do not produce seeds at all.

Purple fringe looks like a pincushion.

An **annual,** by contrast, lives for only one season. During a single summer, an annual has to grow from a seed, produce flowers, and bear its own seeds in order to ensure the continuation of the species the next summer. The tundra's severe weather and short growing season make it difficult for annuals to survive. An exceptionally long, cold winter on the tundra, followed by a very short summer, could wipe out an entire annual species. The only true annual plant that grows on the tundra of the southern Rocky Mountains is koenigia. This tiny member of the buckwheat family, reaching about a half-inch tall, has red stems and blotchy red leaves. It grows in shallow water or in cool, moist areas of the tundra. Curiously, koenigia seeks the cold and cannot grow if the temperature is warmer than about 45°F. It goes through its entire life cycle, from a seed to producing seeds of its own, in less than three weeks—a stark contrast to the six weeks or so required by many annual plants at sea level. Primarily an Arctic plant, koenigia is rare in Colorado, found mostly in the state's northern tundra. It was first discovered on Pikes Peak in 1913 and was not recorded again in Colorado until 1956, on Mount Evans.

Because of the profusion of plants and flowers on the tundra, identifying all of them is beyond the scope of this book. A list of many common species found in Colorado's tundra appears on pp. 65 and 66. Positive identification of plants, especially similar ones, can be difficult. Readers especially interested in plant identification may find the books listed in Appendix C, p. 233, to be helpful. Note that there are more than 300 plant species found on the tundra, and no single book identifies them all.

Water collects in low spots, forming shallow tarns that are encircled by water-loving plants.

Botanists classify any given plant using a two-word Latin (scientific) name: The first word is a noun that describes the *genus,* the second is an adjective that describes the species. Each plant species has a unique Latin name that identifies it wherever it occurs in the world. Although this long-standing and authoritative classification scheme has served well for centuries, it is not absolutely fixed but has evolved with the progress of botanical research over time. Experts can and do still disagree about both larger and finer points of identification and classification. Many species have been significantly or subtly reclassified in the course of this ongoing process.

The bulb of the glacier lily is a favorite of marmots and bears.

The existence of myriad subspecies can also frustrate precise identification, especially for the amateur. To further add to the confusion, a plant can have many different common names, often varying by regional origin, and at times colorfully imaginative. Sometimes, the same common name has even been used for unrelated plants.

King's crown is also called roseroot because of its fragrance.

The list on pp. 65–66, while by no means exhaustive, offers a sampling of some of the plants prevalent at and above treeline in Colorado. For each plant listed, you will find arguably the most popular common name and the scientific name, followed by other common names. Where a scientific name has changed in recent decades, the older name is in brackets after the contemporary one. You may also encounter these older Latin names in some flower-identification books.

A white version of the alpine forget-me-not.

The big head and yellow flowers of alpine thistle.

Alpine avens *(Acomastylis rossii)* *[Geum rossii]*

Alpine clover *(Trifolium dasphyllum):* whiproot clover

Alpine forget-me-not *(Eritrichium aretioides) [Eritrichium argenteum]:* dwarf forget-me-not

Alpine goldenrod *(Solidago multiradiata):* mountain goldenrod

Alpine harebell *(Campanula uniflora)*

Alpine kittentail *(Besseya alpina)*

Alpine lily *(Lloydia serotina):* alplily

Alpine phlox *(Phlox condensata) [Phlox sibirica/Phlox caespitosa]:* cushion phlox

Alpine primrose *(Primula angustifolia):* Fairy primrose

The delicate flowers of the alpine primrose grow about an inch above the ground.

Alpine springbeauty *(Claytonia megarhiza):* big-rooted springbeauty

Alpine sunflower *(Rydbergia grandiflora) [Hymenoxys grandiflora]:* Rydbergia, sun god, old-man-of-the-mountains, alpine goldflower, mountain sunflower, graylocks

Arctic gentian *(Gentianodes algida) [Gentiana romanzovii]*

Avalanche lily *(Erythronium grandiflorum):* snow lily, glacier lily, dogtooth violet, fawn lily, adder's tongue

Bistort *(Bistorta bistortoides) [Polygonum bistortoides]:* American bistort, western bistort, knotweed, snakeweed, bottle-brush

Black-headed daisy *(Erigeron melanocephalus)*

Bog saxifrage *(Micanthres oregana) [Saxifraga oregana]:* alpine bog saxifrage

Colorado columbine *(Aquilegia coerulea) [Aquilegia caerulea]:* Columbine, Colorado blue columbine

Common harebell *(Campanula rotundifolia):* mountain harebell, bluebell, mountain bellflower, witches thimble

Dwarf goldenrod *(Solidago spathulata) [Solidago decumbens]*

Elephantella *(Pedicularis groenlandica) [Elephantella groenlandica]:* elephant head, elephant flower, fernleaf, little red elephant

Frosty ball *(Cirsium scopulorum) [Cirsum hookerianum]:* alpine thistle, woolly thistle, Rocky Mountain thistle, Hooker's thistle

Globeflower *(Trollius albiflorus) [Trollius laxus]:* white globeflower, American globeflower

Jacob's ladder *(Polemonium pulcherrimum) [Polemonium delicatum]:* showy Jacob's ladder, skunkleaf

Jacob's ladder has a skunklike odor when its leaves are crushed.

King's crown *(Rhodiola integrifolia) [Sedum rosea]:* roseroot

Koenigia *(Koenigia islandica)*

Marsh marigold *(Psychrophilia leptosepala) [Caltha leptosepala]:* elk's lip, white marsh marigold, cowslip, meadowbright

Moss campion *(Silene acaulis):* cushion pink, silene, dwarf silene, moss pink, catchfly

Close-up of marsh marigold flowers.

Mountain candytuft *(Noccaea montana) [Thlaspi alpestre]:* wild candytuft, mountain pennycress

Mountain dryad *(Dryas octopetala):* white dryad, alpine avens, mountain avens, alpine rose, white alpine avens

Mountain gentian *(Gentiana calycosa) [Pneumonanthe calycosa]:* blue gentian, bog gentian, mountain bog gentian, explorer's gentian,

Parry clover *(Trifolium parryi):* alpine clover, rose clover

Parry gentian *(Gentiana parryi) [Pneumonanthe parryi]:* Rocky Mountain pleated gentian

Parry primrose *(Primula parryi):* brook primrose

Purple fringe *(Phacelia sericea):* silky phacelia, purple pincushion, scorpion-weed

Pygmy bitterroot *(Oreobroma pygmaea) [Lewisia pygmaea]:* least lewisia, little lewisia, dwarf lewisia

Rocky Mountain columbine *(Aquilegia saximontana):* Alpine columbine, dwarf columbine, dwarf blue columbine

Rocky Mountain nailwort *(Paronychia pulvinata) [Paronychia sessiliflora]:* alpine nailwort paintbrush

Rose crown *(Clementsia rhodantha) [Sedum rhodanthum]:* queen's crown, stonecrop, red orpine

Rosy paintbrush *(Castilleja rhexifolia):* subalpine paintbrush, splitleaf

The true flowers of the rosy paintbrush are an inconspicuous greenish yellow color and are interspersed amid the showy, red-colored "paintbrush," which is made up of bracts, or modified leaves.

Serpentgrass *(Bistorta vivipara) [Polygonum viviparum]:* viviparous bistort, alpine bistort, slender bistort

Sky pilot *(Polemonium viscosum) [Polemonium confertum]:* sticky polemonium, Jacob's ladder, skunkweed, showy polemonium, skunk-leaf, Greek valerian

Snow buttercup *(Ranunculus adoneus):* alpine buttercup, mountain buttercup

Snow buttercups can grow through snow.

Snowball saxifrage *(Micranthes rhomboidea) [Saxifraga rhomboidea]:* diamond-leaf saxifrage

Snowlover *(Chionophilia jamesii):* James' snowlover

Tufted phlox *(Phlox pulvinata)*

Tundra dandelion *(Taraxacum ovinum):* horned dandelion

Weakstem stonecrop *(Sedum debile)*

Western common paintbrush *(Castilleja occidentalis):* yellow paintbrush, lemon paintbrush

Whiplash saxifrage *(Hirculus platysepalus) [Saxifraga flagellaris]*

Woolly actinea *(Tetraneuris brevifolia) [Hymenoxys acaulis]:* woolly sunflower, woolly tetraneuris, goldflower, stemless hymenoxys

The Trees of Treeline

The trees that grow in this ecotone adapt themselves to the varied conditions of Colorado's alpine environment. Limber pine and bristlecone pine thrive in the harshest of conditions—in environments so hostile that other trees offer little competition. Engelmann spruce, on the other hand, flourish in areas with milder climatic conditions.

Trees favor sunny, south-facing, protected slopes, so treeline occurs at a slightly higher elevation on these than on cooler faces and peaks. By the same token, harsh conditions in a north-facing, windy ravine with large amounts of snow accumulation will limit the upward creep of trees, resulting in a treeline several hundred feet lower than the surrounding average. The lowest average summer temperature for successful tree growth is about 50°F, and treeline effectively marks a thermal contour around a mountain, above which the average temperature in the warmest month, July, remains below 50°F. Above this temperature contour, the conditions are too severe for trees to exist.

Temperature determines the speed of the chemical reactions that regulate cell growth within trees. When ambient temperature falls, chemical processes inside a tree either stop or slow down so much that, for all practical purposes, they have ceased. At the top of the subalpine zone—treeline—cell reactions inside a tree effectively cease to function or function

A view of treeline in the San Juan Mountains.

so slowly that the tree can no longer sustain itself. Surprisingly, though, harsh winter temperature is not the major factor that determines treeline, as trees are essentially dormant in winter. Rather, it's the average summer temperature that primarily determines the upper limit at which trees can grow, about 50°F.

Conifers survive at treeline because they tolerate low moisture and drying winds; even so, these trees are smaller than those of the same species growing at more moderate elevations. Mature pine trees at treeline may be only 2 or 3 feet tall. Growth-ring analysis of spruce trees at treeline has shown that a 3-inch-high tree may be 5 to 7 years old, and a 12-inch-high tree may be 25 to 30 years old.

In this transitional zone, young trees may grow up around an isolated mature tree to form a small island. These clumps of trees may eventually appear in rings as the pioneering tree that anchored the island dies, leaving the younger trees that grew up under its protection standing in a circular formation. Exposure to gale-force winds in winter often removes snow from the exposed areas, while just inside the shelter of the trees lie protected areas of high snow accumulation. When the snow melts, wet soil and marshy areas remain between the trees islands.

The Role of Moisture

The internal plumbing of a tree is complex, but basically a tree absorbs water through its roots, draws it up through the trunk into the leaves, and uses it during photosynthesis. Excess water is released back to the environment through tiny pores on the underside of leaves, called **stomata,** in a process called **transpiration.** Since trees need water to carry

A pond along the Mount Elbert Trail.

on this process, the availability of water determines, to some extent, the type of trees that can exist in a given location.

Trees are classified into two general types: broad-leaf and needle-leaf. Almost all broad-leaf trees are deciduous—they lose their leaves in the fall, stand with bare branches throughout the winter, and grow new leaves in the spring. Common examples of deciduous trees in Colorado are the elm, ash, maple, and cottonwood that grow in urban settings all along the Front Range. The leaves of these trees have a large surface area; thus the trees lose a great deal of water back to their environment through transpiration and evaporation. In winter, when an adequate supply of water is not present, a deciduous tree shuts down its internal plumbing system, discards all its leaves, and waits for spring and the return of adequate water supplies before activating photosynthesis again.

Needle-leaf or coniferous trees—so named because they bear their seeds in cones—are specifically adapted to function in environments with low levels of available moisture. The leaves, or needles, have a long, thin shape that creates a small surface area, minimizing moisture loss through evaporation and conserving precious water. Pine needles usually also have an outer coating that is hard and waxy to further protect them from drying out. Common coniferous trees in Colorado are ponderosa pine, limber pine, lodgepole pine, and alpine fir. They are generically called evergreens, because they retain their leaves year-round. Common trees found at treeline are Engelmann spruce, limber pine, alpine fir, and bristlecone (also known as foxtail) pine.

Battled by the Elements

In addition to challenges to proper growth caused by cold temperatures and lack of moisture, the gnarled trees at treeline are constantly buffeted and pounded by wind, hail, ice, sleet, and other extremes of the weather at high altitudes. Typically Engelmann spruce and subalpine fir, they have been molded by the wind into twisted caricatures, hence their name, **krummholz,** German for "crooked wood." They are also sometimes called dwarf trees or elfin timber. Krummholz can be so savagely battered by the elements that they grow almost flat on the ground, forming dwarf forests. Some have lost most of their needles to the wind and stand silhouetted against the sky like gaunt skeletons on ridges or rocky outcroppings. It seems amazing that they can survive, but every summer tiny sprigs of green spring out of the tips of a few of the branches.

Flagged trees, also called **banner trees,** are created by the drying forces of fierce winds at treeline. Flagging occurs when a tree's branches grow straight out from one side of the trunk, resembling a flag flying in the wind. Constant wind sucks the moisture out of the tender young needles on the windward side of a tree, eventually killing them. The wind also carries particles of grit and dirt that abrade bark, needles, and twigs off the windward side of the tree, in a process similar to sandblasting. In winter, snow, sleet, hail, and particles of ice produce the same windborne, scouring effect. The branches and needles on the leeward, or downwind, side of the tree continue to grow in the protection of the trunk. Lone flagged trees are commonly seen on high ridges, their few remaining branches stuck out like streamers in the direction of the prevailing wind, confirming the area's high winds and indicating its usual direction.

The process of creating the dwarf trees at treeline is cyclical. It starts when winter snow falls and accumulates at treeline, completely covering a dormant tree and protecting its delicate needles from the drying and sandblasting effects of winter wind and ice storms. Once the snow melts during the following summer, the tree will slowly grow new twigs, some of which project upward for several inches.

These bristlecone pines on Windy Ridge, near Alma, have been blown into strange shapes by the prevailing wind.

Treeline trees often grow in a dense, tangled mass as protection from the wind.

When the winter snow falls again, these extra few inches of twig may be above the average level of the snow's protection, thus exposing them to the full fury of storms. Hail and ice pound the exposed twigs, winds dry them out, and the cold freezes them. The new growth cannot take this kind of punishment, so the twigs turn brown and die. No matter how hard the tree tries to grow upward, it will not be able to grow higher than the winter's protective snowpack. Evidence of this process can be seen in the brown-tipped upper branches of many trees at treeline.

By contrast, the lower branches, protected in winter by snow cover, continue to extend outward year after year. The result is a short, squat tree that, though it may be mature or even ancient, can never grow higher than the average snow cover.

If several dwarf trees grow close together, they will eventually develop into a dense mat with interwoven branches that reach only a few feet off the ground. These thick carpets of trees are often found in locations where treeline creeps just below a ridge or an exposed rocky area. The scouring effects of the wind and ice in winter make the trees look like they have been mown.

Bushes and trees at treeline find some protection from the elements by growing behind rocks and boulders. If a seed happens to fall behind a rock, it may take root there and grow, sheltered from the prevailing wind. As the tree matures, it will spread outward, shaped like a streamer, downwind from the protection of the rock. This gives some banner trees the appearance of flying out over the side of a ridge in the direction of the prevailing wind.

The cycle of branch growth in summer and die-off in winter produces a phenomenon referred to as **walking trees.** If twigs grow up from behind the shelter of a rock, the branches on the upwind side of the tree may be killed by wind, snow, and cold. These dead branches form a protective windbreak for new growth on the other side of the tree, enabling the downwind branches to continue developing as the upwind part of the tree is being killed. Thus, the living portion of the tree appears to move slowly across the ground over a period of years. These dwarf trees can "walk" as much as 1 or 2 inches per year.

Cold, wind, and a lack of water are not the only tribulations with which the trees of tree-line have to contend. Hikers in early summer may see small coniferous trees with dead branches covered by a brownish black, slimy substance, which hardens in late summer into a solid black crust. This is a fungus called *Herpotrichia,* commonly called **snow mold.** Dark, humid conditions promoted by deep snow cover are favorable for the development of this fungus, which can grow when the temperature is below freezing. Young trees may not survive an attack, but mature trees are usually able to endure snow mold and suffer only a localized destruction of needles.

Bristlecone pine

Bristlecone pines grow in high, windy places at treeline and are often weathered into grotesque shapes. These trees are among the oldest living things in the world, and they commonly reach 300 to 400 years of age, some surviving to be several thousand years old. Bristlecone pines grow at an infinitesimally slow rate—less than 2 inches in diameter every 100 years. Two trees in the Windy Ridge Bristlecone Pine Scenic Area above Alma, in central Colorado, have been documented to be more than 2,000 years old. Bristlecone pine can

The summit of Mount Princeton from the jeep road to Bristlecone Park.

survive with their trunks and limbs mostly stripped bare by the elements, except for the thinnest strips of connecting bark to keep them alive. Bristlecone pines also tend to grow in areas underlaid by limestone. Young bristlecone pine branches are covered with needles 1 to 1.5 inches long that gather at the base in groups of five and have white dots of resin on them. Branches have a brushlike appearance, giving this tree the alternate name of foxtail pine. Bristlecone needles are replaced only every 10 to 15 years, instead of annually like most trees, helping the tree to save energy. Cones are a purplish black and turn brown when mature; covered with sticky resin, they have sharp bristles on the ends of the scales.

Engelmann spruce

Engelmann spruce bark is a reddish brown color, and the tree has a blue-green cast. The needles, which are short, four-sided, rigid, and sharp, are scattered singly over the branches and twigs, and they have a disagreeable, skunklike odor when crushed. Cones are 1 to 2 inches long, with brown, flexible scales. Named after botanist George Engelmann (1809–1884), this tree grows to be from 80 to 120 feet tall at lower elevations, where it is widespread in the montane and subalpine life zones. It attains progressively shorter heights with increasing altitude. Engelmann spruce grows in stands by itself or is mixed with subalpine fir and other conifers. It is long-lived, readily reaching 300 to 400 years in age.

Limber pine

A short, stocky tree, the limber pine received its name because of its flexible branches. These large, vertical branches sport clusters of curved, dark green needles, 2 to 3 inches long, at the ends. Needles grow in groups of five. The bark of young trees is light gray but darkens as the tree ages. The cones, 2 to 5 inches long, are cylindrical and elongated, with thick scales often

covered with pitch. Limber pine grows to be from 25 to 50 feet high at lower elevations but is much shorter at treeline. It grows over a wide range of altitudes, typically on dry, rocky slopes, high summits, and alpine ridgetops. Growth is very slow, and the tree takes 200 to 300 years to reach maturity. The tree grows in groups or mixed in with other conifers.

Subalpine fir

Sometimes called alpine fir or balsam fir, this tree often forms the matted shrubs or flagged trees seen at treeline. It looks quite similar to Engelmann spruce and grows along with it; in young treeline forests, subalpine fir is prevalent, but Engelmann spruce becomes the dominant tree as the forest matures. Subalpine fir typically lives for 150 to 200 years. It has a smooth, light-gray bark marked by dark blisters of resin, and its needles are short, blunt, flat, and soft to the touch. This

Only ruins remain of the town of Mayflower.

tree can be distinguished from other firs because its purplish cones are the only in Colorado that grow upright from the branches rather than drooping down beneath them. At the end of the summer, the cones' scales drop off, leaving pencil-like cores clinging to the branches. A similar species that grows south of Pikes Peak is corkbark fir, which has a grayish, thicker bark with a softer, corklike texture.

Lichen

Lichen are flat, rootless, nonflowering plants that grow on rocks and do not require soil. They can tolerate freezing temperatures, harsh winds, and dry conditions, making them perfectly suited for the alpine environment. They are some of the simplest organisms in the botanical world but are the forerunners of more complex plant forms.

A lichen is not a single plant but consists of two separate organisms: fungus and alga. The fungus attaches itself to a rock surface, surrounding and protecting the alga, and the two live together in mutual assistance; each organism needs the other to survive and grow. The fungus contains no chlorophyll, so it cannot photosynthesize nutrients. The alga contains chlorophyll but requires a moist environment to exist. In their symbiotic relationship, the fungus absorbs and stores water, and the alga makes nutrients.

A lichen is such a simple organism that it can dry out and become dormant in times of severe drought or cold weather. When favorable conditions return, the plant continues growing. Unlike the flowering plants, lichens do not have to grow or reproduce on a set schedule. Even under favorable conditions, lichens grow extremely slowly; thus prolonged inactivity does not hurt the organisms. Scientists have estimated some lichen specimens to be several thousand years old.

Lichen assists in the creation of soil by a combination of methods. It produces acids that slowly eat at the rocks on which it grows. This allows the minerals to be easily extracted for use in producing nutrients. This acid also helps to break down and dissolve rock into a primitive constituent of soil. Lichen absorbs water as it grows, thus keeping the rocks wet, which promotes weathering. The hairlike roots of the lichen work their way into cracks in the rocks, further hastening the weathering process.

The flat, pancakelike form lichen takes when it grows also contributes to soil formation. As it continues to expand outward, the inner core of the plant dies, creating a ring shape. This wreath of lichen traps wind-blown debris, such as sand, dust, and dirt, and combines it with dead organic material from the plant, forming a primitive soil on the rock's surface. After lichen is established on a rock and creates a microenvironment for plant growth, mosses start to grow. Eventually, other plants move in and flourish, more organic debris collects, and soil formation continues.

The pika's nitrogenous waste produces ideal growing conditions for the brilliant, orange-colored jewel lichen.

Animals at Altitude

The temperature extremes and harsh weather conditions of the environment above tree-line are difficult for any form of life to endure, but this habitat is particularly challenging for the animals that make their homes there. Food is scarce and so is moisture, despite the snow. Unlike the forested slopes below, the mountain peaks and the tundra have no trees and few shrubs for shelter, exposing creatures that winter on the tundra to the worst of the weather. Yet, as is nature's way, some animals have adapted to living in this severe environment and even make the tundra their permanent home.

Strategies for Warmth and Survival

Warmth is the key to survival on the tundra. The animals here are driven by the need to produce and conserve body heat. In order to sustain life, most warm-blooded mammals maintain a body temperature that ranges between 97°F and 104°F. Birds have an internal temperature that is a few degrees higher, typically between 100°F and 107°F.

If the surrounding environment is cooler than the animal, heat is lost at the same time it is being generated inside the body, because the science of physics says that heat energy flows from a hot area to a cold one until the temperature difference between the two is equalized. The colder the ambient temperature, the faster heat is lost. Thus, a warm-blooded animal continuously radiates heat through its external body surface and must replenish it in order to maintain the correct internal temperature. Body temperature is maintained by heat generated from metabolic breakdown of nutrients, and as a by-product of exercise.

Marmots make their dens under rocks for protection from predators.

In winter, a mammal's internal body temperature must be maintained in spite of severe drops in the ambient temperature. It is more efficient for the animal to conserve heat than to replace lost energy on a continuous basis. The advantage for the animal is that it does not have to eat as often to replace lost body heat and so does not have to expend as much energy in finding food. Thus, the animals of the tundra have evolved various ways to cope with the loss of body heat, and their seasonal behavior reflects these

Rocky Mountain goat herd. Photo by Wendy Shattil and Bob Rozinski

adaptations. Mountain goats grow heavier coats in the cold winter months to provide additional insulation from the cold, enabling them to stay active all winter. Marmots, on the other hand, hibernate during the winter to escape the cold weather. Pikas and pocket gophers use the thermal insulating properties of snow to their advantage, and spend most of their winter burrowed beneath a blanket of snow.

Ecosystems and Life Zones

Scientists have divided the natural world into different **life zones,** or **ecosystems,** that are shaped by local environmental conditions. While the terms ***ecosystem, life zone, biome,*** and ***habitat*** are often used interchangeably, the first three refer to the total environment, including animals and plants, while the latter should be reserved for the environment in which an animal lives.

Sunlight, wind direction and intensity, available moisture, and soil quality all determine successful plant growth. Since plants and trees are permanently anchored to the soil by their root systems, they grow in environments where they find suitable conditions for their existence. Each ecosystem is defined in terms of the particular species of plants and trees that flourish in it.

Mule deer bucks in krummholz. Photo by Wendy Shattil and Bob Rozinski

Though mobile, animals are tied closely to plant life. Herbivores that depend on certain types of plants for their existence, such as deer with grass, or squirrels with spruce seeds, range in or near areas where these plants exist. Animals higher in the food chain, such as mountain lions, which prey on deer, or pine martens, which hunt squirrels, inhabit areas where their prey live. Thus, both directly and indirectly, animals are tied to particular habitats and ecosystems.

Size and Shape

The size of an animal determines the amount of heat loss it will experience. The amount of heat radiated is proportional to the surface area of the animal, so that the larger the animal's surface area, the larger the amount of heat that will be radiated and lost to the environment. However, heat loss is also related to the size of the animal. The larger the animal, the more mass it has to generate and hold internal heat. As size increases, so does surface area, but at a proportionately slower rate. Thus, in general, a large tundra animal is more efficient at conserving heat than a small one and requires fewer calories per pound of body weight to maintain its internal temperature.

Pikas make their dens in rockslides.

The Rocky Mountain bighorn sheep, which ranges in weight from 150 to 250 pounds, can survive by foraging on short grasses and other tundra plants. By contrast, the masked shrew or the dusky shrew, both of which weigh only a few ounces, have to eat more than their own body weights in food every day or they will starve. As a result, large animals tend to be more active on the tundra in winter than small animals.

However, shape is also a factor in heat conservation, and a small animal with a round, compact shape is efficient at conserving warmth as well. Because a large tail and large ears increase the surface area of an animal's body, increasing heat loss, small alpine animals such as the pika typically have compact bodies, small ears, and small or nonexistent tails.

Insulation

An animal's hair, fur, or feathers reduce heat loss by trapping an insulating layer of air close to its body. Insulation is sometimes erroneously thought to keep out the cold; in reality, it serves to keep body heat in by reducing the amount of heat radiated away. Rocky Mountain bighorn sheep and mountain goats grow thick winter coats, as does the snowshoe hare. The ptarmigan, a bird that inhabits the tundra and subalpine zone, even grows feathers on its feet in winter to reduce heat loss. Animals such as marmots add a layer of insulating fat before hibernating to stay warm during the cold months of winter.

Goats are shaggy and unkempt when they shed their thick coats in summer.

Hibernation

In addition to cold temperatures, another big challenge for animals on the tundra in winter is food supply. For the few short months of the tundra summer, the permanent residents live well, eating grasses, sedges, and herbs that are green, lush, and usually plentiful. During the fall, however, the vegetation shrivels and becomes dormant, loses much of its nutritional value, and soon disappears under layers of winter ice and snow. As a result, another technique for surviving the winter is to sleep through the cold months, eliminating the need to search for food in cold and snowy conditions.

Hibernation is a state of total inactivity, or torpor, in which an animal's metabolic rate, heart rate, and breathing drop to low levels, thereby decreasing its requirement for food. Normal body temperature decreases to within a few degrees of freezing, respiration rate decreases to only a few breaths per minute, and pulse rate may drop to only five or six beats per minute. In this state of near suspended animation, the hibernating animal survives the winter by remaining motionless, requiring only a fraction of its normal summer amount of energy. Tundra inhabitants that hibernate include the marmot and some smaller animals such as the boreal toad.

Migration

Some animals survive the harsh tundra winter by leaving it altogether. Elk are temporary residents of the tundra. They move into the lush alpine meadows during the summer but retreat to lower elevations in winter, seeking shelter and food on the timbered slopes. Mule deer follow a similar pattern of visiting the tundra meadows in the warm months, though they prefer the protection of treeline to the exposed tundra. Some Rocky Mountain bighorn sheep may migrate from the high mountain peaks and alpine meadows to wintering grounds at lower elevations, which offer more protection and forage.

Predators such as mountain lions, badgers, bobcats, red foxes, and coyotes may venture onto the tundra for short periods of time in the summer. Chipmunks scurry about the highest peaks and rocky areas of the meadows. Even an occasional black bear will amble into grassy meadows around, and just above, treeline.

Photo by Wendy Shattil and Bob Rozinski

Elk grazing on the tundra.

Creatures of the Tundra

A variety of animals visit and live in the Colorado tundra. Many have special adaptations that allow them to live in the rugged environment above treeline. Here is a closer look at several of these hardy alpine inhabitants.

Rocky Mountain Bighorn Sheep (Ovis canadensis)

Weight: Male (ram): 150–300 lbs.; female (ewe): 125–300 lbs.

Height (at shoulder): Male: 37–41 inches; female: 32–36 inches

Length: 5–6 feet

Lifespan: Male: 15 years; female: 18 years

Offspring: 1, sometimes 2

Designated Colorado's official state animal in 1961, the Rocky Mountain bighorn sheep is often considered the most majestic of permanent tundra inhabitants. Also called mountain sheep, bighorns range over slopes, crags, and steep hills, where they feed on grasses and sedges. Although deficient in the senses of smell and hearing, the sheep compensate with phenomenal eyesight. The wide expanses above treeline enable them to spot danger in time to flee long before a predator approaches. Even so, these impressive animals, once prevalent all over the mountains, have largely withdrawn to the high peaks because of encroachment by humans and domestic animals.

Bighorns sport a thick coat of gray or brown hair (not wool as with domestic sheep), with a pale belly and white rump, and have sharp, cloven hooves that let them dig into ice and adjust to uneven surfaces. They are agile and sure-footed, even in the most rocky terrain. Weighing up to 300 pounds, the males, or rams, sport heavy (up to 35 pounds) horns that are highly prized by trophy hunters.

Tough, hollow sheaths that fit over a short, bony core, the horns are composed of keratin, a fibrous protein, and continue to grow throughout a sheep's life, gradually curling around and outward. Along the horns, a pattern of rings develops, similar to those of a tree trunk. A ram with a three-quarter curl is typically about eight to ten years old; a ram whose horns may form a complete circle has attained an old age of about 12 years.

A fascinating time to observe bighorn sheep is during the mating season, or rut, in late fall. Rams challenge one another to determine which will propagate the species, effectively determining dominance and territory. Courtship battles start with rounds of posturing and kicking. Then, starting from a distance of 20 feet or more, two males will rear up and charge one another, slamming their heads together with a violent crash. A series of bouts ends when one ram concedes defeat and ambles (or staggers) away. Two or three head-bashes over several minutes are usually enough to settle the matter.

One might think rams would batter their brains out with such stunning blows, but serious injury is rare. Even so, broken horns and bleeding ears and noses are common. The horns of mature, dominant males are usually "broomed": chipped, splintered, or broken off at the tips.

Female bighorns, or ewes, have smaller, sharper horns that stick up from their heads and curve slightly backward. Ewes and juvenile rams are sometimes confused given their similar builds and horns. Lambs are born in late spring, usually one per ewe. They can walk soon after birth and within a few days are scaling slopes with relative ease. However, their mortality rate—from disease, inadequate nutrition, climatic adversity, and predation—is high.

When winter snows arrive, herds follow well-defined migration routes to feeding grounds in lower, more sheltered places, or to exposed ridges where winter winds have swept off the snow to expose forage. In winter, weaker animals often starve or are taken by a waiting predator. Ticks, lice, worms, and disease may afflict the sheep. Lungworm has taken a huge toll on sheep populations in the past, although some wildlife-management techniques, including treatment with drugs, have helped reduce bighorn deaths.

Like their domestic cousins, bighorn sheep are herd animals. Despite the social order in the herd, sheep are rarely seen alone. In the warmer months, rams range in small groups, grazing to fatten up for the rut and winter season, at slightly higher elevations than the ewes and lambs, who live in larger groups. At the mating season, the mature rams migrate down to the females and spend winter near the ewes and their young.

Both bighorn sheep and mountain goats also seek out salt licks—whether naturally occurring or salt spills along old railbeds—and paw through the top layers of the soil to expose them. Left undisturbed, a herd tends to stay on the same ranges generation after generation, which has proven to be a dangerous habit. If humans or other animals move in on its territory, the shy bighorn does not stake out new ground but simply retreats from the threat, which can cause overcrowding, overgrazing, and even starvation.

Colorado's bighorn herds are considered healthy, however, numbering about 7,500 animals in more than 70 herds (by contrast, an estimated 300,000 elk inhabit the state). Stewardship efforts have helped, including relocating sheep to new ranges to prevent over-crowding. Beyond the highest peaks, some 350 desert bighorns inhabit the eastern plains and the canyon country near the Utah border.

Photo by Wendy Shattil and Bob Rozinski

Bighorns on tundra in Rocky Mountain National Park.

Viewing Guide for Bighorn Sheep

National Forest	Location
Arapaho	• Georgetown Bighorn Viewing Site, 45 miles west of Denver. • Mount Evans
Gunnison	• Almont Triangle, bordered by CO 135, FR 742, and FR 813, northeast of Gunnison. • Red Creek, at the end of FR 723 on the north side of Blue Mesa Reservoir between Gunnison and Montrose.
Pike	• Pikes Peak • Castle Concrete Quarry on the west side of Colorado Springs (restricted land; use binoculars from the north end of Garden of the Gods park). • Tarryall Reservoir area, north of US 24, west of Lake George. • Dome Rock State Wildlife Area, north of Cripple Creek. • Buffalo Peaks, west of the junction of US 24 and US 285. • Between Grant, on US 285 southwest of Denver, and the top of Guanella Pass. • Waterton Canyon, southwest of Denver. • The Shelf Road, County Road 88, south of Cripple Creek.
Rio Grande	• Trickle Mountain, north of CO 114, about 15 miles west of Saguache. • Natural Arch area, up La Garita Creek north of Del Norte.
Roosevelt	• Poudre Canyon, around The Narrows, on CO 14, about 25 miles west of Fort Collins. • Big Bend Campground on CO 14 about 40 miles west of Fort Collins. • Big Thompson Canyon, along US 34 west of Loveland. • Rocky Mountain National Park, particularly around Sheep Lakes in Horseshoe Park and in the adjacent Never Summer Range.
San Isabel	• Sheep Mountain, north of Cottonwood Lake, west of Buena Vista on FR 344. • Sangre de Cristo Mountains, on the high peaks and in basins from the Arkansas River Canyon on the north to Medano Pass on the south. • Greenhorn Mountain Wilderness, southwest of Pueblo.
Uncompahgre	• Ouray, north and south of town 3 miles in each direction on US 550.
White River	• Crystal River Canyon, south of Carbondale on CO 133, between Nettle Creek/FR 313 and the Redstone Campground.
Miscellaneous	• Arkansas River Canyon on US 50 between Salida and Parkdale. • Dinosaur National Monument, around Lodore Canyon, Harpers Corner Road, and Echo Park. • Cottonwood Canyon, west of Campo.

Wildlife watchers may also wish to consult the Colorado Division of Wildlife's Bighorn Sheep Watching Guide and its Bighorn Sheep & Mountain Goats brochure, both of which are available from Division of Wildlife field offices.

Mountain Goat (Oreamnos americanus)

Weight: Male (billy): 150–250 lbs.;
female (nanny): 100–200 lbs.

Height (at shoulder): Male: 40–44 inches;
female: 35–40 inches

Length: Male: 5–6 feet; female: 4–5 feet

Lifespan: Male: 14 years; female: 18 years

Offspring: 1, sometimes 2

Like bighorn sheep, mountain goats are grazing animals that live above treeline year-round, ranging in rocky areas and feeding on the herbaceous plants and grasses of the tundra. They are most at home in the high cliffs, which they bound across with graceful agility, but they also sometimes venture onto alpine meadows. Prized trophy animals, the goats are not popular as edible game because of their musky taste.

The mountain goat is not a true goat but is properly a mountain antelope, related to those in Africa and to the chamois of the European Alps. The animal is roughly the same size as a bighorn sheep, standing 3 to 3.5 feet tall and weighing between 150 and 250 pounds, but the resemblance ends there. The goat has a distinctive shoulder hump, a white goatee (long hairs hanging from the throat), and side whiskers. To protect it against wind, rain, and snow,

Photo by Wendy Shattil and Bob Rozinski

Mountain goat kids on Mount Evans.

the mountain goat sports a yellowish white outer coat of thick, shaggy guard hair about 7 inches long and a woolly undercoat at least 3 inches thick, which keep the animal warm and enable it to survive above treeline all year. In early summer, goats look shaggy and unkempt as they shed their thick winter coats and new hair grows back underneath.

Both male and female goats have short, sharp, spiky black horns, about 8 inches long, that stick straight up from the tops of their heads and curve backward at the tips. The horns of males are larger at the base than those of the females and curve more gradually. The females' horns are thinner and more widely spaced, with sharper curves near the tips. Adult male and female goats, however, can be difficult to differentiate.

Like bighorns, mountain goats have keen eyesight and can spot a human or animal moving at great distance. Consequently, goats are difficult to approach, and sightings are rare. Startling a goat, however, particularly one with young, may provoke a threat response. Skilled climbers, goats can traverse almost vertical slopes with ease. Also like bighorns, mountain goats have cloven hooves and flexible leg joints, and enjoy superior traction. Goats may jump between ledges but generally do not run, even when disturbed.

In the summer, mountain goats feed on dwarf grasses and sedges of the tundra and on the lichens and mosses that cling to rocks of the high summits. In the winter they also eat willow and alpine fir trees. Their multiple stomachs allow them to extract nourishment from poor food with great efficiency. Goats descend below treeline only to seek temporary shelter from the bitterest of winter storms. They may paw through the snow with the points of their hooves to reach the plants below or graze in areas blown clear of snow.

Male mountain goats, or billies, challenge other males to win females, or nannies, during the rut, which occurs in late fall. A male may scent-mark a female with a musky oil produced by glands at the base of his horns. Unlike bighorns, whose mating battles rarely result in serious injury, a billy will aim with its daggerlike horns for the chest and belly of its rival and may even try to butt him over a cliff. Fortunately for the species, more posturing than actual fighting takes place.

The winners then breed with the nannies; the young, or kids, are born in the spring and can follow their mothers within hours of birth. Kids may fall prey to raptors and other predators, but the goats' attraction to remote mountain ledges is more often their undoing: More goats perish from avalanches, falling snow cornices, and rockslides than from predation. Billies typically range alone or in groups of two or three and on higher, rockier terrain than the nannies and kids.

Since the goats will not venture long below treeline, places such as South Pass in southern Wyoming, where the Continental Divide dips below treeline, form natural barriers that prevent their expansion into different ranges. Although bighorns and mountain goats live in similar habitats, the herds don't mix. If goats expand into the range of a sheep herd, the sheep will often seek a different part of the range. Such habitat limitation can create overcrowding and stress for the sheep.

The mountain goat is not a Colorado native but was transplanted from the northern Rockies of Montana, Idaho, and South Dakota to mountains in Colorado from 1948 to the 1970s. These goats have flourished, reaching a population of about 1,600 animals statewide.

Yellow-Bellied Marmot (Marmota flaviventris)

Weight: 8–10 lbs.
Length: 18–22 inches
Lifespan: 3 years
Offspring: 3–8

A type of ground squirrel related to the woodchuck, or eastern groundhog, the marmot typically lives in rocky slopes close to alpine meadows. Its body is about 18 inches long, with a long furry tail that adds another 6 inches or so. The animal's fur is usually yellowish brown with the fur along the belly a lighter yellow, hence their name. A mature marmot typically weighs about 8 to 10 pounds. Although marmots occupy various habitats in Colorado, as low as the shrublands and pine forests at 6,000 feet, they are most prevalent in subalpine and alpine environments at elevations above 8,000 feet. Stocky and bowlegged, they either waddle or bound when crossing the tundra.

Marmots are herbivores, spending their summers eating grasses, sedges, forbs, clover, berries, and roots—and sitting in the sun. The rocks close to their burrows are particularly convenient for sunbathing: It is not unusual for hikers to spot a fat marmot lolling on a rock with its legs spread out in all directions. As soon as it sees an intruder, however, all semblance of laziness vanishes. It leaps up and eyes the perceived danger warily. If the hiker stops and is quiet, the animal may simply watch with its head cocked to one side. These curious animals can often be approached and viewed at close range.

When danger lurks or an intruder is near, a marmot will whistle a warning to its fellows—the closer the danger, the more noise. At last the long sound degenerates into a series of short, sharp, worried-sounding whistles as the marmot bolts for safety into the depths of its burrow. This characteristic alarm signal has earned the marmot the nickname of whistle-pig.

A territorial creature, the marmot will vigorously defend its terrain of several hundred square yards. Males and females live in separate territories, and although a female marmot will be receptive to a male during mating season, she will drive him away once her litter is born. Fiercely competitive, the females may even kill the young of others in order to assert territorial dominance.

Marmots make their dens under boulders or in rocky areas (earning them another nickname, rockchuck), using their sharp claws to dig a deep burrow, usually with several entrances and exits. They line it with soft grasses and hair to make a comfortable den, where they spend an estimated 80% of their time. If rock piles are not available, marmots may dig burrows directly into the rock-strewn hillsides. Bears and mountain lions eat marmots, but the rocks make it difficult for these predators to dig their way into a marmot den.

During late summer and early fall, marmots are prolific eaters. They gorge themselves on grasses and berries, building up a heavy layer of fat to insulate their bodies. Marmots then retreat to their dens, which are deep enough in the rocks and soil to prevent them from freezing, and hibernate for the eight-month tundra winter. The fat not only protects the marmot from the cold, but it also serves as a food reserve to keep the animal alive and its body functioning during hibernation. The animals lose about 40% of their fat reserves over the course of the winter, and if the season is particularly long, the mortality rate for hibernating marmots may be high.

Though some females are monogamous, a male often gathers a harem and may hibernate in the same den with several females, all of them effectively sharing body heat. When spring returns to the tundra in late May, the marmots emerge. Soon after, litters of four or five babies are born.

Pika (Ochotona princeps)

Weight: 4–8 ozs.
Length: 6–8 inches
Lifespan: 6 years
Offspring: 2–5

An alpine rodent that also calls the talus slopes and rock piles of the high mountains home, the brownish gray pika is about 6 to 8 inches long, typically weighs about 4 to 6 ounces, and has small, round, white-rimmed ears, short legs, and a vestigial tail. This compact design minimizes the pika's loss of body heat during winter. Even the soles of the animal's feet are covered with hair to help conserve internal warmth. As mountaintop dwellers, pikas have no trouble surviving in the cold mountain environment at and above treeline, but they are rarely seen below it and they cannot survive temperatures much higher than 90°F.

Pikas live in the subalpine and alpine zones, next to mountain meadows full of the grasses, sedges, and alpine avens they like to eat. Talus slopes provide them with protected sites for dens and safe hiding places from hungry weasels, martens, hawks, eagles, and coyotes. Using prominent rocks for lookout perches, pikas can safely survey an area for predators and warn other rock-pile residents when danger approaches. In contrast to the mournful whistle of the marmot, the pika's warning is a sharp squeak, sounding somewhat like a creaky floorboard or a door with rusty hinges. Distinct courting vocalizations are heard during the mating season.

Among the most territorial of tundra animals, the adult pika will guard sections of talus slopes from 50 to 100 feet across around its den. Aggression diminishes only during the brief mating season in the spring, from about April to June. A spring litter of four or five young is typical, although a second litter may be born before September, and may not survive an early winter.

Throughout the winter, pikas do not hibernate but stay active in rock piles beneath the snow. During the summer, pikas harvest grasses and herbs and leave them to dry on rocks in the warm air. When this vegetation has dried, which happens quickly in the tundra climate, they gather it in their mouths and store it in their dens. During the summer a pika may gather 40 to 50 pounds of dried plants. This food keeps the pika alive during the long winter months and is vital to the animal's survival. Pikas chase intruders away from their hay piles and mark the area around the food with urine and feces, or with scent from the glands underneath their chins.

Large splashes of white material deposited on rocks in fellfields, often surrounded by bright orange lichen, also indicate an active pika population. Because they live in rocky areas of the tundra, pikas do not have the opportunity to drink much water—and given their specialized metabolism, they do not need to. Consequently, the pika's urine is concentrated and viscous, with a high nitrogen content. The animals frequently deposit their waste on rock outcroppings, creating large splashes of white, chalky material that is almost crystalline. Brilliantly colored jewel lichen, which thrives on nitrogen, is nourished by the pikas' urine and grows on the animal's favorite rock perches.

The name for the pika comes originally from Siberia, where it is pronounced "pee-ka." The name has been Americanized and is often pronounced "pie-ka"; thus either pronunciation is correct. Other names for the pika include cony, in reference to an animal mentioned in the Bible (probably the rock hyrax), and rock rabbit. The pika is a close, but not closely resembling, relative of the rabbit and hare, and shares several physical attributes characteristic of the rabbit family, including chisel-shaped teeth and stomachs that contain bacteria to assist in digestion of grasses and sedges. Its squeaking noise—a sharp eek!—has earned it the other nicknames of piping hare and whistling hare.

Hikers on the tundra often hear the shrill, piping squeaks of the pika's warning to its neighbors as they approach rockslides. As danger comes closer, the little animal changes its tune to an even shorter, sharper series of cries. When it feels that danger is imminent, it bolts into its den in a nearby rock pile, uttering a series of staccato shrieks.

Northern Pocket Gopher (Thomomys talpoides)

Weight: 3–6 ozs.
Length: 8–10 inches
Lifespan: 5 years
Offspring: 3–8

Another permanent resident of the tundra, the northern pocket gopher is a brownish-gray rodent, about 8 to 10 inches in length, with large incisor teeth, long, curved front claws, a short, almost hairless tail, short legs, small ears, and a bullet-shaped face. The gopher's habitat ranges from low-elevation grassland to the mountaintop alpine zone. Though the gopher primarily lives underground in burrows and is itself rarely seen, distinctive piles of dirt give evidence of its presence in the tundra. The rodent occasionally ventures into the open but usually only at night for short periods of time to gather grasses, herbs, and forbs, which it quickly pulls back down into its burrow. It seldom eats all the material it stores in its tunnels.

Melting snow reveals earthen casts, or eskers, made by a pocket gopher digging under the snow.

The pocket gopher can seal its eyes tightly shut and close flaps over its ears and mouth to keep the dirt from flooding its mouth and throat when it's digging. It is named for the fur-lined pouches, or pockets, on either side of its face, which are used to carry food and can be turned inside out to eject the contents. The gopher fills its cheek pouches with dirt, which it deposits at the surface in mounds that mark entrances to the tunnel system. Shallow tunnels, 2 to 8 inches beneath the surface of the ground, serve as thoroughfares for traveling and gathering food. Deeper tunnels, 10 to 18 inches under the ground, lead to nesting chambers below frost line. Other chambers are used for food storage or body waste. Burrows may be up to 500 feet long, and a system of tunnels will typically range over several hundred square yards.

Both males and females are highly territorial and fight to keep intruders from their dens. During the mating season, however, males seek females by digging underground into the females' burrows. After mating, they seal the connecting tunnels to separate the burrows again.

Using its powerful, enlarged front claws to find the roots and bulbs it eats, gophers spend most of their lives underground. The subterranean networks and mounds of dirt left on the surface of the ground serve to redistribute and aerate the soil, allowing water to better percolate into the ground. Gophers also fertilize the soil by churning up roots, uneaten food, and waste matter to produce humus. The resulting flower-strewn sections of alpine vegetation have been nicknamed gopher gardens.

Like the pika, the pocket gopher doesn't hibernate but remains active throughout the tundra winter, using the insulating quality of snow to survive the winter cold. Though the air on the tundra may fall to as low as 50°F below zero, the temperature in the gopher's den stays constant at about 26°F. The gopher stays under this insulating blanket during the winter and does not venture out onto the exposed tundra.

When the top layers of the soil freeze, a gopher will tunnel between the snow and the ground looking for the plants and roots it needs for survival. The animal leaves piles of debris behind it as it goes, and when the snow melts in spring, sausage-shaped cores of dirt called eskers remain. These dirt casts are several inches in diameter and meander across the tundra. After several months of exposure to the elements, weathering reduces these earthen snakes to ground level again. Eskers also help to alter the soil patterns, encouraging new plants to grow.

Long-Tailed Vole (Microtus longicaudus)

Weight: 1.5–2 ozs.
Length: 5–7 inches
Lifespan: 1 year
Offspring: 2–8

A dark gray, mouselike animal about 6 inches long, the long-tailed vole also inhabits alpine meadows. In summer it lives in underground burrows, often in wet places such as bogs, streambanks, and willowed areas, and feeds mostly on grasses and seeds. Like the pika, it also cuts and stores grass to eat during the winter months. Also called the meadow mouse, the vole survives the winter in a nest under the snow on the ground's surface and changes its diet to roots and bark when other vegetation is not available. Voles tunnel beneath the snow, like gophers, while the wind and snowstorms rage above. The small strings of dirt and grass they leave behind them are similar to gopher eskers.

This tiny creature has a reputation for having a bad temper. Voles do not tolerate other voles or humans, often biting when handled. Because of this characteristic, at one time this animal was known by the scientific name of *Microtus mordax,* the "cantankerous vole." Given their short gestation period and multiple litters each year, voles often experience crowding in suitable environments. Most adults carry scars from the bites of other voles, the frequency of bites increasing as overcrowding occurs in a particular area.

Long-Tailed Weasel (Mustela frenata)

Weight: 5–10 ozs.
Length: 12–22 inches
Lifespan: Less than 5 years
Offspring: 3–9

A predator of the pocket gopher and the vole, the long-tailed weasel is the largest of the three North American weasels. With a body 12 to 22 inches long, a black-tipped tail of 4 to 6 inches, and short legs, the weasel suffers poor heat efficiency; thus it searches constantly for food, consuming one-third or more of its body weight each day. The most widespread carnivore in the Western Hemisphere, the weasel ranges from low-altitude farmland up to the mountaintops, where it inhabits alpine meadows.

Its long, slender body allows the weasel to tunnel both for shelter and prey under the snow and down into burrows. On the tundra, it frequents rocky areas and streams, which environments host most of its prey. Changing color with the seasons, weasels don a dark brown coat in summer and a completely white one in winter—except for the tip of the tail, which remains black year-round. A weasel may feed on pikas and shrews, although its primary food source consists of voles and pocket gophers. It also can and will attack animals its own size and even larger, such as rabbits, dispatching its victim by biting it on the neck at the base of its skull.

Photo by Wendy Shattil and Bob Rozinski

Weasels often make their dens in burrows of other animals, such as those of the pocket

Long-tailed weasel

gopher. The nest is lined with grass and fur—either its own or that of other animals that it consumes. It uses a wide variety of calls, including screeching, squealing, and purring, depending on its mood. When a weasel is irritated or alarmed, it exudes a nasty odor from a gland at the base of the tail. This odor is thought to be used as a warning to other animals.

Snowshoe Hare (Lepus americanus)

Photo by Wendy Shattil and Bob Rozinski

Weight: 3–4 lbs.
Length: 14–20 inches
Lifespan: 5 years
Offspring: 2–7

Though the snowshoe hare can be found in the tundra, it is not, strictly speaking, a permanent resident. It is a subalpine dweller and is usually found at treeline and below in coniferous forests, living in simple depressions in the ground, called forms, at the base of trees or under shrubs. The hare owes its name to its disproportionately large hind feet, which can be up to 6 inches long. Relying on its camouflage to protect it from predators, the hare changes color with the seasons, giving it the alternate name, varying hare. In summer, its coat is a brownish color that blends with the surrounding vegetation; in fall and spring, a mottled brown and white; and in winter, white—although the tips of its ears remain black. The change in color is triggered by decreasing hours of daylight in the fall, not by the approach of cold weather, so the hare is vulnerable to being easily visible to predators if an early snowstorm occurs.

The hare's coat also grows heavier in winter and fluffs up to trap air pockets, which provide extra insulation against the cold. In wintertime, insulating mats of coarse hair grow on and in between its toes, which, like snowshoes, help keep the hare from sinking into deep snow. The hare's ears are heavily furred and relatively small so as to reduce heat loss. By contrast, its cousin, the white-tailed jackrabbit of the Colorado foothills, has large ears to help it stay cool by radiating excess heat from its body. Sometimes the snowshoe hare is inaccurately called the snowshoe rabbit.

The snowshoe hare's diet consists of grasses, forbs, sedges, herbs, and willows. These plants are plentiful throughout the summer, but competition for food increases during the winter months. However, the snowshoe hare has an advantage that other small animals do not: In winter, its "snowshoes" enable it to walk on top of snowdrifts in search of food. Once summer comes to the tundra again, it looks as if a tall animal has eaten the tops of the willows. However, it was a snowshoe hare, lifted by the deep winter snow, that feasted on the tender willow tips.

Hares can stand upright, sometimes prancing in the air and cuffing one another during courtship rituals. This ability to stand on their hind legs also allows them to reach food beyond the grasp of shorter residents of the tundra.

Snowshoe hares can have up to four litters per year, with up to seven young per litter. Their relative abundance makes them a favorite of many predators.

White-Tailed Ptarmigan (Lagopus leucurus)

The only bird that remains on the tundra all year-round is the white-tailed ptarmigan, the smallest member of the grouse family. It is about 12 inches tall, the size of a small chicken, which has given it the alternate name of rock chicken. Large flocks of these birds were reported in Colorado in the latter half of the 19th century, but early settlers found them easy to catch and quite tasty, so their numbers declined severely by the early 20th century. Their seeming inability to escape also gave them the dubious title of fool hen.

Though it can fly well, the ptarmigan prefers the ground. It feeds and travels on the ground, even to escape from predators, though it will sometimes erupt into an erratic flight across the tundra. Females generally stay below treeline during the winter months. Males sometimes join them in unusually severe weather but spend the rest of the year on the tundra. During winter storms, ptarmigan may huddle together in groups to stay warm, often using willow thickets as protection from the wind or burrowing in the snow.

The white-tailed ptarmigan frequents talus slopes and alpine meadows close to dwarf alpine willow bushes. It eats insects, berries, seeds, forbs, and tender willow buds, as well almost every other part of the willow bush during fall and winter, including leaves, shoots, bark, and twigs. The ptarmigan must compete for the willows with snowshoe hares and elk, more and more of the latter of which are wintering above treeline.

Since there are no trees on the tundra, the ptarmigan nests on its cream-colored belly on the open turf or under a willow shrub. In June, it lays four to eight eggs—buff-colored with darker spots—in a depression in the ground lined with grass, lichen, and its own feathers. The incubation period is about 3 weeks. The mortality rate for chicks is high, and only an average of two out of five survive the first year of life.

Like the snowshoe hare, the ptarmigan is notable for its adaptive coloration. In summer its plumage is a mottled combination of brown, white, and tan that looks like a lichen-covered rock and blends in with the tundra landscape. In winter it turns white, with the bird's black beak and thin red combs over its black eyes all that keeps it from disappearing seamlessly into the snow. Its feathers grow thick for insulation, and it even grows feathers on its legs and feet to prevent heat loss. These feathers also act as tiny snowshoes, helping the bird move around easily on top of the snow. In spring, the ptarmigan molts to continue the cycle.

Ptarmigan are so confident of their camouflage that it is easy to get quite close to them—intentionally or unintentionally—before they run away. It is not unusual to be hiking on the tundra and suddenly see what looks like a rock scuttling across the grass. Sometimes the birds make cackling and clucking noises when danger approaches, and females will try to draw a perceived predator away from her nest or chicks by running along the ground with her wings spread. Males strut and posture to rebuff an intruder.

Like pikas, white-tailed ptarmigan are so well adapted to their environment and so well insulated that they are unable to tolerate warm weather. They pant when they are too hot, and they cannot survive in temperatures higher than 100°F for more than about an hour.

Other Birds

White-tailed ptarmigan are the only birds that live on the Colorado tundra year-round. Like many of the mammals of the forests, most birds go above treeline during the summer but are not permanent residents of the tundra. The white-crowned sparrow usually nests just below treeline and ranges both above and below treeline during the summer. Other part-time residents are the gray-crowned finch, the black finch, and the brown-capped rosy finch, as well as the horned lark, the American pipit, and the water pipit. All of these birds migrate above treeline in early summer to breed and nest on the tundra but return to the warmer climates of the lower elevations in the fall in order to escape fierce alpine winters. Rufous and broad-tailed hummingbirds contribute to wildflower pollination on the tundra in the summer. The spurs of the Colorado blue columbine flower form nectar reservoirs for both hummingbirds and long-tongued insects.

Photo by Wendy Shattil and Bob Rozinski

White-crowned sparrow

Large predatory birds such as golden eagles and hawks fly above treeline in the summer, hunting for marmots, pikas, shrews, or bighorn lambs. Ravens, bluebirds, and jays also visit the mountaintops in summer. However, all of these birds nest in the trees below.

Gray-crowned finch

Cold-Blooded Animals

Animals such as snakes and frogs do not generate and regulate their internal temperature like mammals but instead take on the temperature of their surroundings. On the tundra, however, the average ambient temperature, even in summer, is too low for the life processes of most cold-blooded animals to function properly. For this reason, there are no snakes on the tundra.

One of the few cold-blooded animals to exist on the tundra is the boreal toad, a small amphibian about 4 inches long with brownish black, warty skin and a bright white or yellow stripe down its back. It is most common between 8,500 and 11,000 feet; however, it is sometimes found at elevations up to 12,000 feet, in and around subalpine and alpine ponds. It is sometimes hard to find because it does not call frequently or loudly like other toads and frogs. Sometimes called the western toad, the boreal toad is rare in Colorado and considered an endangered species.

Other amphibians found up to 12,000 feet are the northern leopard frog, the chorus frog, and the tiger salamander.

A colorful boreal toad

Photo by Wendy Shattil and Bob Rozinski

Insects

Even though they're cold-blooded, some insects live above treeline. Clouds of gnats and mosquitoes may appear in the early morning sun, especially around tundra pools and marshy areas, and flies, bees, spiders, ants, grasshoppers, beetles, and butterflies will move about on warm, sunny days in the summer. Butterflies often fly up (or blown up) to the tundra in summer from lower elevations but generally do not lay eggs there, because the low summer temperatures would retard egg development. Spiders

Phoebus parnassian

commonly spin webs between rocks in tundra boulder fields to catch the numerous insects that live in and use sun-heated rocks as a source of warmth. The requirement for tempera- tures high enough for insect activity means that they are visible during sunny daylight hours. Early morning, evening, and night are too cold for them to be active.

Many tundra insects are dark in color, which helps them to absorb heat from the sun, and they are generally hairy or fuzzy to trap an insulating layer of warm air next to their bodies. Insects such as bumblebees and butterflies can also raise their body temperatures by muscular motion in a process analogous to shivering in humans. Bumblebees' flight muscles must be at about 85°F to function properly, which they can attain by shivering. This allows them to fly while ambient temperatures dip below 50°F, when bees would otherwise

Aphrodite fritillary

be unable to move. Flies also play an important role in pollinating tundra flowers, because they can move about at lower ambient temperatures than bees. Bees are attracted to flowers, with strong odors, such as clovers, whereas flies generally prefer flowers that are flat and open without an odor.

Insects of the tundra tend to remain close to the ground because the temperature near the soil is warmer than it is several feet above and there is less chance of being blown away by the wind. Insects also seek out the warmer micro-climates found near tundra plants and flowers. Sedges and grasses are primarily pol-linated by the wind, but many tundra flowers are pollinated by insects. Tundra flowers are usually bright and showy to attract their pollinators.

Insects, such as this spider, are active for about two months during the summer.

If the sun goes behind a cloud, tundra insects often drop to the ground, paralyzed by the abrupt change in temper-ature. Butterflies and bees become immobile, and flies vanish into hiding places in the rocks and soil. When the cloud moves on and the sun reappears, insects spring to life again. At night, they crawl into crevices along the ground and in rocks and stay dormant during the hours of darkness. Bumblebees may also use the abandoned burrows of mice, voles, and pocket gophers as places to hide at night or when the weather is cold or windy.

Because they are cold-blooded and at the mercy of their environment, insects have evolved ways to allow themselves to survive the drop in ambient temperature as winter approaches and until the warmth of the following summer returns. Depending on the par-ticular species, they may live out the tundra winter as eggs, larvae, pupae, or adult insects. Bumblebees, for one, die off at the end of the summer, except for the fertilized queen, who survives the winter in a hole in the ground.

Cold temperatures are particularly harmful to insects if ice forms in their tissues. In order to avoid damage, some species synthesize a type of "antifreeze" in their cells to prevent water-filled parts of their bodies from freezing. Others have adapted to allow parts of their bodies to freeze and are able to thaw without harm when the warm weather returns.

SCENIC DRIVES

All of the following drives offer fine hiking options along the way and are suitable for passenger cars. On the Guanella Pass, Boreas Pass, and Greenhorn Mountain drives, you will encounter dirt surfaces and poor stretches that should be traveled with caution. The top section of the Pikes Peak Toll Road and the west side of Cottonwood Pass Road are both well-maintained and made of hard-surfaced dirt. The rest of the drives are along paved roads.

Mining ruins above treeline.

CONTENTS

Opposite: *The thin, crisp air on top of a fourteener produces an intense blue sky.*

TRAIL RIDGE ROAD

LOCATION: Trail Ridge Road links the towns of Estes Park on the east side of Rocky Mountain National Park and Granby on the west side.

HIGHLIGHTS: The highest continuous paved highway in the United States, Trail Ridge Road provides unparalleled views of the tundra, along with pullouts and short trails to scenic overlooks, and is well suited to those who cannot hike.

ACCESS: This paved, two-lane highway forms US 34 through Rocky Mountain National Park. Admission is charged to enter the park. The road is closed by snow in winter.

LENGTH: From Estes Park to Grand Lake is approximately 49 miles.

MAPS: Roosevelt National Forest. Rocky Mountain National Park brochure and map are available at entrance stations.

HOW TO GET THERE: From US 36 in Estes Park, follow signs for Rocky Mountain National Park to the west edge of town. The highway enters Rocky Mountain National Park at Beaver Meadows Visitor Center. Follow US 36 to Deer Ridge Junction inside the park, where the road rejoins US 34 and becomes Trail Ridge Road. Follow the road to the west entrance of the park. Allow three to four hours to complete the drive one-way across the park.

At Kawuneeche Visitor Center, near Grand Lake at the west entrance to the park, you can alternatively retrace your miles back to Estes Park or drive south to Granby, then drive south on US 40 over scenic Berthoud Pass to join I-70 heading east. This makes a 240-mile loop from Denver.

The view from Forest Canyon Overlook shows the previous route of a hanging glacier stepping down the mountainside opposite.

One of the most easily accessible areas of alpine tundra in Colorado, Rocky Mountain National Park is also one of the most scenic. The easy drive on a paved highway across the tundra in the park is perfect for those who are unable to sustain the exertion of hiking. With a maximum elevation of 12,183 feet, Trail Ridge Road remains above 11,000 feet for 11 miles and above 12,000 feet for 4 miles, weaving through beautiful expanses of tundra. An ideal introduction to the tundra, the road was named for a Ute Indian trail across the Continental Divide.

About 14 miles from the Beaver Meadows Entrance Station, stop at the Forest Canyon Overlook at 11,716 feet, which offers an outstanding view across the valley to Gorge Lakes. These scenic lakes are stair-stepped down the mountainside on the previous route of a hanging glacier. Marmots are common around the parking area, and elk and Rocky Mountain bighorn sheep may be visible on nearby meadows and hillsides.

After about 2 more miles, stop at the Rock Cut pullout at 12,210 feet. On the north side of the parking area is the Tundra Communities Trailhead and the 0.5-mile Toll Memorial Trail, a pleasant walk over a paved path with interpretive signs that illustrate many features of the tundra. Driving up the road again, you will pass in about 2.5 miles Iceberg Lake at 11,900 feet, which often still has ice on the surface in July. Between Rock Cut and Iceberg Lake, the road crosses

Rocky Mountain National Park

The human history in the vicinity of Longs Peak and Rocky Mountain National Park is a storied one. Early inhabitants included Ute Indians, who lived on the west side of the mountains, and the Cheyenne and Arapaho, who lived at lower elevations on the east side. In summer, these tribal peoples crossed the mountains; traces of their presence include trails and low stone walls, used for herding game at high elevations. The written history of the park dates from 1859 when Joel Estes, a Kentuckian who participated in the California gold rush, migrated with his family to settle in the wide valley that now bears his name. Albert Bierstadt, one of the outstanding painters of the Rocky Mountain West, produced several fine, romantic canvases of the area after visits in the 1870s, helping to widen its fame. Writer, mountain guide, and conservationist Enos A. Mills, who had first come to the park in 1884 when he was 14 years old, spent much of his life on Longs Peak. Through his writings and speeches, he promoted the grandeur of the area, campaigned ceaselessly for its protection, and was instrumental in its designation by Congress as Rocky Mountain National Park in 1915.

The high country encompassed by the park was among the least affected by the mining boom in the Colorado mountains. The ghost town of Lulu City, in the northwest corner of the park, was founded as a "gold" town, but miners soon concluded that there were no paying quantities of gold there. The Eugenia Mine, off the Longs Peak Trail on the east side, was another short-lived gold strike; visitors to it today can enjoy a pleasant day hike.

The Alpine Visitor Center

11,827-foot Iceberg Pass, where you travel for a short distance on top of the route of the former Ute Trail.

Driving on again, a must stop is the Alpine Visitor Center, at 11,796 feet, where the road crosses Fall River Pass. The visitor center contains interpretive displays about the tundra and excellent views from the balcony. Behind the building, the Alpine Ridge Trail, a short hike of a quarter mile and some 350 feet of elevation gain, leads to an overlook and views of the canyons far below.

The park is excellent for viewing bighorn sheep at any time of year. Stop at one of the visitor centers and ask if sheep have been sighted recently at any particular location. The best places to view sheep in summer are from Trail Ridge Road around Specimen Mountain and Milner Pass, and in the Mummy Range in the northern section of the park. In winter, bighorn sheep are often seen at Sheep Lakes, a natural salt lick in Horseshoe Park. Sheep may come down as low as the entrance road on the Estes Park side in the wintertime and are often seen around the visitor center or alongside the road just outside the park boundary.

HIKES ALONG THE WAY Ute Trail and Timberline Pass

FEATURES: This hike and pass on the old Ute Indian trail in Rocky Mountain National Park links Trail Ridge Road on the west and Windy Gulch on the east.

HOW TO GET THERE: The trailhead is on Trail Ridge Road at Ute Crossing, about 1 mile east of the Forest Canyon Overlook and 13 miles west of Beaver Meadows Visitor Center.

HIKE DIFFICULTY: EASY TO MODERATE: The trailhead is at 11,420 feet and the high point at 11,484 feet, making this a fairly level hike. The paltry elevation gain makes the hiking relatively easy, but because the route is all above treeline, the hike may require extra exertion for those unused to high altitude.

LENGTH: From Trail Ridge Road to the top of Timberline Pass is a little less than 2 miles. Continue about 4 miles to reach the Upper Beaver Meadows Trailhead.

The Ute Trail is sometimes called the Dog Trail, because American Indians used sleds called travois, pulled by dogs, to transport supplies over this route. Timberline Pass is the only pass above treeline on the old Ute Indian trail. This crossing of the Continental Divide has been in use for at least 6,000 years. The narrow trail goes southeast along Tombstone Ridge, named for the odd rock formations found there. In places where the trail appears indistinct, it is marked by rock cairns. The pass can also be hiked from the east through the timber from the Upper Beaver Meadows Trailhead, but this route is considerably more strenuous because of the large elevation gain as it climbs to the pass. Arranging for a shuttle to drop you at Trail Ridge Road and hiking down to Beaver Meadows makes for a less taxing adventure. Another section of the Ute Trail is accessible from the Alpine Visitor Center.

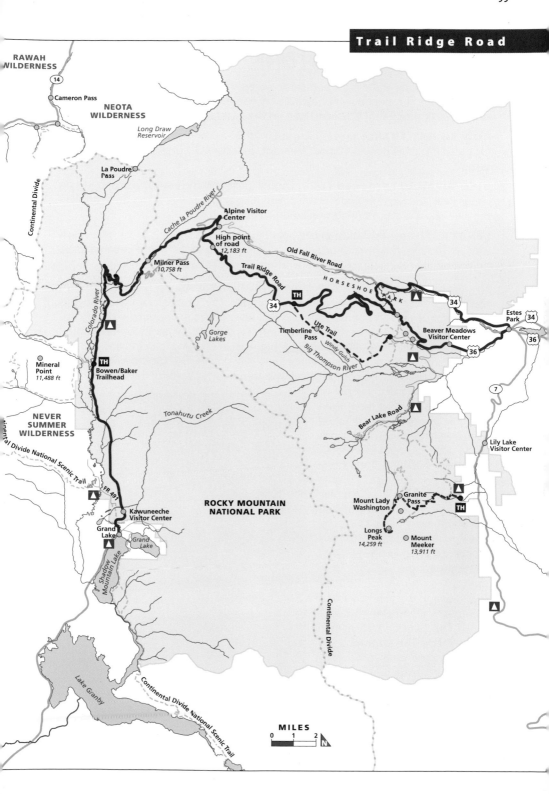

RAWAH
WILDERNESS

(14)

Cameron Pass

NEOTA
WILDERNESS

Long Draw
Reservoir

Continental Divide

La Poudre
Pass

Cache la Poudre River

Alpine Visitor
Center

High point
of road
12,183 ft

Old Fall River Road

Milner Pass
10,758 ft

Trail Ridge Road

HORSESHOE PARK

(34)

Estes
Park

(34)

(36)

TH

Gorge
Lakes

Ute Trail

Timberline
Pass

Windy Gulch

Beaver Meadows
Visitor Center

Big Thompson River

(7)

Mineral
Point
11,488 ft

Colorado River

TH

Bowen/Baker
Trailhead

NEVER
SUMMER
WILDERNESS

Tonahutu Creek

Bear Lake Road

Lily Lake
Visitor Center

Continental Divide National Scenic Trail

FR 49

Kawuneeche
Visitor Center

ROCKY MOUNTAIN
NATIONAL PARK

Grand
Lake

Grand
Lake

Mount Lady
Washington

Granite
Pass

TH

Longs
Peak
14,259 ft

Mount
Meeker
13,911 ft

Shadow Mountain Lake

Continental Divide

Lake Granby

Continental Divide National Scenic Trail

MILES

0   1   2

N

OTHER NEARBY HIKES | Longs Peak

FEATURES: One of the most popular fourteener hikes in Colorado is the Keyhole Route. Technical mountaineers, however, choose among dozens of climbs up the almost-vertical, 945-foot "Diamond" cliff on the east face.

HOW TO GET THERE: Take CO 7 south from Estes Park for 9 miles to the turnoff for the Longs Peak Ranger Station. Alternatively, take CO 7 west from Lyons to the turnoff.

HIKE DIFFICULTY: STRENUOUS: Though probably the easiest of the routes up Longs Peak, the Keyhole Route is still a hard hike and requires being on the trail in the wee hours of the morning, well before sunrise.

LENGTH: The Longs Peak Trail (Keyhole Route) to the summit is 7.5 miles each way, spiraling up the peak. Shorter trails, including Chasm Lake and Eugenia Mine, branch off the main trail for those preferring a less demanding day hike.

The northernmost of Colorado's fourteeners, Longs Peak stands majestically above the rest of the skyline to the west of Longmont. The 14,259-foot mountain was named for Major Stephen H. Long, who described the mountain during his exploratory expedition of 1820—although he did not climb it. Archaeological clues suggest that the summit was climbed earlier by American Indians, but the most famous early ascent by a white man was in August 1868 by Major John Wesley Powell. The one-armed Civil War hero and Western adventurer later explored the Grand Canyon.

Estimates are that more than 100,000 people have reached the top of the mountain, which is the only fourteener in Rocky Mountain National Park. Most climbers ascend the 7.5-mile Keyhole Route, an easy, popular, nontechnical trail that winds up from the west face. Over the years, many mountaineers have pioneered and described dozens of routes to the summit. More than 75 of the most difficult routes are on the almost-vertical 945-foot wall on the east face called The Diamond, so named for its shape. This approach was not attempted until 1960, partly because of restrictions on rock climbing within the park.

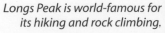

Longs Peak is world-famous for its hiking and rock climbing.

Elk at Play

It had been one of those July weeks along the Front Range when the temperatures hovers in the high eighties. To escape the plains, my wife and I had sought the cool of the mountains and were now parked alongside Trail Ridge Road in Rocky Mountain National Park. In front of us, the carpet of green grass and flowers that made up the tundra dropped sharply to the timber at the end of a long valley. It was mid-afternoon, and at 12,000 feet I could feel the sun's rays burning through the thin air onto my face and neck.

My wife touched my arm. "Over there," she said, pointing to the hillside across the valley as she lifted her binoculars to her eyes. I lifted my own binoculars to scan the ridge to the south of where we were standing and trained the lenses on the area she had indicated. Coming over the top of the ridge, their brown bodies standing out in sharp contrast against the green grass, were five large elk.

Photo by Wendy Shattil and Bob Rozinski

Because of the distance and the time of year, I couldn't tell if they were bulls or cows. (Bull elk lose their antlers in the winter, regrowing them over the summer in time for the fall rutting season.) As I watched, the five started to move slowly down the steep slope that led into the valley.

Though most of the snow had melted, a large snowbank still lay a short distance below the crest of the ridge on the steep, north-facing slope across from us. Snow must have drifted into a low spot over the winter and was late to melt because of its orientation to the sun. The snowfield looked to be several hundred yards long and perhaps a hundred wide. From where we stood I couldn't gauge the depth, but it looked to be at least several feet.

The elk picked their way down the slope until they reached the top of the snowbank. Once there, they stood and looked at it. Then one of them, obviously braver than the others, stepped gingerly up onto the brilliant white sheet of snow and started to amble slowly downhill. Then it started to race. Through the field glasses I could see its hooves sinking into the soft surface of the snow and sending up wet sprays of slush. At the top of the snowfield another elk started to follow it.

I held my breath. I was sure that one of them would stumble and break a leg. But no. With surefooted ease, both continued down the snowy slope in a headlong rush. As the first elk reached the lower edge of the snowbank, it slowed, then stepped off onto the grass again, before turning to start ambling back uphill. It skirted the edge of the snowfield until it reached the top. There, it paused and then stepped onto the snow again. Again it started to dash downhill.

By this time, three of the elk were in various stages of charging down the snowbank. The other two had wandered to the side and were now lying contentedly on the snow, obviously enjoying their version of elk air-conditioning.

My wife and I watched with fascination as the elk repeated their performance several times. As soon as one of them finished its gallop down the snowfield, it turned and climbed back up to the top, then launched itself down the white slope again.

Then, just as quickly as it had started, the show was over. The three frisky elk apparently lost interest in their game and stayed on the green grass, where they lowered their heads to graze. The two lying on the snowbank struggled awkwardly in the slush to their feet and rejoined the others.

Speechless at these antics, my wife and I looked at each other. We had been in just the right place, at just the right time, to observe this fascinating animal display.

BERTHOUD PASS

LOCATION: About 45 miles west of Denver, this 11,315-foot pass accesses Winter Park and the Fraser Valley.

HIGHLIGHTS: Historic road across the Continental Divide with scenic sections of tundra above the pass.

ACCESS: This paved all-weather road is open all year.

LENGTH: From Empire to Winter Park is 26 miles.

MAPS: Arapaho National Forest.

HOW TO GET THERE: Drive west of Denver on I-70 to the turnoff for the town of Empire and US 40. Follow US 40 about 13 miles west and north to the summit of the pass.

The road to Winter Park and the mountains of Rocky Mountain National Park in the distance from the top of Berthoud Pass.

This pass was named for Captain Edward L. Berthoud, who conducted the first survey of the area in 1861 while he was looking for a possible railroad crossing. The pass was made into a toll road in 1874 and was eventually purchased by the state of Colorado to become the first free crossing of the Divide. Colorado's oldest ski area (now closed) was established at the summit in 1937, the year before it was paved. The road is in the process of being widened and improved.

The scenery along the drive up Berthoud Pass may be more impressive than at the summit, but the pass does provide good hiking access to the tundra above. The old Berthoud Pass ski area and lift stand near the pass marker. To the south is a fine view of the cirque and the long, impressive ridge that makes up part of 13,362-foot Engelmann Peak. To the north are the west side of the Indian Peaks Wilderness and, farther in the distance, the long range of mountains that make up the backbone of Rocky Mountain National Park.

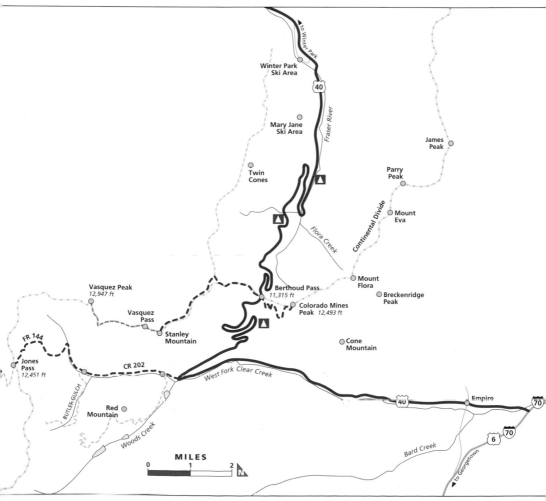

HIKES ALONG THE WAY **Vasquez Pass and Vasquez Peak**

FEATURES: At 12,947 feet, Vasquez Peak is the highest summit in the area, providing superb views.

HOW TO GET THERE: Park at the summit of Berthoud Pass and look for an old maintenance road that climbs up through the former ski area, directly on the west side of US 40. The road turns into a trail after about 0.75 mile.

HIKE DIFFICULTY: MODERATE: Starting at 11,315 feet, and after an initial climb of about 1,000 feet, this trail has a relatively gentle grade along the crest of the mountain.

LENGTH: From the trailhead on Berthoud Pass, the summit of Vasquez Peak is 5.5 miles.

Climb up to the ridge, turn (left) south, and continue for about 2 miles above treeline to a junction with the Mount Nystrom Trail (TR 13), which comes up from the Mary Jane ski area in the valley below to the north. Continue west on TR 13 across Vasquez Pass (12,521 feet) to Vasquez Peak. Both are on the Continental Divide Trail on the south edge of the Vasquez Peak Wilderness. For a shorter hike from the summit of Berthoud Pass, 12,493-foot Colorado Mines Peak on the east side of US 40 also provides fine views. Look for a modern, gated, broad gravel access road that climbs up to a communications complex on the east side of US 40, behind the old ski-area building.

OTHER NEARBY HIKES **Jones Pass**

FEATURES: This scenic 12,451-foot pass offers great views to the east and south from the summit and accessible backcountry crossings of the Continental Divide.

HOW TO GET THERE: At the first big switchback on the way up the south side of Berthoud Pass, find CR 202 going west. Follow the road past the Henderson Mine (molybdenum mining and processing), turn right at the signs for Jones Pass, and follow FR 144 to the top of the pass.

HIKE DIFFICULTY: MODERATE: There is a steady elevation gain of about 2,000 feet from the Henderson Mine to the summit.

LENGTH: From the turnoff on US 40 to the summit is 6 miles; from the Henderson Mine to the summit is about 4 miles.

This out-and-back route may be driven in a 4WD, biked, or hiked, though at times the road is maintained enough by the Denver Water Board for cars with high clearance and sufficient power to make it to the top. Note that during some years the top of the pass may be blocked by snowbanks until late in August. Across the Divide, the road on the west side of the pass drops steeply down through the timber into the Williams Fork river valley to a locked Forest Service gate, which is the end of the drivable portion of the road. From here, you can hike on TR 66 to the South Fork and Sugarloaf Campgrounds. If you do not wish to hike, you may prefer to turn around at the top of the pass and avoid the drive or hike down the west side, because you will have to turn around anyway at the bottom and drive back up the pass to return to US 40.

LOVELAND PASS

LOCATION: This tundra stretch of US 6 lies some 50 miles west of Denver, between Loveland Ski Area and Dillon.

HIGHLIGHTS: Hiking trails leave from the pass summit, which is at 11,990 feet, to lovely stretches of tundra on the Continental Divide. Be prepared for outstanding views of peaks not visible from I-70.

ACCESS: This scenic, two-lane, paved highway is open year-round, weather permitting.

LENGTH: Driving distance on US 6 from the east portal of the Eisenhower Tunnel on I-70 to Dillon is 19 miles.

MAPS: Arapaho National Forest on the east side, White River National Forest on the west side.

HOW TO GET THERE: From Denver and the east side of the Continental Divide, follow I-70 to the turnoff for US 6 (Exit 216), just before Eisenhower Memorial Tunnel. From the west side, exit I-70 at Silverthorne/Dillon (Exit 205) and follow US 6 past the ski area at Keystone to the top of the pass.

The summit of Loveland Pass, with Grizzly Peak in the background.

The pass was named for William A. H. Loveland, a retail merchant and founder of the city of Golden, who diversified into mining and railroads. He built a toll wagon road over the pass in 1879, but his plans for a subsequent railroad route never came to fruition. Because of the harsh winter weather on the pass, the road was essentially abandoned by 1900 and remained in a primitive state until it was rebuilt in 1927–1929. Winter storms and avalanches frequently forced closure of this portion of US 6 when it was the major route through the mountains. The need for a reliable connection between towns on the eastern and western slopes led to the construction of the Eisenhower Memorial Tunnel, opened in 1973, which bores under the Continental Divide. Today, the scenic stretch of US 6 over the Divide to Dillon accesses two ski areas and is used by truckers to carry hazardous loads not allowed through the tunnel. The road is open year-round, except during the fiercest winter storms.

The drive over Loveland Pass offers staggering views. Social trails from the parking area at the summit go north to various overlooks and also down into Loveland Basin. One trail from the parking area goes east up to and along the ridge of the Continental Divide. Pass Lake, at 11,835 feet just below the summit on the west side, makes a good place for a scenic lunch, despite the rather dilapidated picnic tables. The lake provides an ideal sampling of the tundra for those who do not wish to hike. Flowers, small mammals, an alpine lake, a sweeping view of Arapahoe Basin, and examples of over-hanging snow cornices in late July can all be seen from the lake's small, blacktopped parking area. Two smaller tarns are less than 0.25 mile up a short trail west of the Pass Lake parking area.

HIKES ALONG THE WAY **Mount Sniktau**

FEATURES: A brisk climb up a 13,234-foot peak that lies close to a major highway.

HOW TO GET THERE: Park at the summit of Loveland Pass. The trailhead takes off almost directly east up the edge of the ridge.

HIKE DIFFICULTY: MODERATE TO STRENUOUS: Steep climb.

LENGTH: From the parking area at the top of the pass to the top of Mount Sniktau is a little less than 2 miles.

On a historical note, Mount Sniktau was key to Colorado's bid for the 1976 Winter Olympics: The plan was to develop two courses on the north-facing slope for down-hill races, with the finish at I-70 below. However, further study showed that the upper slopes were usually scoured free of snow by the wind.

The trail of Mount Sniktau climbs very steeply for a mile up the open ridge to the east to 12,915 feet, then turns and goes to the northeast for another mile to reach the summit of the mountain. Be aware that there is a false summit of 13,152 feet, about halfway up to the true summit. Atop the small peak you'll reach after the first mile, another trail heads southeast along the Continental Divide for 2 more miles to the summit of Grizzly Peak (13,427 feet), offering fine views of the Arapahoe Basin ski area. You may also ridge-hike along 12,448-foot Baker Mountain, lying to the east between Mount Sniktau and Grizzly Peak, which is accessed from the trail between Loveland Pass and Grizzly Peak.

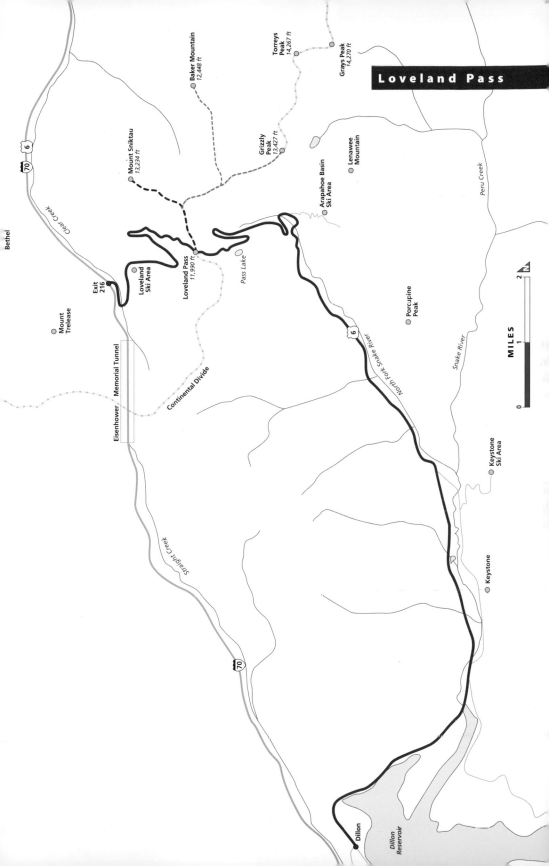

Loveland Pass

Bethel

70 6

Clear Creek

Mount Trelease

Exit 216

Loveland Ski Area

Loveland Pass
11,990 ft

Eisenhower Memorial Tunnel

Continental Divide

70

Straight Creek

Mount Sniktau
13,234 ft

Baker Mountain
12,448 ft

Torreys Peak
14,267 ft

Grays Peak
14,270 ft

Grizzly Peak
13,427 ft

Pass Lake

Arapahoe Basin Ski Area

Lenawee Mountain

Peru Creek

North Fork Snake River

6

Porcupine Peak

Snake River

Keystone Ski Area

Keystone

Dillon

Dillon Reservoir

MILES

0   1   2

MOUNT EVANS

LOCATION: About 35 miles west of Denver, south of Idaho Springs.

HIGHLIGHTS: This 14,264-foot summit can be driven by a passenger car, or even pedaled by an intrepid bicyclist. The trip features outstanding examples of tundra as well as breathtaking views.

ACCESS: A paved, two-lane road leads to the top of the mountain. Return the same way. The road is closed in winter. A fee is charged at the Forest Service entrance station.

LENGTH: From Idaho Springs to the entrance station is 13 miles, from the entrance station to Summit Lake is 9 miles, and from the entrance station to the top of Mount Evans is 14 miles.

MAPS: Arapaho National Forest.

HOW TO GET THERE: From Idaho Springs, drive south on CO 103, then turn right onto the Mount Evans Highway (CO 5) just past Echo Lake. Follow the road to the top.

Standing some 35 miles west of Denver and clearly visible from downtown, Mount Evans offers a popular day-drive to the top of a fourteener. As well as being one of Colorado's favorite tourist attractions in the mountains, Mount Evans is the site of scientific studies on subjects ranging from alpine plants to cosmic rays.

Thousands of tourists drive the road to the top each year on one of the highest paved roads in the world. Those who are in a hurry to climb a fourteener but have no appetite for mountain hiking can reach the 14,264-foot summit from the parking area at the end of the road—a climb of about 130 vertical feet! On a clear day, the Mount of the Holy Cross is visible from the summit. Bighorn sheep frequent the ridges above Summit Lake. Mountain goats are common along the last couple of miles of highway below the summit as well as around the pit toilets at Echo Lake, where they are attracted by uric acid salts.

Bristlecone pines at the Mount Goliath Natural Area.

Mount Evans

The mountain was given the name Mount Rosalie in 1863 by noted Rocky Mountain landscape artist Albert Bierstadt, after his wife. In 1870, a suggestion was made to change the peak's name in honor of John Evans, the second territorial governor of Colorado, and the new designation was approved in 1895 by the Colorado state legislature. To compensate for the name change, a nearby 13,575-foot peak located southeast of Mount Evans was christened as Rosalie Peak. In 1914, a 14,060-foot mountain that

The Sawtooth connects Mounts Evans and Bierstadt.

connected to Mount Evans by a 1.5-mile ridge was named after Bierstadt. The ridge has a dramatic, jagged section appropriately called The Sawtooth, a feature clearly visible from Guanella Pass.

Crest House, the original Mount Evans summit house and gift shop built in 1940, was destroyed by a propane explosion and fire on September 1, 1979. In 1992, the stone ruins were converted into an observation platform. An observatory owned by the University of Denver also stands at the summit.

HIKES ALONG THE WAY Mount Goliath Natural Area

FEATURES: Easily accessible bristlecone pine forest and alpine garden trails on the tundra.

HOW TO GET THERE: Drive 3 miles on the Mount Evans Highway from the entrance station to a paved parking area on the left.

HIKE DIFFICULTY: EASY: Hiking ranges in difficulty from strolls around two loops at either end of the trail to a steeper section that connects the two.

LENGTH: A round-trip hike from either trailhead is 3 miles; it's 1.5 miles one way if you arrange a vehicle shuttle between trailhead parking areas.

A 0.25-mile loop at the lower trailhead leads through a bristlecone pine forest. At the upper trailhead, 0.5-mile TR 49, also known as the Alpine Garden Trail, loops through tundra plants and wildflowers. The 1.5-mile M. Walter Pesman Trail, previously known as Mount Goliath Trail, connects the two trailheads, starting in the bristlecone pine forest at 11,540 feet, climbing through treeline, and finishing with the alpine garden at the upper trailhead. Elevation gain on this trail is 612 feet in 1.5 miles, with most of the climbing takes place in the first 0.5 mile of the trail. Pikas, marmots, mountain goats, bighorn sheep, and ptarmigan frequent this area.

Mount Evans

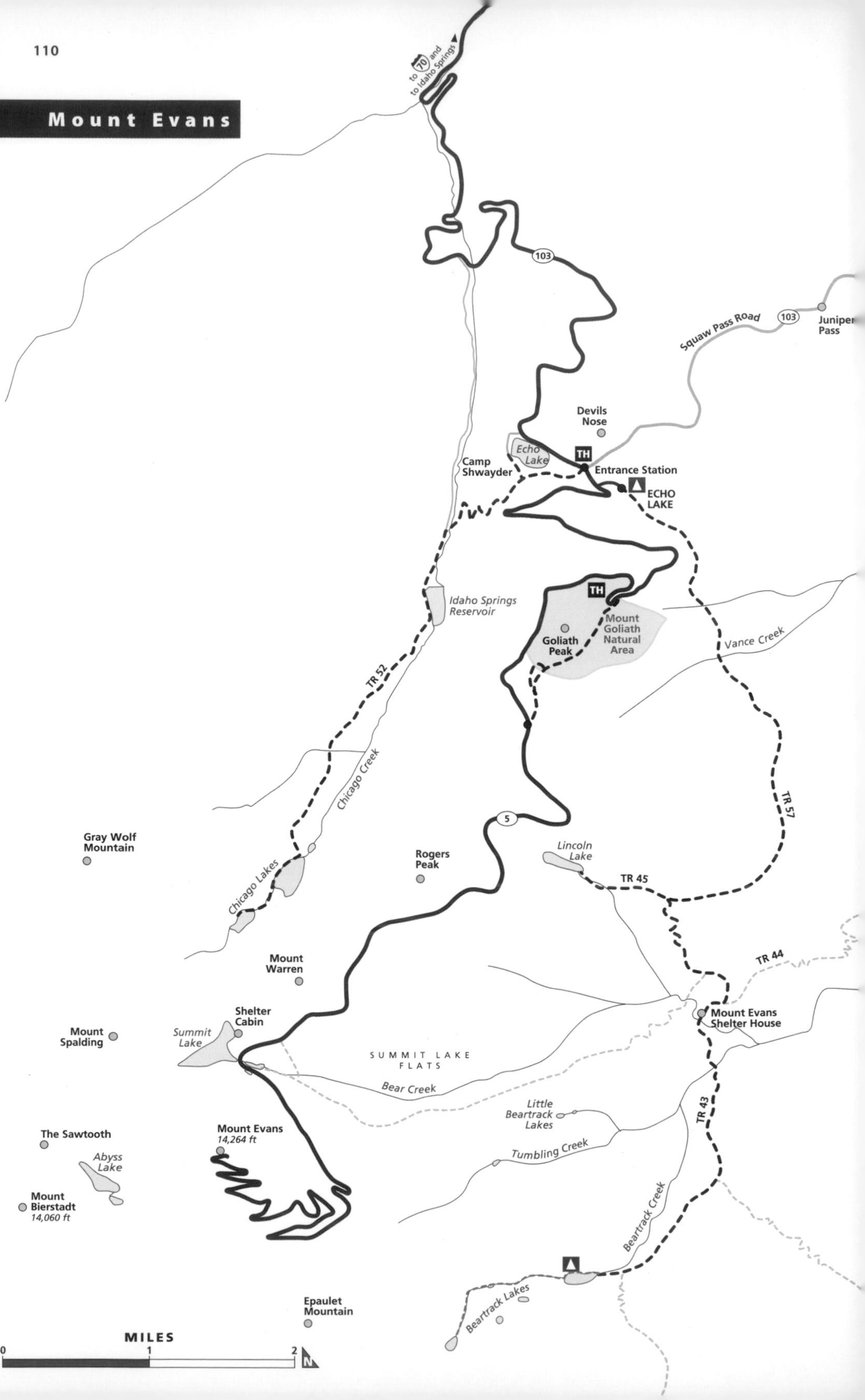

to 70 and to Idaho Springs

103

Squaw Pass Road 103 Juniper Pass

Devils Nose

Echo Lake

TH

Camp Shwayder

Entrance Station

ECHO LAKE

Idaho Springs Reservoir

TH

Mount Goliath Natural Area

Goliath Peak

Vance Creek

TR 52

Chicago Creek

TR 57

Gray Wolf Mountain

Chicago Lakes

5

Rogers Peak

Lincoln Lake

TR 45

Mount Warren

TR 44

Shelter Cabin

Mount Evans Shelter House

Mount Spalding

Summit Lake

SUMMIT LAKE FLATS

Bear Creek

Little Beartrack Lakes

TR 43

The Sawtooth

Abyss Lake

Mount Evans 14,264 ft

Tumbling Creek

Mount Bierstadt 14,060 ft

Beartrack Creek

Epaulet Mountain

Beartrack Lakes

MILES

0   1   2   N

A young mountain goat on Mount Evans.

HIKES ALONG THE WAY **Chicago Lakes**

FEATURES: Two lakes with a good example of a glacial cirque behind them.

HOW TO GET THERE: Follow the Mount Evans Highway for about 13 miles from Idaho Springs to Echo Lake. The trail starts at the entrance to the campground.

HIKE DIFFICULTY: MODERATE: Moderate climb up a glacial valley to the lower lake; steep hike (350 feet in a quarter of a mile—a 26% grade) from there to the upper lake.

LENGTH: From the trailhead to the lower lake is 4 miles; the second lake is 0.25 mile farther.

Hike from Echo Lake on TR 52 past the Idaho Springs Reservoir to the two lakes at 11,400 feet and 11,750 feet, respectively, in a high glacial valley.

HIKES ALONG THE WAY **Lincoln Lake and Beartrack Lakes**

FEATURES: A series of high, remote lakes in the Mount Evans Wilderness.

HOW TO GET THERE: Follow the Mount Evans Highway for about 13 miles from Idaho Springs to Echo Lake, park, then follow TR 57 to the south. After a few miles, spur TR 45 veers right (west) to Lincoln Lake. Back on TR 57, about 0.5 mile farther, a short jog takes you onto TR 44 for a short distance; from here, continue on TR 43 for another couple of miles south to Lower Beartrack Lake.

HIKE DIFFICULTY: MODERATE TO STRENUOUS: The trail climbs slowly through heavily forested slopes, only breaking out above the trees at the lakes.

LENGTH: From Echo Lake to Lincoln Lake is 7 miles; from Lincoln Lake to Lower Beartrack Lake is 3 miles; from Lower Beartrack Lake to Upper Beartrack Lake is 3 miles; from Echo Lake to Beartrack Lakes is 13 miles.

A string of lakes in a remote corner of the wilderness, Beartrack Lakes makes a good backpacking destination.

GUANELLA PASS

LOCATION: 40 miles west of Denver and about 12 miles south of Georgetown.

HIGHLIGHTS: This north-south pass crosses over the tundra at its 11,669-foot summit and is the start of several good hikes.

ACCESS: Though nominally graded and passable for passenger cars, this erratic and potholed dirt road is best driven in a high-clearance vehicle. With work having started in 2004, the road is being reconstructed and rehabilitated. The project is expected to be complete by 2006; expect weekday delays.

LENGTH: The drive between Georgetown and Grant is 24 miles.

MAPS: Arapaho National Forest on the north side, Pike National Forest on the south side.

HOW TO GET THERE: From Georgetown, the Guanella Pass road (CR 381/FR 381) starts at the southwest edge of town. From the south, at the town of Grant on US 285, head north on the pass road (here, FR 118).

Mount Evans from the Guanella Pass road.

Originally buffalo used this low spot among the mountain peaks to cross between South Park and the Clear Creek valley. Today's pass is named for Byron Guanella, a county commissioner who had championed building the road over the pass.

Tundra trails from the summit of Guanella Pass lead in many directions. Trails to the east lead into the Mount Evans Wilderness, with hikes to Mount Bierstadt (14,060 feet) and Mount Evans (14,264 feet). The top of the pass is one of the best places in the state for viewing ptarmigan. Also watch for bighorn sheep, mountain goats, and elk on open meadows. On a hillside west of the road, about 2.5 miles down the south side of the pass and about 1 mile below Duck Lake, are the open slopes of the former Geneva Basin ski area.

NEARBY STOPS **Georgetown Bighorn Viewing Site**

FEATURES: Bighorn sheep gather on the hillsides on the north side of I-70.

HOW TO GET THERE: From I-70 Exit 228 at Georgetown, follow the brown binocular signs to the wildlife viewing area, 1 mile east on Alvarado Road.

Bighorn sheep may be seen in this vicinity at almost any time of the year, but sightings are more frequent in the late fall, winter, and early spring, when the sheep have left the high peaks because of the weather. The herd numbers about 150 to 200 animals. Sheep are often sighted at other locations around Idaho Springs and Georgetown, including the junction of US 6 and CO 119, the slopes along I-70 between the two towns, and particularly the slopes near the junction of I-70 and US 40.

Some bighorn sheep have identifying eartags as part of herd management.

Silver Dollar Lake

FEATURES: An attractive lake in a high alpine basin with sweeping views.

HOW TO GET THERE: The trailhead for Silver Dollar Lake (11,950 feet) is about 0.5 mile up a rough dirt road to Naylor Lake (private property) that goes to the west about 1.5 miles below the summit on the north side of Guanella Pass. A high-clearance vehicle is preferable to reach the trailhead parking. Alternatively, park at the turnoff on the Guanella Pass road and hike the entire distance to the lake.

HIKE DIFFICULTY: EASY TO MODERATE: Steep but short hike along a former sheep trail.

LENGTH: 1.5 miles from the trailhead to Silver Dollar Lake.

The trail climbs up through the evergreen forest to the lake, which is on a shelf above treeline. About 0.5 mile farther on, at 12,080 feet, is Murray Lake, some half the size of Silver Dollar Lake.

Square Top Lakes

FEATURES: Two scenic tundra lakes in a shallow bowl at 12,110 feet.

HOW TO GET THERE: The trail to the lakes starts from FR 381/118, just south of the summit of Guanella Pass.

HIKE DIFFICULTY: EASY TO MODERATE: Relatively flat with a slight final climb up to the lakes.

LENGTH: Under 2 miles from the trailhead to the first lake; the second is about 0.25 mile and 250 vertical feet above the first on a tundra shelf to the northwest.

The trail initially goes slightly downhill into a stretch that may be boggy in early summer, then climbs to the depression that holds the lakes. The trail is entirely above treeline, which allows good views back at Mount Evans and Mount Bierstadt.

Abyss Lake

FEATURES: A high alpine lake in a glacial basin between Mount Bierstadt and Mount Evans.

HOW TO GET THERE: The trail to Abyss Lake starts from the summit of Guanella Pass. Follow TR 603 until it intersects TR 602 in about 4.5 miles. Turn north on TR 602 for another 4 miles to the lake.

HIKE DIFFICULTY: STRENUOUS: Long hike with steep sections on the final approach to the lake.

LENGTH: 8.5 miles from the trailhead to the lake.

This attractive lake lies at 12,500 feet, nestled high above treeline between Mount Evans and Mount Bierstadt, right under The Sawtooth. Strong hikers may hike down from the summit of Mount Evans to the lake, or climb from the lake up to the summit of Evans.

Guanella Pass

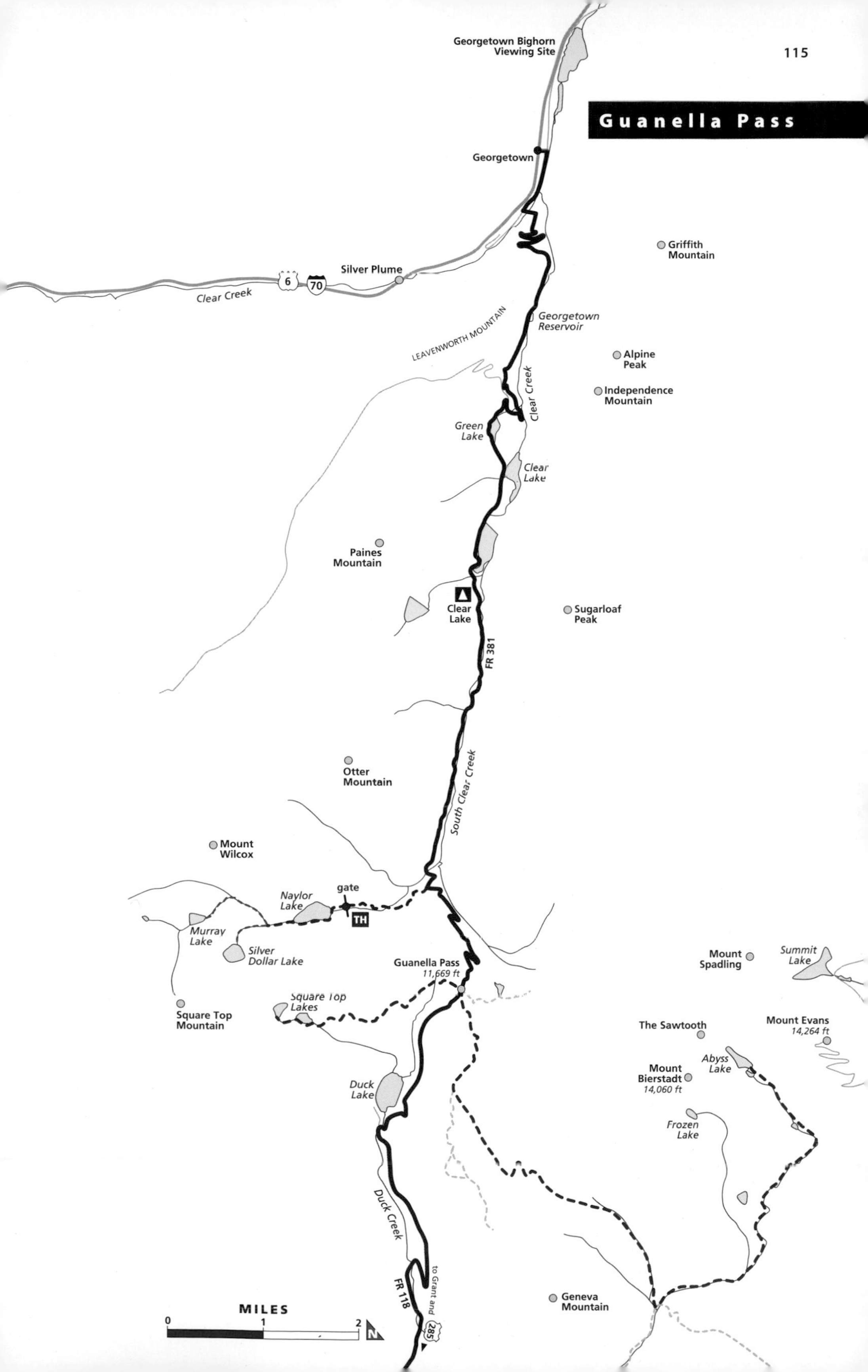

Georgetown Bighorn Viewing Site

Georgetown

Griffith Mountain

Silver Plume

6 70

Clear Creek

LEAVENWORTH MOUNTAIN

Georgetown Reservoir

Clear Creek

Alpine Peak

Independence Mountain

Green Lake

Clear Lake

Paines Mountain

Clear Lake

Sugarloaf Peak

FR 381

South Clear Creek

Otter Mountain

Mount Wilcox

Naylor Lake

gate

TH

Murray Lake

Silver Dollar Lake

Square Top Lakes

Guanella Pass 11,669 ft

Mount Spadling

Summit Lake

Square Top Mountain

The Sawtooth

Mount Evans 14,264 ft

Duck Lake

Mount Bierstadt 14,060 ft

Abyss Lake

Frozen Lake

Duck Creek

FR 118

to Grant and 285

Geneva Mountain

MILES

0   1   2

N

BOREAS PASS

LOCATION: About 10 miles southeast of Breckenridge.

HIGHLIGHTS: This picturesque route follows an old railroad bed, and historic railroad structures and a visitor center are on the summit. This drive is particularly attractive in mid- and late September when the aspen trees display their colors.

ACCESS: The dirt road between Como and Breckenridge is generally suitable for passenger cars with good clearance, but there may be difficult stretches in wet weather.

LENGTH: It is about 10 miles from Breckenridge to the top of the pass and then another 10 miles down to Como on the south side.

MAPS: Arapaho National Forest on the north side, Pike National Forest on the south side.

HOW TO GET THERE: From CO 9 in Breckenridge, turn east onto the Boreas Pass Road (CR 10) on the south side of town and follow the road across the pass. If traveling from the south side of the pass, take US 285 southwest from Denver to Como. Drive through Como and head northwest on CR 33 for about 3.5 miles to a junction in the road that was the railroad stop of Peabodys. At the junction make a right turn and continue along CR 33 to the top of the pass.

The restored section house at the summit of Boreas Pass is now a Forest Service visitor center.

Boreas Pass is a popular driving and bicycling route out of Breckenridge in summer. In winter the road is closed to traffic and heavily used as a cross-country ski trail. From November to May, the restored section house at the summit is available for overnight rental by skiers. Across the road from the section house stand a couple of historical relics: a railroad car and the foundation of the stone engine house. All around on the hillsides are tree stumps that remain from when railroad workers cut wood to construct the buildings at Boreas and to fuel fires in winter. Conservation attitudes were different in the 1880s than today; unfortunately, some of the felled trees were centuries-old bristlecone pines.

The Pass Now Known as Boreas

Long before it became a railroad route, this tundra pass was a Ute Indian trail. As a wagon road, it was used in the 1860s by white settlers in the Blue River Valley and by prospectors traveling from South Park to the mines around Breckenridge. Dubbed Breckinridge Pass (note the original spelling, after John Breckinridge, vice president under James Buchanan) by white men, the 11,481-foot pass was later renamed, more aptly, after the god of the north wind.

In 1880, construction began over the pass on a branch of the Denver, South Park & Pacific Railroad between Como and Breckenridge, with its terminus in Leadville. The Como–Leadville branch extended 64 miles and cost $1.1 million. (For the other highlight of the railroad, the Alpine Tunnel, see p. 173.) By 1882, the tracks had crossed the pass, and the community of Boreas sprang up atop the summit to serve railroad crews and travelers. Boreas consisted of a station, a telegraph office, a stone engine house, an engine turntable, and a bunkhouse. It's been estimated

Bakers Tank supplied water for trains.

that 150 people lived there year-round; its post office, in operation from 1896 to 1906, was the highest in the United States. Winters were so severe on top of the pass that the railroad built 10 snowsheds (destroyed by fire in 1934) to protect the track.

The rail route was abandoned in 1937, the railroad was dismantled in 1938, and in 1952 the railbed was converted into a road. In 1996, the old section house at the summit was restored as a Forest Service visitor center, complete with historical displays. In Como, which had been a major division point for the railroad, the old roundhouse still stands. Used for housing and repairing engines, it is in the slow process of being restored.

When starting or leaving the road at Breckenridge, stop to see the rotary snowplow interpretive display. Plows like these ran up and down the tracks constantly in winter to keep them free from snow. About 6 miles up the road from Breckenridge, on the way to the summit, you will also pass the restored Bakers Tank, a huge water tank that was used to supply thirsty steam engines climbing the pass. When full, the tank held 9,305 gallons of water. It was moved to this location from the Alpine Tunnel branch of the railroad in 1910 when the size of the original tank proved to be inadequate.

On the south side of the pass, amid panoramic views of South Park and Mount Silverheels to the west, stop for a few moments at the marked Davis Overlook to enjoy the view out into South Park and the Tarryall Creek drainage. Below in the valley are huge piles of rock and gravel left over from placer gold mining with dredges, which operated around the towns of Tarryall and Hamilton in the 1860s. Tarryall prospectors were so protective of their mining claims that late arrivals called the town "Grab-all." As a sarcastic poke at these Tarryall prospectors, frustrated would-be miners moved 10 miles or so farther west and founded a town that they named Fair Play Camp, to emphasize fair play for fellow newcomers. This camp eventually became the modern town of Fairplay.

HIKES ALONG THE WAY

Those wanting to experience the tundra close-up can choose among several short hikes from the summit of the pass. From the Forest Service gate, a short hike leads west for about 0.5 mile to the top of Hoosier Ridge along the Continental Divide. Or hike to the northeast up aptly named Bald Mountain: As there is no designated trail on this route, the climb involves bushwhacking east from the pass summit to a low spot (12,815 feet) on the north-south ridge on the skyline, followed by a steep hike to the north up a rocky ridge to the 13,684-foot summit, for a total distance of about 2.5 miles.

The old engine roundhouse of the Denver, South Park & Pacific Railroad still stands at Como.

ckenridge

enridge

Goose
Pasture
Tarn

Blue River

9

Indiana Creek

Boreas Pass Road

B A L D

M O U N T A I N

13,684 ft

13,634 ft

Continental Divide

French
Pass

CR 10

TH

12,159 ft

Dyersville
townsite

Warriors
Mark Mine

12,815 ft

Boreas Pass
11,481 ft

Boreas
Mountain

12,029 ft

R I D G E

H O O S I E R

12,231 ft

Continental Divide

CR 33

North Tarryall Creek

Tarryall Creek

TR 614

South Tarryall Creek

FR 405

TH

Peabodys
townsite

285

to Como

to Como

Mount
Silverheels
13,822 ft

Little Baldy
Mountain

MILES

0   1   2

N

HIKES ALONG THE WAY   Dyersville

FEATURES: Stroll around an old townsite, then hike up to the Continental Divide.

HOW TO GET THERE: About 1.5 miles north of the summit of Boreas Pass, an old road turns back south and descends on a steep grade. After about 0.5 mile, with the trail swinging to the northwest, it takes a hairpin turn back to the south and shortly leads to the site of the former settlement of Dyersville in the trees.

HIKE DIFFICULTY: EASY TO MODERATE: Walk downhill to Dyersville for an elevation loss of about 300 feet, then climb steeply uphill to the ridge behind it for an elevation gain of 1,000 feet in a mile.

LENGTH: About 2 miles from the Boreas Pass road to the top of the divide.

The hike from the Boreas Pass road is gently forested to the site of the ghost town of Dyersville, founded in the 1880s. The town was named for Methodist minister Father John Dyer, who preached at small towns and mining camps in the Fairplay area. He also carried mail over Mosquito Pass. In winter, he traveled on Norwegian snowshoes (what we now call skis). Often he traveled at night, when frozen conditions made his journey easier. Dyer staked a mining claim here, and others moved in and settled along Indiana Creek which formed Dyersville. The trail goes south past the townsite for 1 mile as it climbs steeply up to the Continental Divide at above 12,000 feet on Hoosier Ridge, west of the summit of Boreas Pass.

HIKES ALONG THE WAY   Mount Silverheels

FEATURES: A hardy climb on the tundra to stunning views of South Park and the mountains behind Fairplay to the west.

HOW TO GET THERE: Follow the page 116 description of the Boreas Pass road (CR 33) from the south to reach Peabodys. Instead of turning up the hill on CR 33, keep straight on FR 405. After about 1.5 miles the road splits again. The road ahead is FR 406 to the Selkirk Campground. Turn left and stay on FR 405 for another 0.25 mile to a turnoff to the left. Walk across Silverheels Creek (footbridge) up this road for a couple hundred yards and find the trailhead for TR 614, which is on national forest land on the left. After about 2.5 miles the trail crosses a saddle (11,300 feet) between Mount Silverheels and Little Baldy Mountain. At this point, leave TR 614, which goes down into the Trout Creek drainage below, and follow the ridge about 2.5 miles to the top of Mount Silverheels.

HIKE DIFFICULTY: MODERATE TO STRENUOUS: A steady, steep climb of about 3,700 feet in 5 miles.

LENGTH: From the trailhead to the summit of Mount Silverheels is 5 miles.

At 13,822 feet, Mount Silverheels juts against the western skyline as you descend the south side of Boreas Pass. Look for Rocky Mountain bighorn sheep as you hike. The mountain was named for a dance-hall girl known for her slippers' silver heels. When a smallpox epidemic hit the town of Buckskin Joe, she helped nurse sick miners back to health. Supposedly she got the disease and left the area, her beautiful face ravaged by scars. As thanks, grateful miners gave her name to the most beautiful mountain in the area.

INDEPENDENCE PASS

LOCATION: About 16 miles southwest of Leadville and 21 miles east of Aspen.

HIGHLIGHTS: This scenic drive across the Continental Divide crosses a lovely stretch of tundra with good mountain views.

ACCESS: CO 82 is a two-lane, paved highway. Vehicles over 35 feet in length are not permitted because of tight switchbacks as the pass approaches the summit and because of several narrow—essentially one-lane—sections on the west side. The road is closed in winter.

LENGTH: From the junction of CO 82 and US 24 to Aspen is 44 miles. From US 24 to the summit is 23 miles; from the summit down to Aspen is 21 miles.

MAPS: San Isabel National Forest on the east side; White River National Forest on the west side.

HOW TO GET THERE: From US 24 to the east, about halfway between Buena Vista and Leadville, turn west onto CO 82. Follow the highway through the historic village of Twin Lakes and across the pass to Aspen.

Linkins Lake sits on a high shelf to the west of Independence Pass.

Named for the old mine and town of Independence on the west descent from the summit toward Aspen, Independence Pass was also called variously Hunter's Pass and Ute Pass, and Aspen was originally Ute City. Its current name dates from the founding of the town of Independence on July 4, 1879. For a time the route was a toll road, and remnants of the old toll gate, the foun-

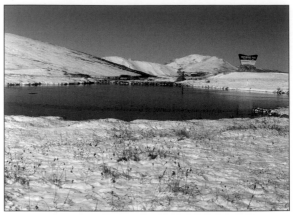

The summit of Independence Pass after a September snow.

dation of the gatekeeper's house, and a section of the original steep pass road remain on the uphill side of CO 82 about 3 miles below the summit on the east side. After gold was found near Aspen, the pass route became popular with prospectors pouring into the Roaring Fork Valley to find their fortunes. Its popularity waned after 1887, when the railroad reached Aspen through the Hagerman Tunnel (see 4WD Trips, p. 162), making travel to Aspen easier and cheaper.

Those not used to mountain driving are sure to find the switchbacks on both sides of this pass to be thrilling. Views at the impressive 12,095-foot summit usually include lingering snowbanks and many wildflowers. Stop for a short tundra walk on the nature trail to an overlook with interpretive signs.

For experienced hikers, an old, closed-off jeep road starts to the south at the parking area at the summit, then turns into a faint trail that continues up the ridge for 3 miles to an unnamed 13,020-foot peak on the Continental Divide. On the north side of the road, a strenuous, faint trail heads across the tundra and up the ridge for 2.5 miles to Twining Peak (13,711 feet) with fine views in all directions.

STOPS NOT TO MISS Independence

FEATURES: A visit to this historic and picturesque ghost town at the edge of an alpine meadow is well worth the time.

HOW TO GET THERE: Independence is located beside CO 82, about 4 miles west of the summit of the pass.

Founded on Independence Day, 1879, to support various mines nearby, this ghost town is partially restored and provides an intriguing glimpse into local history. At one time, more than 2,000 people are said to have lived in this community, which, like many of the early mining towns, supported several gambling halls and saloons. The boom was short-lived, however, and by 1888 most of the inhabitants had moved away.

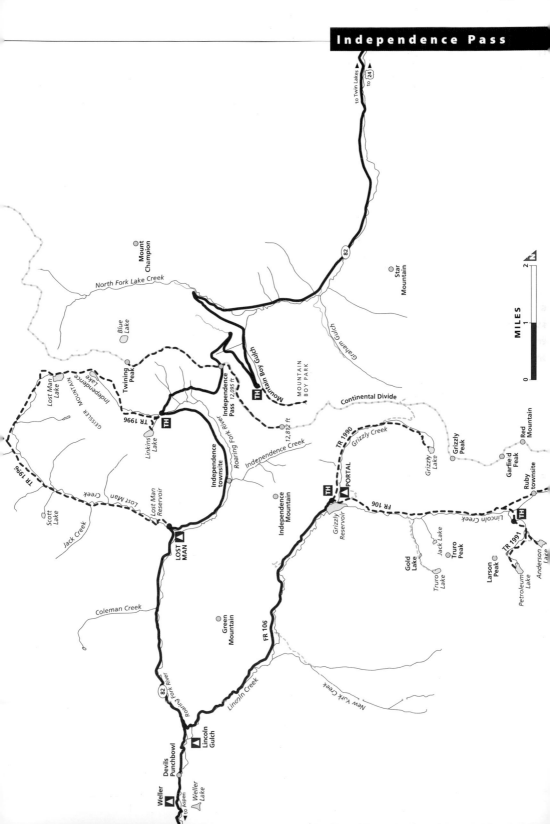

to Twin Lakes
to 24

82

Mount Champion

Star Mountain

North Fork Lake Creek

Blue Lake

Twining Peak

Mountain Boy Gulch

MOUNTAIN BOY PARK

Graham Gulch

Lost Man Lake

Independence Lake

GEISSLER MOUNTAIN

Independence Pass 12,095 ft

TH

Continental Divide

Red Mountain

TR 1996

Linkins Lake

TH

Independence townsite

Roaring Fork River

Independence 12,821 ft

Independence Creek

TR 1990

Grizzly Creek

Grizzly Peak

Grizzly Lake

Garfield Peak

Ruby townsite

TH

Scott Lake

TR 1996

Lost Man Creek

Jack Creek

Lost Man Reservoir

Independence Mountain

TH

PORTAL

Grizzly Reservoir

FR 106

Lincoln Creek

TR 1991

Anderson Lake

LOST MAN

Gold Lake

Jack Lake

Truro Peak

Larson Peak

Petroleum Lake

Coleman Creek

Green Mountain

FR 106

Truro Lake

82

Roaring Fork River

Lincoln Creek

New York Creek

Devils Punchbowl

Lincoln Gulch

Weller

Weller Lake

to Aspen

MILES

0   1   2

HIKES ALONG THE WAY   Linkins Lake & the Lost Man Loop

FEATURES: A short, steep hike leads to scenic Linkins Lake on the tundra at 12,008 feet, with an extended loop shuttle-hike option.

HOW TO GET THERE: From the summit of Independence Pass, drive about 2 miles west to the bottom of the first large switchback. The trailhead is on the north side of the road. After starting up the trail a few hundred yards, watch for a steep fork up the hill to the left that climbs to Linkins Lake. The trail that follows straight ahead beside the creek is TR 1996, which goes to the head of the valley, passing first Independence Lake then Lost Man Lake at 12,490 feet, and then climbs to South Fork Pass in the saddle above the lakes.

HIKE DIFFICULTY: MODERATE TO STRENUOUS: The effort that is required depends on how far and to which lake you choose to hike.

LENGTH: From the trailhead on CO 82 it is about 0.5 mile up a steep slope to Linkins Lake. From CO 82 to Lost Man Lake is about 2.5 miles. To South Fork Pass is about 2 more miles.

Picturesque views of the valley below and of Independence Pass above punctuate the hike to Linkins Lake in the Hunter-Fryingpan Wilderness. The adventurous with a vehicle shuttle can continue by making a loop hike, past Lost Man Lake and over South Fork Pass. Stay on TR 1996 down the Lost Man Creek drainage to Lost Man Reservoir, which returns you to CO 82 on the west side of Geissler Mountain. The entire loop on TR 1996 to Lost Man Reservoir is about 8 miles.

HIKES ALONG THE WAY   Mountain Boy Gulch

FEATURES: The trail through this alpine valley passes through fields of summer wildflowers and ends with scenic views.

HOW TO GET THERE: Look for a parking pullout about 2 miles east of the summit of Independence Pass at the second large hairpin switchback, just below treeline. The hike is up the valley across the creek. The trail starts from the highway and goes initially downhill to where it crosses the creek.

HIKE DIFFICULTY: MODERATE: This hike is not difficult but starts at treeline and climbs to above 12,500 feet in 1.5 miles, for an elevation gain of 1,200 feet.

LENGTH: From the highway to the top of the gulch is 1.5 miles.

A faint trail on the south side of the creek, across from the road, parallels the highway at the edge of the timber. Access to the trail from the highway may be difficult to find. If you can't find the faint trail across the creek, bushwhack across to intersect the trail farther up the valley. As the trail climbs toward treeline, it joins an old, well-defined wagon road. The road ends at the ruins of miners' shacks about halfway up the gulch; from here, the narrow hiking trail resumes to the top of an unnamed saddle, then curves to the south. From the saddle, options are to climb to the top of the hill to the east, where you can see the relics of old snow fences and enjoy the view, or continue on a faint trail down into the gulch ahead. The latter trail leads steeply downhill, which means an uphill climb on the way back.

Grizzly Lake

FEATURES: High in a tundra bowl below the Continental Divide, this alpine lake is often still covered with ice in July.

HOW TO GET THERE: About 10 miles west of Independence Pass, turn south off CO 82 at the sign for the Lincoln Gulch Campground (9.5 miles east from Aspen) and drive up the Lincoln Gulch Road (FR 106) for 6 miles to Grizzly Reservoir. Park passenger cars at the trailhead, opposite the reservoir caretaker's house, or by Portal Campground, a few hundred yards farther on.

HIKE DIFFICULTY: MODERATE TO STRENUOUS: Fairly level walking alternates with some switchbacks to make this a fairly strenuous but exhilarating hike.

LENGTH: From Grizzly Reservoir to Grizzly Lake is 3.5 miles.

The first part of this hike switchbacks up through the timber on TR 1990, then follows Grizzly Creek for 2 miles up a broad, open valley. At the head of the valley, the trail ascends several tundra shelves before climbing steeply up a series of switchbacks and cresting a final, small saddle beside the lake. Enthusiastic skiers hike up the steep slope behind the lake in summer to ski down the snowfield.

Petroleum Lake

FEATURES: This trail passes through fields of alpine flowers in the summer on its way to the tundra and Petroleum Lake at 12,300 feet.

HOW TO GET THERE: About 10 miles west of Independence Pass, turn south off CO 82 at the sign for the Lincoln Gulch Campground (9.5 miles east from Aspen) and drive up the Lincoln Gulch Road (FR 106) for 6 miles to Grizzly Reservoir. Past this point, you will need a high-clearance vehicle to access the trailhead to Petroleum Lake; park passenger cars by Portal Campground. High-clearance vehicles can continue another 3.5 miles up FR 106 to an unmarked fork in the road just before the ghost town of Ruby. Hike a few hundred yards down the road to the right (west) and cross Lincoln Creek. Continue on the road into the trees, walk around the locked Forest Service gate, and follow the trail, which is an old jeep road at this point, to the lake.

HIKE DIFFICULTY: MODERATE TO STRENUOUS: Not difficult if you start at the trailhead, but adds significant distance if you park at Grizzly Reservoir.

LENGTH: From CO 82 to Grizzly Reservoir is 6 miles; the trailhead at the Lincoln Creek crossing is another 3.5 miles; from the trailhead to Petroleum Lake is 2 miles.

Even if you don't drive all the way to the trailhead, the hike up this forested alpine valley is enjoyable. Look for the remains of a waterwheel hidden in the bushes next to the creek alongside the road at the site of a former sawmill about 3 miles from Grizzly Reservoir, about 0.25 mile before the crossing of Lincoln Creek.

The first segment of TR 1991 to Petroleum Lake is an old jeep road that climbs to Anderson Lake (11,840 feet) at treeline. This lake is usually green with glacial flour. Above Anderson Lake, the jeep road changes into a hiking trail that continues east about 1 mile to the shelf above, circles past several unnamed tarns, and ends at beautiful Petroleum Lake, high on the tundra.

Tundra Close-up

The tiny blue flower almost touching the tip of my nose fluttered momentarily in the breeze, then was still. Seizing this moment of repose, I gently pushed the shutter release button on my camera, and the image of the alpine forget-me-not bloom was frozen in time on my film. I pushed myself up on my elbows and rose stiffly to my knees.

From ground level, the tundra looks different. The cushion plants of the alpine zone are so small that lying on your stomach is the best way to absorb their detail. As I stood upright, the force of the wind strengthened. My right ear, which had begun to feel normal while I was lying down and out of the wind, started to numb again in the cold. Just as I had been warmer photographing plants at their level, the cushion plants of the open, windswept ridges hug the ground to stay below the strongest of the wind.

It was late June on the tundra, and I was trying to photograph alpine wildflowers at their peak. The growing season is so short that these plants bloom for only a few weeks before the cold of approaching winter turns them brown again until the following spring.

Though the sun was out when I parked at the top of Cottonwood Pass, the early morning wind on the summit was bitter. As I hiked along the trail following the alpine ridge to the south, I could feel the icy blast leaking under the hood of my coat and around the edges of my wool hat to nip at my cheeks and ears. It was making my pant legs flutter and slap.

Ahead of me the ground looked barren and bare, punctuated by outcroppings of gray, dull

A good way to photograph and observe tundra flowers is on your elbows and knees!

rock pushing through bright patches of green grass. A few lingering snowbanks still clung to the ridge, straggling down from the crest like white icing dripping from a cake. Crossing a flat, open spot, I found what I was looking for. The ground was dotted with clumps of tiny blue blossoms that contrasted sharply with the yellowish, sandy soil in which they grew.

Cushion plants grow with agonizing slowness. The plant I had just photographed was probably 15 or 20 years old but was mere inches in diameter. Many summers had gone by as it formed itself into the low-growing cushion shape that slowed the wind's vigor and allowed the sun to warm its interior.

Plants are not the only tundra life-forms that take advantage of the added warmth offered by staying close to the ground. As I was walking back toward the parking area and my jeep, a huge bumblebee, about an inch long, zoomed unsteadily past me, swaying precariously as gusts of wind buffeted it from side to side. About 15 feet ahead of me, it suddenly dropped out of my sight to the grass. Curious, I lengthened my pace, watching the ground to see what had happened to it. Had it been dashed out of the air by an extra gust of wind? How could it fly anyway in this cold?

But my fears were groundless; the bumblebee was all right. It was crawling through the grass, though not without a struggle. I knelt down to observe its progress. As I watched, it crawled toward a hole in the ground that was about an inch in diameter—perhaps an old vole burrow—and paused for a moment on the lip, then crawled headfirst down into the depths and vanished. I was captivated. I had read that these giant insects used the abandoned burrows of small tundra animals to protect themselves from the wind and cold, but I had never seen one entering its hiding place.

Though I waited and watched a little longer, wishing that my camera had been at the ready, the bee did not reappear. I straightened up into the wind and started back to my car, hunching my shoulders against the ever-present chill. It had been a good morning.

COTTONWOOD PASS

LOCATION: About 15 miles west of Buena Vista.

HIGHLIGHTS: Enjoy sweeping panoramic views of the tundra and towering mountains from the top of this pass on the Continental Divide.

ACCESS: A paved road leads to the summit on the east side, and a gravel road continues down the west side to Taylor Reservoir. The road is paved from the reservoir to Gunnison. The pass and the approach roads are closed in winter.

LENGTH: From Buena Vista to the summit of the pass is 20 miles. From Buena Vista to Taylor Park Reservoir is 33 miles, then it is an additional 35 miles from the reservoir to Gunnison.

MAPS: San Isabel National Forest on the east side; Gunnison National Forest on the west side.

HOW TO GET THERE: From the east, turn west at the traffic light in the center of Buena Vista on US 24 and follow paved CR/FR 306 west to the top of the pass. Either return by the same route or continue on to Gunnison. From the west, follow CR 209/FR 742 from Gunnison to Taylor Park Reservoir, then continue on CR/FR 209 to the summit of Cottonwood Pass.

A view west from the pass summit.

The spectacular scenery along this drive makes keeping your eyes on the road a challenge! Mountain goats are often visible on Jones Mountain, about 16 miles up on the east side of the pass. The summit of the pass, at 12,126 feet, offers several hiking options. Advanced hikers can head south from the parking area, staying above treeline along the crest of the Continental Divide on a very faint trail for 6 strenuous miles to the top of Mount Kreutzer (13,094 feet). On the north side of the road, across from the parking lot, TR 417 goes (steeply downhill!) into the Texas Creek basin.

This route, like many others, was originally an Indian trail over the mountains, since this pass was a relatively easy crossing. It was also popular because of the hot springs that lie at the east end of the pass. At one time, along with Taylor Pass at the north end of Taylor Park, this pass was a main supply route into Aspen, until the improved Independence Pass route took away much of the toll business after 1881. The road subsequently fell into disuse and became a rough 4WD road. It was not used for recreational travel until it was rebuilt in 1959 by the Forest Service as a direct way to reach Taylor Reservoir and Gunnison from the east.

This lake north of Cottonwood Pass is colored with suspended particles of glacial flour.

Cottonwood Pass

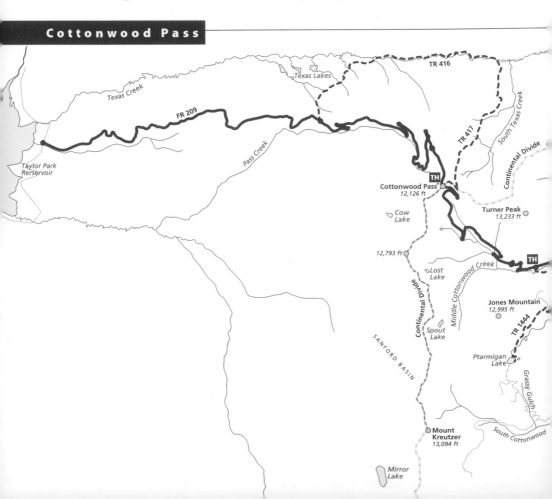

HIKES ALONG THE WAY **Browns Pass**

FEATURES: This hike up the Denny Creek valley is flanked by summer wildflowers and leads to excellent views from the 12,010-foot summit.

HOW TO GET THERE: The Denny Creek trailhead is on the right, 12 miles west of Buena Vista along CR/FR 306 to Cottonwood Pass. Also the Mount Yale trailhead.

HIKE DIFFICULTY: MODERATE: Not particularly difficult but a steady climb to the top of the pass.

LENGTH: From the trailhead to the top of the pass is 3.5 miles.

This hike passes through diverse mountain ecosystems before ending with incredible views of alpine valleys. The trail splits after about 1.25 miles: Mount Yale Trail goes to the right and Browns Pass Trail (TR 1442) continues straight ahead. Enjoy views of Texas Creek and the back of the Three Apostles from the top, then visit the collapsed ruins of historic Browns Cabin and the remains of a mine and mill about 0.5 mile below the pass on the north side. Advanced hikers can continue on the trail downhill to Magdalene Gulch, across the valley to the north. From the summit of Browns Pass, another trail leads up the ridge to the northeast, then drops to beautiful Kroenke Lake 2 miles away in the North Cottonwood Creek drainage.

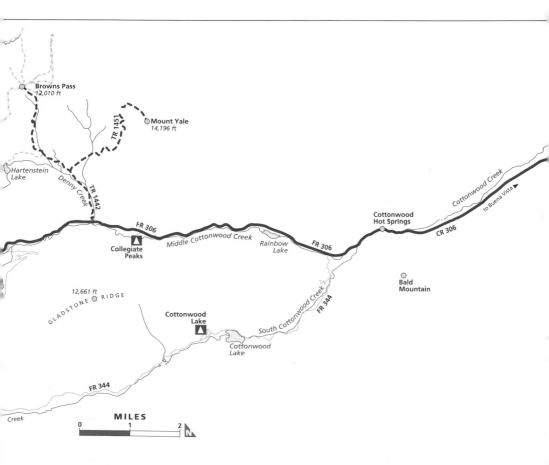

HIKES ALONG THE WAY Mount Yale

FEATURES: A climb up a 14,196-foot peak.

HOW TO GET THERE: The Denny Creek trailhead is located on the right (north), 12 miles west of Buena Vista along CR/FR 306 toward Cottonwood Pass.

HIKE DIFFICULTY: MODERATE TO STRENUOUS: Not particularly difficult, but rated for a high-altitude trail to the top of a fourteener.

LENGTH: From the trailhead on FR 306 to the summit is 4 miles.

Mounts Yale, Columbia, Harvard, Princeton, and Oxford form the backbone of the Collegiate Range. Not considered a challenge by mountain climbers, this pleasant hike to the summit of a fourteener is popular with families. Start on Browns Pass Trail (TR 1442) and hike for about 1.25 miles. Mount Yale Trail (TR 1451) splits off to the right and climbs steeply for another few miles to the summit. On the way down, be sure to stick to the trail you came up. Some climbers have died in falls when they attempted to pioneer shortcuts back to the trailhead, especially on the old trail that climbs up Denny Gulch, and found themselves on slopes too steep to negotiate with safety.

HIKES ALONG THE WAY Ptarmigan Lake & Jones Mountain

FEATURES: A large herd of mountain goats inhabits the Jones Mountain area, and bighorn sheep are often seen on the north side of the Cottonwood Pass road.

HOW TO GET THERE: From Buena Vista, follow paved CR/FR 306 toward Cottonwood Pass. Look for the trailhead for Ptarmigan Lake just off the road on your left (south) on a small loop about 14.5 miles west of Buena Vista.

HIKE DIFFICULTY: MODERATE: A steep initial stretch is followed by a flatter final approach to the lake.

LENGTH: Ptarmigan Lake is 3 miles from the trailhead.

The hike on TR 1444 first climbs steeply through the forest, then flattens out as it passes into the rocky cirque that holds Ptarmigan Lake (12,132 feet). The meadow area below the lake may be marshy in early summer—a prime habitat for wildflowers. Also watch for mountain goats on the high slopes of Jones Mountain to the west. Enthusiastic hikers can follow the trail past the lake to the top of the pass behind it. Just over the final ridge, the trail meets a rough jeep road (FR 349) that comes up Grassy Gulch from FR 344 past Cottonwood Lake, which is another way to access Ptarmigan Lake. From the junction of the road and trail, it is possible to hike east along Gladstone Ridge, which is a likely area for spotting mountain goats. Those who don't hike can use binoculars to spot mountain goats on Jones Mountain from the Cottonwood Pass road. Also be on the lookout for bighorn sheep on the north side of the road.

PIKES PEAK

LOCATION: 12 miles west of Colorado Springs.

HIGHLIGHTS: Scenic sections of tundra, wildlife, and sweeping views draw thousands of visitors each year to the accessible summit of one of the most famous mountains in America.

ACCESS: The first 10 miles of the road are paved, then a wide, graded, two-lane dirt road continues to the summit. The section of the road beyond Glen Cove to the summit usually closes in late fall when the snow becomes too deep to plow, but the road may be kept open as far as Glen Cove if weather and road conditions permit.

LENGTH: The driving distance from the tollgate to the summit is 19 miles.

MAPS: Pike National Forest

HOW TO GET THERE: From Colorado Springs, drive west up Ute Pass on US 24. When you reach the traffic light at Cascade, turn left and follow the signs for the Pikes Peak Toll Road and toll station.

Pikes Peak, one of America's most famous mountains, seen from the Rampart Range Road.

Join the thousands of annual visitors who either drive up the well-maintained toll road, ride to the summit on the cog railway, or hike up Barr Trail to the summit of Pikes Peak. Driving up the Pikes Peak Toll Road provides an excellent introduction to the high mountains. The 19-mile journey passes through the foothills, montane, and

Cog Railway car.

subalpine ecosystems before reaching the grand finale of the alpine zone at the summit. The east face of Pikes Peak is mostly rocky alpine bowls and provides a good example of weathering (see p. 37). The west side and back slopes of the mountain reveal open, rolling tundra ridges, covered in summer with wildflowers. Look for marmots, pikas, and bighorn sheep all over the mountain.

Stop at any of the numerous viewing pullouts and trailheads along the toll road, and give yourself time to explore a bit. Glen Cove, just below treeline at mile marker 13, has a gift shop and snacks, and offers ranger talks. At mile marker 17, Bighorn Sheep Overlook has outstanding views and promises a good chance to view these mountain dwellers. Look for sheep on the rocky areas and steep cliff faces to the north side of the road, and also scan the ridges and valleys to the west and south with binoculars. On a very clear day (which is unfortunately increasingly rare), it is possible to see New Mexico to the south, Kansas to the east, and Wyoming to the north from the top of Pikes Peak.

"Pikes Peak or Bust"

About 10 miles west of Colorado Springs, 14,110-foot Pikes Peak was first noted by Lieutenant Zebulon Pike during an exploratory expedition: He and three others attempted the summit in November 1806 but were turned back by deep snow. Pike named the mountain Grand Peak and estimated it to be 18,581 feet high, claiming that it could never be climbed. The first documented climb of Pikes Peak by Euro-Americans, however, occurred July 14, 1820, when Edwin James and two of his companions reached the summit. James was a botanist with Major Stephen H. Long's expedition, which was searching for the headwaters of the Platte River. The rallying cry "Pikes Peak or Bust" rang out among early gold seekers, who hoped to strike it rich in the Cripple Creek area. (Plenty of them went "bust.") By the 1850s, climbing Pikes Peak had become a popular pastime.

In the 1870s, the U.S. Army Signal Corps for a time operated a weather station on top of Pikes Peak. To combat boredom, one of the operators delighted in sending down tall tales to be printed in the local newspaper: snowdrifts covering the weather station, a sea serpent in Lake Moraine, a simmering volcano on top of the peak, voracious giant rats that ate everything in sight. Such stories caused a big sensation among news readers until further investigations were made.

The view from the top of Pikes Peak inspired Katharine Lee Bates, a professor of English at Wellesley College, to pen the poem "America the Beautiful" in July 1893. The words were later set to the music of a traditional hymn, which has remained among the best-loved unofficial anthems of the United States.

The Summit House offers snacks, a gift shop, and an oxygen bar for those feeling the altitude at 14,110 feet!

The exertion-free alternative for those averse to driving is to take the Manitou and Pikes Peak Cog Railway from Manitou Springs at the base of the mountain. Be sure to inquire about tickets in advance during the popular summer season. Families especially will enjoy taking in the views and leaving the navigation to others. Watch for bighorn sheep, which commonly graze alongside the tracks above treeline.

HIKES ALONG THE WAY Devils Playground

FEATURES: A shorter option to reach the summit of Pikes Peak.

HOW TO GET THERE: Pay the toll and drive up the Pikes Peak Toll Road; when you have ascended to just above the switchbacks, look for a large parking area to the right, down a short, steep section of unmarked side road. Park, then walk back and cross the road to a sign that marks the trail.

HIKE DIFFICULTY: MODERATE: Entirely above treeline, this hike removes much of the elevation gain by starting at the top of the switchbacks. You will still climb about 1,200 vertical feet to the summit.

LENGTH: Approximately 2.5 miles to the summit.

Hikers can follow this tundra trail to the summit; alternatively, they can walk to the southwest corner of the Devils Playground parking area and follow the traces of one of the early roads that now forms the top part of the trail from Crags Campground. Look for bighorn sheep in the open alpine meadows and on the ridges that extend to the south from the Devils Playground area.

OTHER NEARBY HIKES Crags Campground Trail

FEATURES: A west-side approach to Pikes Peak that climbs steeply to Devils Playground and the summit.

HOW TO GET THERE: From Divide on US 24, drive south on CO 67 toward Cripple Creek. After about 4 miles, turn left (east) onto FR 383, signed to Crags Campground, and drive about 3 miles on a gravel road. The trail up the peak starts at the far end of the campground, where there's an outhouse and trailhead parking.

HIKE DIFFICULTY: STRENUOUS: Elevation gain of about 3,000 feet to reach Devils Playground on the Pikes Peak Toll Road.

LENGTH: From Crags Campground to the summit is 7 miles.

This has become a popular trail for climbing Pikes Peak in recent years because it is not as long, or crowded, as Barr Trail. The trail ascends steeply up a bowl well above treeline on the west side of the mountain. Once you have reached Devils Playground, you will cross the Pikes Peak Toll Road, then make another strenuous climb to the summit.

Pikes Peak

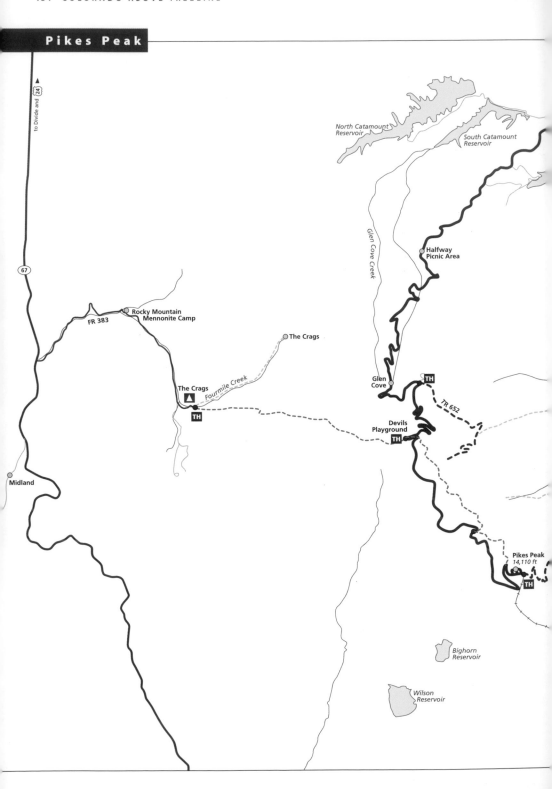

to Divide and (24)

(67)

FR 383

Rocky Mountain
Mennonite Camp

The Crags

The Crags

Fourmile Creek

TH

Midland

North Catamount
Reservoir

South Catamount
Reservoir

Glen Cove Creek

Halfway
Picnic Area

Glen
Cove

TH

TR 652

Devils
Playground

TH

Pikes Peak
14,110 ft

TH

Bighorn
Reservoir

Wilson
Reservoir

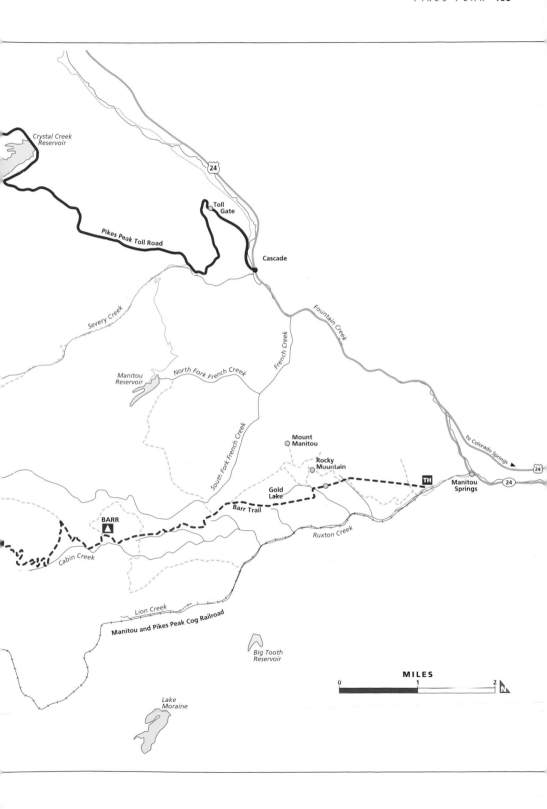

Crystal Creek
Reservoir

24

Toll
Gate

Pikes Peak Toll Road

Cascade

Severy Creek

Fountain Creek

French Creek

Manitou
Reservoir

North Fork French Creek

South Fork French Creek

Mount
Manitou

Rocky
Mountain

Gold
Lake

Barr Trail

TH

Manitou
Springs

to Colorado Springs

24

24

BARR

Ruxton Creek

Cabin Creek

Lion Creek

Manitou and Pikes Peak Cog Railroad

Big Tooth
Reservoir

MILES

0   1   2

Lake
Moraine

OTHER NEARBY HIKES **Barr Trail**

FEATURES: This popular hiking trail up Pikes Peak is long and steep in sections.

HOW TO GET THERE: From Colorado Springs, drive CO 24 west to Manitou Springs. In the center of town, turn left up Ruxton Avenue. Drive past the cog railway depot to an old brick building on the right (a historic hydroelectric station, still in use). Make a sharp right turn up the hill to the signed parking lot for Barr Trail (TR 620). The parking area is quite small and often fills up early in the day. Overflow parking is not in the railway parking lot but farther down Ruxton Avenue.

HIKE DIFFICULTY: STRENUOUS: A long hike, beginning with 4 steep miles.

LENGTH: From Manitou Springs to Barr Camp is 7 miles; the summit is 5 miles farther, for a total of 12 miles.

This 12-mile National Scenic Recreation Trail goes up the east side of the peak. The first 4 miles of trail climb steeply up the side of Rocky Mountain (often mistakenly called Mount Manitou, which is actually the next mountain peak to the northwest). Here the trail doubles back at a marked sign for the top of the old Mount Manitou Inclined Railway: Do not take this turnoff, but continue straight ahead for another half-mile or so to a three-way intersection. Take the trail uphill to the left, which continues to Barr Camp (the trail straight ahead eventually goes back down to Ute Pass). Backpackers can stay overnight at Barr Camp for a modest fee.

  Barr Trail hikers enjoy many options for summiting Pikes Peak—and evading the full 24-mile hiking route. For those disinclined to complete the entire epic hike, one alternative is to arrange to have a driver meet their party in a car on the summit, which halves the hike—still an energetic day. Others may be successful in hitching a ride back down from the summit with a sympathetic motorist. A third choice is to ride the cog railway either on the way up or back down, on a space-available basis. Be aware that unless you purchase a full-price ticket, there may not be any space available, given the popularity of the train at peak summer times; to use this option, be sure to stop by the train depot in Manitou Springs. Some hikers who have ridden the train up and walked the entire distance down feel that hiking downhill is easier on the lungs—but much harder on the legs.

OTHER NEARBY HIKES **Elk Park Trail**

FEATURES: Interesting mining ruins at the end, along with views of the lower reaches of Pikes Peak and the eastern plains, distinguish this hike.

HOW TO GET THERE: At Cascade on US 24, take the Pikes Peak Toll Road. The trailhead for the Elk Park Trail (TR 652), lies about 1 mile above Glen Cove, on the side road that leads to Elk Park Knoll. The turnoff is abrupt and just before a hairpin turn, so be careful as you approach, and turn off onto it.

HIKE DIFFICULTY: EASY TO MODERATE: This trail is one of those that hikers dread most: downhill on the way in, uphill on the way out! Elevation loss on the first part is about 1,000 feet, gaining back about 500 feet at the end, making for actually a short, steep uphill climb both ways.

LENGTH: From Elk Park to the Oil Creek Tunnel is about 2 miles.

The trail goes to the Cincinnati Mine and Oil Creek Tunnel in Ghost Town Hollow. Good views of Colorado Springs and Pikes Peak when you're above treeline.

GREENHORN MOUNTAIN

LOCATION: About 30 miles southwest of Pueblo.

HIGHLIGHTS: This isolated alpine wilderness area lies in the Wet Mountains, west of Pueblo.

ACCESS: Graded dirt road that becomes rougher at the end.

LENGTH: From the turnoff on CO 165 to the parking area at the end of the road is 24 miles.

MAPS: San Isabel National Forest

HOW TO GET THERE: Access the secluded road that climbs up Greenhorn from the north by taking CO 165, which crosses the heart of the Wet Mountains and links McKenzie Junction to Colorado City, southwest of Pueblo. From McKenzie Junction, travel south on CO 165 for about 12 miles; alternatively, from Exit 74 on I-25, travel west and north on CO 165 for about 27 miles. Either of these will put you at Fairview and the turnoff for Ophir Creek Campground onto FR 400, which lies at the bend of a tight hairpin turn. Take dirt FR 400 west and pass the campground; after about 1 mile, the road hairpins sharply back to the left, and you are on your way. After about 6.5 more miles, you will reach an open meadow, where the road splits. Take the left fork, headed southeast (the other road goes south to Gardner, in the Wet Mountain valley below). Follow FR 403 to the road's end on top of 12,347-foot Greenhorn Mountain.

North Peak from Blue Lakes.

T he road up Greenhorn originally extended into the large bowl below the peak on the west side. After the area was declared the Greenhorn Mountain Wilderness, the Forest Service dismantled the last 2 miles of the old road and re-vegetated it. If you should visit this little-known high-country wilderness, you are apt to find solitude. Your only company might be an elusive, resident band of Rocky Mountain bighorn sheep on the higher slopes, as well as mule deer, elk, black bear, and other creatures that thrive in this concentrated alpine zone.

HIKES ALONG THE WAY **Greenhorn Summit**

FEATURES: Though it makes for a fine drive, Greenhorn Mountain is best enjoyed by exploring on foot at the end of the road.

HOW TO GET THERE: The summit trail starts up the slope behind the parking lot at the end of FR 403.

HIKE DIFFICULTY: MODERATE: The summit trail climbs steeply, but a walk along the old road is an alternative, less strenuous option.

LENGTH: From the trailhead parking area to the summit is 2 miles.

It is not necessary to climb to the top of the mountain to enjoy an alpine experience on this trip. Though the last 2 miles of the old road are closed to motorized travel, the hike to the end of the road on the west side of the mountain is fairly gentle and is an excellent way to enjoy Greenhorn if time and effort allow. The road is wide and fairly level, making for easy walking.

HIKES ALONG THE WAY **Greenhorn Trail**

FEATURES: A steeper, much more invigorating way to reach the top of Greenhorn Mountain than driving up access road FR 403.

HOW TO GET THERE: Though this is the same mountain, this trail starts quite some distance away in the foothills town of Rye. To reach Rye, turn west off I-25 at Exit 74 south of Pueblo. Take CO 165 past Colorado City to the west side of Rye on CR 250 toward Cuerna Verde (Spanish for Greenhorn) Park. Before reaching the park, find TR 1316, the Greenhorn Trail.

HIKE DIFFICULTY: STRENUOUS: Steep, usually hot, and over 5,000 feet elevation gain.

LENGTH: From the trailhead to the summit of Greenhorn Mountain is 7 miles.

This trail leads up alongside North Peak, which forms the northernmost peak of the Greenhorn massif, and joins FR 403 for the final ascent of Greenhorn Peak, to the south. Pack in your water, because there are no significant water sources on this route.

Ophir Creek Road   Fairview

FR 400

FR 403

165

Saint Charles Peak   *11,784 ft*

Amethyst Creek

Saint Charles River

Lake Isabel

W E T

M O U N T A I N S

to Rye

Greenhorn Creek

Cuerna Verde Park

CR 250   TH

TR 1316

North Peak   *12,220 ft*

Blue Lakes

TH

Road Closed

TH

Greenhorn Mountain   *12,347 ft*

MILES

0   1   2

N

Black Bear Feast

Though winter had not yet arrived, it was definitely coming. The crisp fall morning on Greenhorn Mountain had a cool nip to the air that called for a heavy jacket. I was hiking along the old road that wound up onto the tundra from the primitive parking area at the edge of the trees. Far below me, on the floor of the Wet Mountain valley to the west, I could see patches of aspen gleaming gold in the mid-morning sunlight.

Though relatively unknown, this small wilderness area in the mountains southwest of Pueblo is rich in wildlife. Elk, deer, and a small band of resident Rocky Mountain bighorn sheep were the targets of my camera today. Ahead of me, the grassy slopes were disappointingly lacking in suitable photo subjects. I turned and scanned the rocky hillside above me: no luck there, either. No telltale brown bodies with white rumps that would give away the bighorn sheep.

Today's subjects may be flowers, I said to myself, though by this time of year, most of the tundra plants had already turned brown in preparation for the long winter above timberline. I had seen only a few Arctic gentian, one of the last flowers to bloom on the tundra each year. So it might be a day of few photographs.

I was approaching a lone clump of large bushes growing just below the trail when an unexpected rustling made me jump. I stopped and peered gingerly around the foliage. What I saw made me jump again. A black bear was pawing at the other side of the bushes. I am a poor judge of animal size, but I sensed this was a large bear. Some black bears can weigh up to 600 pounds, and I judged that this one was on the high end of the range.

And it was getting fatter by the minute.

Bears gain about one-third of their body weight in preparation for hibernation.

And if a bear weighs 500 pounds to begin with, that's a lot of berries. Bears eat up to 20,000 calories a day when preparing for their long winter sleep. Though we don't always follow our own advice, we humans should limit ourselves to some 1,500 to 2,000 calories a day on a healthy diet. At 20,000 calories a day, I would soon look like this porker in front of me.

While these thoughts all flashed through my head, I didn't linger to complete this mental review of bear science; bears bother me. Though I have inadvertently come across them on several occasions in the wild and have photographed them at close range, I also have a strong instinct for self-preservation. In this case, with this large a bear, my self-preservation was kicking into high gear. Hoping that it didn't smell me, I walked quietly to the uphill side of the road and tried to judge the wind direction. Usually when tracking large animals it is wise to walk into the wind, so that you can smell them before they smell you. However, an old tracker once told me that the exception is in bear country. In that case, you want to walk with the wind—and hope the bear smells you first and escapes before you run into it by mistake. Perhaps that's the basis for the old joke that you can tell grizzly bear scat from black bear scat because the grizzly's contains little bear-warning bells and smells of pepper spray.

Acutely aware of these factors, I retreated silently up the hill and made a wide berth around the bushes. It wasn't until I was several hundred yards up the hill that I decided it was safe to proceed back toward the road. When I felt that I was at a safe distance, I peered warily over the edge back at the bushes. The bear was still happily gorging itself on whatever it had found—probably some berries. I pulled out my field glasses, sat down on the side of the road, and watched.

The bear never even saw me.

Opposite: *Greenhorn Mountain and the old road around the base.*

4WD ADVENTURES

These trips should only be attempted by experienced drivers. Four-wheel drive (4WD) here refers to a high-clearance vehicle with off-road tires, a transfer case, and a low gear range—not to a generic truck or an all-wheel-drive vehicle. Note that the author cannot second-guess specific vehicle capability, individual driving ability, or risk; if you're not comfortable with road conditions, turn back or park and walk the rest of the way. Another option is to take a commercial jeep tour, leaving the navigation to seasoned operators.

Some trips listed here simply require a high-clearance vehicle, such as a pickup truck; these instances are noted under the Access heading for the trip. Options for the adventurous who lack a 4WD are to drive as far on the access road as you feel comfortable, then hike, ride a bicycle, or travel by ATV.

CONTENTS

Opposite: *4WD vehicles should stay on established roads to avoid damage to the tundra.*

ROLLINS PASS

Offering panoramic views and excellent subalpine and tundra wildflowers in summer, Rollins Pass crosses the Continental Divide just south of the Indian Peaks Wilderness. The mile-long stretch of closed road on the east side of the summit should be no obstacle; hikers can easily cross from one side to the other. Stretches of tundra and several historic railroad trestles highlight hikes on either side of the closure. Yankee Doodle Lake beside the east approach is worth a stop and makes a scenic picnic spot, with backdrops of flowers on the hillsides in the summer.

LOCATION: About 25 miles west of Boulder.

HIGHLIGHTS: Picturesque views, wildflower-strewn meadows, and railroad history distinguish this former Continental Divide crossing.

ACCESS: Much of this route, the old Moffat Road (FR 149), is suitable for any vehicle with adequate power and high clearance, given good road conditions, but proceed with caution. A 4WD or pickup truck makes the trip easier on the east side, but note that a mile of road just east of the summit is closed indefinitely, so the route can no longer be driven from start to finish. Access to the west side is via US 40 at Winter Park and to the east side via CO 119 at Rollinsville, between Central City and Nederland.

LENGTH: On the east side, it is about 15 miles from the east portal of the Moffat Tunnel to the summit. On the west side, the summit is about 14 miles from the turnoff on US 40.

MAPS: Arapaho National Forest on the east side; Roosevelt National Forest on the west side.

HOW TO GET THERE: Drive from Rollinsville on CO 119 and take CR 16 west to the Moffat Tunnel. Just before the tunnel, switchback up the road to the right (north) onto FR 149. The road about 1 mile below the summit on the east side is closed because of the unsafe Needles Eye Tunnel and Twin Trestles, but it is also possible to hike or ride a bicycle on these stretches. Access on the west side of Rollins Pass is also via FR 149, which heads east (right) for about 0.5 mile north of the little town of Winter Park on US 40.

One lonely telephone pole stands by the road to the summit.

HIKES ALONG THE WAY **Corona Lake**

FEATURES: An 8-acre lake nestled in a scenic alpine bowl at 11,185 feet.

HOW TO GET THERE: A little less than a mile below the summit of Rollins Pass on the west side, an old 4WD road heads northwest (left), just north of Pumphouse Lake. Follow the trail, bearing right, about 1 mile to Corona Lake.

HIKE DIFFICULTY: EASY TO MODERATE: The trail is slightly downhill and ends approximately 300 feet lower than the start, but is above 11,000 feet all the way.

LENGTH: About 1 mile from FR 149 to Corona Lake.

When the railroad was operating, Pumphouse Lake was the source of water for the railroad engines and for the station and hotel at Corona. In winter, the pump operator was often cut off from the rest of civilization for weeks at a time by snows that drifted 20 to 30 feet deep.

The Moffat Road

Rollins Pass was originally an Indian trail, then a wagon crossing in 1865 for Mormon pioneers traveling to Utah, and rebuilt in 1873 as a toll road into Middle Park. After its glory days as part of the historic Denver, Northwestern & Pacific Railway, the pass is now an auto road on the abandoned railbed. During its early days, Rollins Pass was called Boulder Pass and, once the railroad was established, Corona Pass, after the former railway station on the summit. At one time, Corona had a workers' bunkhouse, hotel, and restaurant.

The Denver, Northwestern & Pacific Railway started laying tracks across the mountains in 1903. The route started in Denver and was originally planned to go to Salt Lake City; however, the tracks never went farther than Craig, Colorado. This railroad was more popularly known as The Moffat Road after its founder, David Moffat, a Colorado banker. Moffat had hoped to build a 2.5-mile-long tunnel under the Continental Divide so the route could bypass winter storms; in the meantime, a "temporary" railroad track with 2 miles of snowsheds was constructed over 11,671-foot Rollins Pass.

An old railroad trestle on the west side of Rollins Pass.

Moffat died in 1911 without seeing his tunnel built. The railroad continued to run over the weather-beaten pass until 1927, when the Moffat Tunnel was finally completed, cutting travel time across the Divide from seven hours to twelve minutes. The Moffat Tunnel still carries trains under the mountains, including the Winter Park Ski Train from Denver's Union Station. In 1937, the railroad route over Rollins Pass was dismantled and made into an auto road.

Rollins Pass

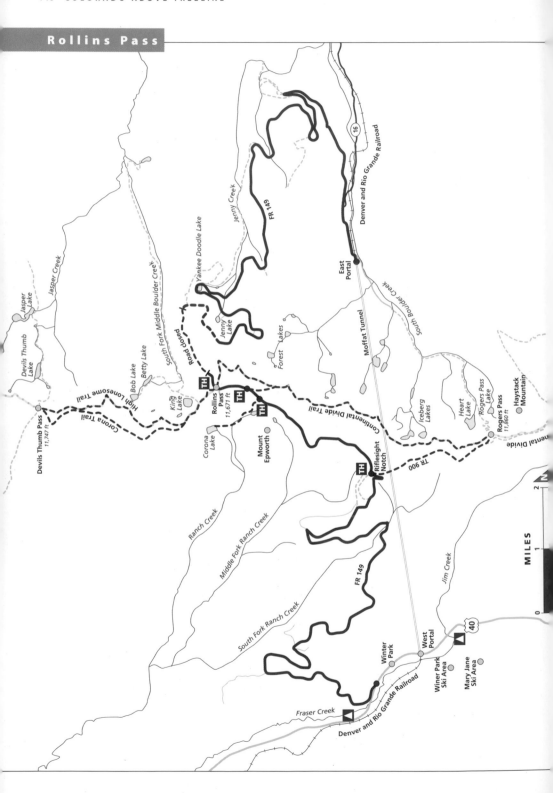

HIKES ALONG THE WAY   Corona Trail & Devils Thumb Pass

FEATURES: A hike near the crest of the Continental Divide to 11,747-foot Devils Thumb Pass, named for a curious rock formation that sticks up on the skyline.

HOW TO GET THERE: From the summit of Rollins Pass, follow the Continental Divide Trail (CDT; here called High Lonesome Trail) north. About 0.3 mile up, the trail splits; bear left for the less-improved Corona Trail, which parallels the CDT to the west along a contour just below the crest for a couple of miles. The trails rejoin to continue north to Devils Thumb Pass.

HIKE DIFFICULTY: MODERATE: The trail lies entirely above 11,600 feet. After an initial climb to the ridge to the north of Rollins Pass, the trail is relatively flat and stays at roughly the same elevation all the way.

LENGTH: From the summit of Rollins Pass to Devils Thumb Pass is about 3.5 miles.

Devils Thumb Pass was reportedly an early wagon crossing of the Continental Divide, and was even suggested as the location for a major highway; looking at it now, this seems amazing. The "thumb" is not obvious from the pass because of the angle of view from the summit but is sharply delineated on the skyline from Devils Thumb Lake below, on the east side of the pass.

HIKES ALONG THE WAY   Rogers Pass

FEATURES: Rewarding views on either side of the Continental Divide and of the four Arapaho Lakes below.

HOW TO GET THERE: Find a parking spot near the Riflesight Notch trestle and abandoned Tunnel No. 3 on the west side of the Continental Divide (3 miles south of Rollins Pass), about 10.5 miles up the road from US 40. An old, rough 4WD road (now TR 900) goes due south and climbs for about 2 miles to Rogers Pass. An alternative route from FR 149 is described below.

HIKE DIFFICULTY: MODERATE TO STRENUOUS: The first part of the hike climbs steeply up to the Continental Divide; from there, enjoy an easy walk along the crest; the alternate route is more strenuous.

LENGTH: From the Riflesight Notch trestle on TR 900 south to Rogers Pass is about 2 miles. From the turnoff on FR 149 to Rogers Pass is about 4.5 miles.

This 11,860-foot pass was named for Andrew Rogers, an early mayor of Central City, who proposed a tunnel under the Continental Divide at the pass that now bears his name. Those who want a more strenuous hike can take a longer route to the summit. Start by parking on the right (east) side of FR 149, 0.25 north of the left turnoff to Corona Lake (0.5 mile below the summit of Rollins Pass on the west side), to pick up the Continental Divide Trail (CDT) heading south up the ridge, then continue along the Divide crest to Rogers Pass. Within 0.75 mile from the road, you'll reach the high point of this stretch of the Divide at 12,072 feet. This approach adds another 2.5 miles or so to the hike.

WALDORF

LOCATION: About 6 miles southwest of Georgetown.

HIGHLIGHTS: A high alpine basin rich in history that offers many side trips onto the tundra from an old townsite.

ACCESS: Not too many years ago, passenger cars could make the trip to Waldorf; however, today several rough spots and rocks littered over the roadbed make this suited to 4WD. Alternatives are to hike or ride a bicycle.

LENGTH: The total drive from Georgetown to Waldorf is 9 miles; it is 2.5 miles from Georgetown to the turnoff from FR 381 onto FR 248.1, and then 5.5 more miles on FR 248.1 to Waldorf.

MAPS: Arapaho National Forest.

HOW TO GET THERE: From Georgetown, drive south through town and find the Guanella Pass Road (CR 381/FR 381), which exits the southwest corner of town. After about 2.5 miles, take the dirt road west to Waldorf (FR 248.1). There are many side roads, so be careful to stay on FR 248.1.

View of Grays Peak (left) and Torreys Peak (right) from the ridge above Waldorf.

W hen you reach the end of the road, you will arrive at the Waldorf Mine (11,594 feet). The townsite of Waldorf is 400 feet higher up the hill to the northwest, after a switchback. Keep an eye out for mountain goats that inhabit these rocky slopes. Use caution when hiking in this area in late summer, as this remote basin is prone to severe electrical storms.

Established in 1868, Waldorf once had the highest post office in the country. This company town grew up around the Waldorf Mine and boasted a boarding-house, hotel, mill, machine shop, stables, and various mine-related structures. Even at such an unlikely alpine locale, the town was also served by a railroad.

A trail up Grays Peak zigzags over talus slopes to the summit at right.

Only 16 miles in length, the Argentine Central Railway was a narrow-gauge steam line built in 1905 to carry silver ore. The track had many switchbacks and the grade occasionally approached 7%, very steep for a conventional railroad. Second in height only to the cog railway up Pikes Peak, the Argentine Central enjoyed a good tourist business. From Waldorf the line climbed to 13,110 feet, just below the summit of McClellan Mountain. Due to steep grades, engines were fitted with both air and steam brakes to guard against mechanical failure.

HIKES ALONG THE WAY **Argentine Pass**

FEATURES: The state's highest pass road crosses the Divide amid outstanding alpine scenery and views of Grays and Torreys Peaks and the Peru Creek valley.

HOW TO GET THERE: From the first switchback on FR 248.1 at the Waldorf Mine, take the road south and climb several switchbacks across the tundra to the visible summit of the pass ahead.

HIKE DIFFICULTY: MODERATE: If the road is open, 4WD vehicles can maneuver to the top of Argentine Pass from the Waldorf Mine on the east side; the west side of the pass is a narrow, steep shelf trail closed to all vehicles.

LENGTH: From the Waldorf Mine to the summit of the pass is about 2 miles.

Like many pass routes, 13,207-foot Argentine Pass was built in 1871 to access gold and silver deposits, like Peru Creek on the west side of the pass. The pass was the highest wagon road ever built on the Continental Divide.

Hikers can approach Argentine Pass from the west side with a little easier vehicle access but substantially more elevation gain. They are also likely to encounter mountain bikers. From just east of the Keystone ski area on US 6, take FR 5 (Montezuma Road) east up the Snake River valley. After about 4.5 miles, take FR 260 (Peru Creek Road) east. You will see the pass road angling up the mountainside ahead. After about 5 miles, find TR 77, which goes steeply up the west side of Argentine Pass in one giant switchback for 2 miles to the summit.

Waldorf

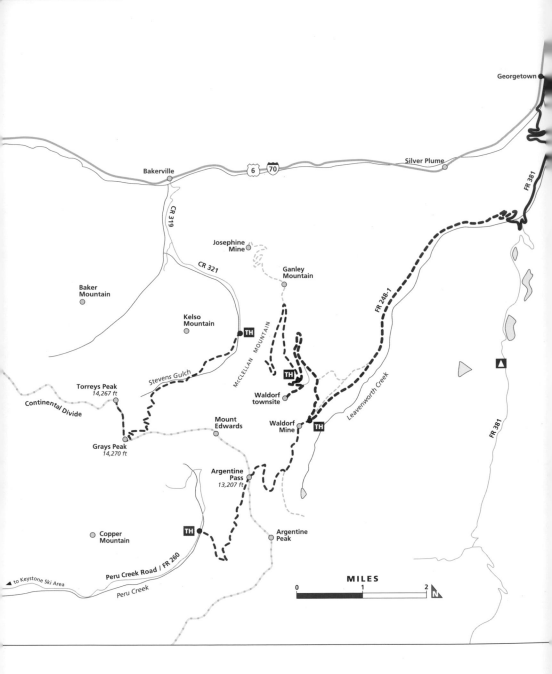

Georgetown

Silver Plume

Bakerville

6 70

FR 381

CR 319

Josephine Mine

CR 321

Ganley Mountain

Baker Mountain

Kelso Mountain

TH

McCLELLAN MOUNTAIN

FR 248-1

Stevens Gulch

Torreys Peak
14,267 ft

Continental Divide

Waldorf townsite

TH

Leavenworth Creek

Mount Edwards

Waldorf Mine

TH

Grays Peak
14,270 ft

FR 381

Argentine Pass
13,207 ft

Copper Mountain

TH

Argentine Peak

Peru Creek Road / FR 260

to Keystone Ski Area

Peru Creek

MILES
0   1   2
N

HIKES ALONG THE WAY **McClellan Mountain**

FEATURES: Grand views of Mounts Evans and Bierstadt from the end of the tracks of the Argentine Central Railway.

HOW TO GET THERE: From the Waldorf Mine, follow the bed of the old railroad as its switchbacks north to the crest of McClellan Mountain.

HIKE DIFFICULTY: MODERATE: Steady but gentle climb up the switchbacks of the old railroad bed.

LENGTH: From the Waldorf Mine to the end of the railroad track is 4.5 miles.

In 1909, plans were under way to extend the tracks of the Argentine Central Railway to the summit of Grays Peak, where a hotel was to be built for tourists. The owners had laid only about 500 feet of track, however, before the entire venture went bankrupt and was sold at foreclosure. Today, the last switchback on the abandoned railway brings the hiker to a little above 13,000 feet on the final ridge.

It has been said that one-sixth of the state of Colorado can be seen from the summit of McClellan Mountain. On a clear day, the Mount of the Holy Cross is visible in the distance. The trail splits below the summit of Ganley Mountain (12,902 feet). The branch to the north starts down to a tributary of Clear Creek and reaches a dead end at some old mine works. The branch to the south continues to the ridge at the top of McClellan Mountain, named for Civil War general George McClellan.

OTHER NEARBY HIKES **Grays Peak and Torreys Peak**

FEATURES: These twin fourteeners west of Waldorf are usually climbed together on the same day.

HOW TO GET THERE: From Georgetown on I-70, drive west 6 miles and take Exit 221 to Bakerville, heading south up the Stevens Gulch road (CR 319). After 1 mile, the road splits. Take the left fork (CR 321) to the marked trailhead for the climb. Passenger cars can reach the trailhead under most conditions. From there, follow the old jeep road past the closed gate. The Stevens Mine ruins are across the creek to the east. The road you are on eventually turns into a trail that leads to the summit of Grays Peak. Most people climb Grays Peak first, then descend 500 feet to the saddle between the two peaks and climb Torreys Peak, a half mile to the north.

HIKE DIFFICULTY: MODERATE TO STRENUOUS: The first part of the hike is relatively level on the old road to the head of Stevens Gulch; from there, the trail climbs steeply up Grays Peak.

LENGTH: From the trailhead to the summit of Grays Peak is about 3.5 miles.

Often called by climbers' shorthand "Grazentorreys," these two mountains have been popular since the 1870s. They were named after leading 19th-century botanists Asa Gray and John Torrey. In the early days, parties including children and women in long skirts made the climb. Because of the similar pointed shapes of the peaks, some American Indians referred to them as "The Ant Hills." Grays, at 14,270 feet, and Torreys, at 14,267 feet, have only a 3-foot difference in height but are separated by a saddle that drops 500 feet.

Another way to climb Grays Peak is to go to Waldorf, then follow the old railbed to the top of McClellan Mountain. From here, the hike follows along the rocky ridge to the south and attains 1,200 feet of elevation gain to reach the summit.

MOSQUITO PASS

LOCATION: About 10 miles northwest of Fairplay, between Alma and Leadville.

HIGHLIGHTS: One of the highest in the nation, this 13,186-foot pass offers spectacular views east and west, and is steeped in Colorado history.

ACCESS: Though still shown on some maps as an auto road, this rugged mountain pass requires a 4WD. On the Fairplay (east) side, passenger cars can often manage (but should proceed with caution) for the first 6.5 miles, as far as the stream crossing just beyond the ruins of the North London Mill. Above this point, the steep and rough road to the summit demands a 4WD. Those without one can park at the mill ruins and climb to the summit. The descent on the Leadville (west) side of the pass also requires a 4WD.

LENGTH: On the east side it is 10 miles from Alma Junction to the summit (6.5 miles to as far as the North London Mill ruins), and on the west side, another 8 miles down to Leadville.

MAPS: Pike National Forest on the east side; San Isabel National Forest on the west.

HOW TO GET THERE: From Fairplay, drive north about 4 miles on CO 9 to the Mosquito Pass turnoff at Alma Junction, about 1 mile south of Alma. Turn west onto CR 12, and follow this road toward the pass. After about 4.5 miles, the road splits; take the right fork. (The road on the left goes to the South London Mine, on private property. A tunnel does connect the mines through London Mountain, but you can't see it.)

Where the road forks, a sign declares that the road beyond is 4WD only; however, under good conditions, passenger cars can proceed safely for about another 2 miles to the ruins of the North London Mill. From the fork in the road, the summit of the pass is 5.5 miles. From the summit, the road drops steeply down from the tundra into Evans Gulch, past the famous Matchless Mine, and into Leadville. To summit the pass from the Leadville side also requires 4WD.

Mosquito Pass road and London Mountain from the beaver ponds at the base of the pass.

The ruins of the North London Mill in the valley by Mosquito Creek, the North London Mine higher up on London Mountain, and a few remaining towers of the derelict ore tramway (the first in Colorado) that connected them are still visible. Several lakes bordered by fields of summer wildflowers lie nestled in spectacular basins against the Continental Divide to the north; also look for beaver ponds just north of the Mosquito Pass road, about 0.5 mile north of the North London Mill.

The stone memorial at the top of the pass honors the Reverend John L. Dyer (see Dyersville, Boreas Pass, p. 120). Every summer, Mosquito Pass is the route of the World Championship Pack Burro Race from Fairplay to Leadville.

The Highway of Frozen Death

Legend has it that Mosquito Pass and the Mosquito Range were named for a squashed mosquito discovered in a ledger that recorded area prospectors' names and claims. An Indian trail originally, the pass connected South Park to early placer gold mines in California Gulch, near present-day Leadville (then called Oro City). Once Leadville was established in 1878, the pass was improved as a toll road to accommodate wagons and stagecoaches en route to the silver boomtown. Though now closed in winter, the pass was originally a year-round route, earning it the lugubrious nickname "Highway of Frozen Death." Because it was such a hazardous crossing in winter, the pass declined in use after the Denver & Rio Grande reached Leadville in 1880, having made the journey far easier.

In 1882, the London, South Park & Leadville Railroad made plans to lay track over Mosquito Pass—or under it, through a tunnel—to Leadville. Tracks were laid in Mosquito Gulch from London Junction (present-day Alma Junction, where it connected with the Denver, South Park & Pacific Railroad) to the North London Mill. Here, a 4,500-foot-long tramway led down from the North London Mine, perched at 12,400 feet on a shelf on the tundra; processed ore from the mill left on the railroad. But the Mosquito Pass railway crossing never materialized, and the railroad spur was abandoned in 1884. The railbed is still obvious in the gentle rise of the road up the gulch.

Oliver Twist Lake and the North London Mine.

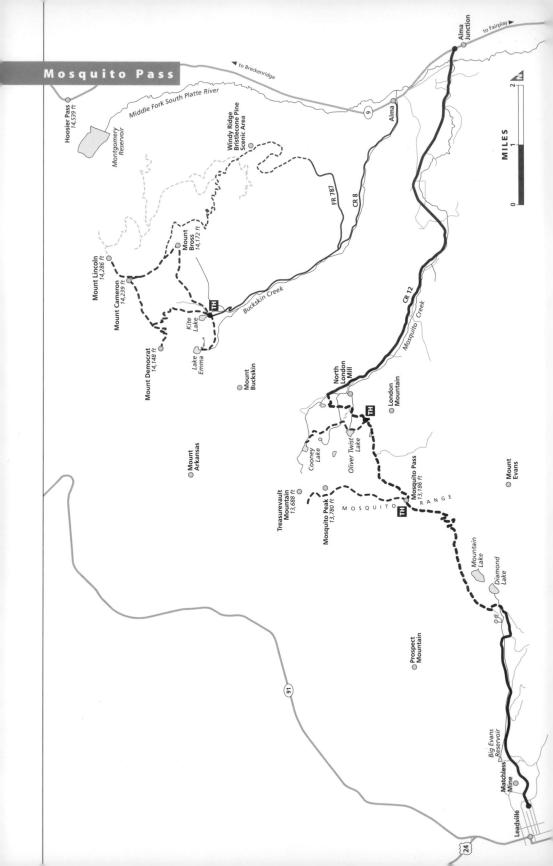

to Breckenridge

Hoosier Pass
14,539 ft

Middle Fork South Platte River

Montgomery
Reservoir

Windy Ridge
Bristlecone Pine
Scenic Area

to Fairplay

Alma
Junction

Alma

9

FR 787

CR 8

Mount Lincoln
14,286 ft

Mount
Bross
14,172 ft

Mount Cameron
14,239 ft

Buckskin Creek

CR 12

Mosquito Creek

Kite
Lake

North
London
Mill

Mount Democrat
14,148 ft

Lake
Emma

Mount
Buckskin

London
Mountain

Mount
Arkansas

Cooney
Lake

Oliver Twist
Lake

Treasurevault
Mountain
13,688 ft

Mosquito Peak
13,780 ft

Mosquito Pass
13,186 ft

Mount
Evans

M O S Q U I T O

R A N G E

Mountain
Lake

Diamond
Lake

Prospect
Mountain

91

Big Evans
Reservoir

Matchless
Mine

Leadville

24

MILES

0   1   2

Oliver Twist Lake and Cooney Lake

FEATURES: Two alpine lakes on the tundra.

HOW TO GET THERE: About 0.25 mile west of the North London Mill ruins, where the road makes a turn, an old jeep road takes off north across the tundra for about 0.33 mile to Oliver Twist Lake.

HIKE DIFFICULTY: EASY TO MODERATE: The old road to Oliver Twist Lake is almost flat, then the trail climbs steeply to Cooney Lake.

LENGTH: From the Mosquito Pass road to Cooney Lake is about 1.5 miles.

The starting point is at 12,175 feet, and Oliver Twist Lake is at the same elevation— but a small rise of about 70 feet hides the lake until you are almost upon it. From Oliver Twist Lake, the trail climbs steeply for the next mile to Cooney Lake, which is nestled about 500 feet higher up the mountain, under a high ridge to the north.

Mosquito Peak

FEATURES: A trail along the Continental Divide to a high peak with fine views.

HOW TO GET THERE: From the summit of Mosquito Pass, follow an old road north along the ridge to 13,780-foot Mosquito Peak.

HIKE DIFFICULTY: EASY TO MODERATE: This is a high-altitude, fairly flat ridge walk until the last quarter mile's final ascent of the peak.

LENGTH: From the summit of Mosquito Pass to Mosquito Peak is about 1.5 miles.

This old road route ends at the site of the abandoned Corrine Mine, then becomes a footpath that descends the slope to the west to abandoned prospect holes. By bushwhacking about 0.5 mile farther along the ridge, you can also ascend to the summit of 13,688-foot Treasurevault Mountain. To the west is a fine view of Leadville, Turquoise Reservoir, and the Sawatch Range. To the northeast is the massif that comprises Mounts Democrat, Lincoln, Cameron, and Bross.

Mount Lincoln

FEATURES: Old mining remnants and a system of old roads characterize this southern approach to the top of Mount Lincoln (14,286 feet).

HOW TO GET THERE: The road continues north from the parking area for the Bristlecone Pine Scenic Area (see p. 157).

HIKE DIFFICULTY: MODERATE: If you park at the Bristlecone Pine area at treeline, it is an easy hike to the top of Mount Lincoln along old mine roads. It is possible, though not recommended, to drive to the final shelf on the tundra below the summit; hikers may be vocal about what they consider a discourtesy.

LENGTH: Depending on how far you choose to drive, the summit is about 4 miles.

From Bristlecone Pine Scenic Area, hikers can continue north, exploring the old mine roads in the area leading up to the summit. The mountain slopes are dotted with old mine works. In the 1800s, several eminent authorities put the height of Mount Lincoln at above 17,000 feet; some believed it the highest peak in Colorado.

*The stone memorial
to Father Dyer at the
Mosquito Pass summit.*

OTHER NEARBY HIKES | # Kite Lake and Mount Democrat

FEATURES: A scenic lake in a 12,000-foot alpine basin, complete with campground, provides access to three fourteeners.

HOW TO GET THERE: From Alma, drive west on graded dirt CR 8/FR 416 (Buckskin Road). The first 4 miles or so of the road are good; as of this writing, the last 1.5 mile had been repaired and is in reasonable shape for most cars to drive all the way to the lake. Expect a fee to park in the parking area or to camp.

HIKE DIFFICULTY: MODERATE TO STRENUOUS: Though relatively easy in terms of fourteeners, this climb still involves a steep hike at high altitude and requires some stamina.

LENGTH: The drive to the lake from Alma is 5.5 miles. The hike up Mount Democrat, on the marked trail behind and to the northwest of the lake, is 2 miles.

The breathtaking drive up to the lake should not be missed, even if hiking a fourteener is not your goal. Campers and visitors can take their pick among Mounts Democrat, Lincoln, and Bross. Mount Democrat is considered one of the easiest fourteeners and is worth a try. Looking back at Kite Lake from the trail, you'll see why it received its name—it has the four-sided shape of a child's kite. The campground at Kite Lake is the highest developed campground in the United States—but don't expect any extras.

Advanced hikers may wish to attempt all three fourteeners in a single trip. To reach Mount Lincoln and Mount Bross, return down the ridge from the summit of Democrat (14,148 feet) to the saddle—0.5 mile and a 750-foot elevation drop—as if descending to Kite Lake, then continue east for about 1 mile on the ridge to climb Mount Cameron (14,239 feet). Though above 14,000 feet, Mount Cameron is technically considered to be a part of Mount Lincoln and not a separate fourteener. The trail to Mount Lincoln (14,286 feet) leads north; the trail to Mount Bross (14,172 feet) is to the south. The return to Kite Lake from Mount Bross can be made down a steep (more than 2,000 vertical feet in a little over 1 mile), rocky trail that drops briskly to the lake. Most hikers can climb all three peaks in about 6 to 8 hours.

For those with less time or less energy, a shorter, lower hike is the tundra footpath to Lake Emma, also a scenic adventure. Lying a bit higher and 0.75 mile to the west of Kite Lake, this lake is reached by a trail that leads west from the Kite Lake parking area.

NEARBY STOPS Windy Ridge Bristlecone Pine Scenic Area

FEATURES: Enjoy superb views of Hoosier Pass and environs while exploring a unique bristlecone pine forest at treeline.

HOW TO GET THERE: A graded dirt road changes to a high-clearance 4WD road before it reaches the scenic area. From Alma, turn west up CR 8/FR 416 (Buckskin Road) toward Kite Lake. After about 3 miles, just past the abandoned Paris Mill, turn sharply to the right (north) onto FR 787 (Dolly Varden Road) and climb steeply through the trees. The first part of the road is good, but it becomes poorer and potholed farther up. After about 2.5 miles, the road passes the ruins of a mine site, then climbs 0.5 mile up a steep 4WD section to treeline. Pull off at the primitive parking area on the right (east).

LENGTH: It is a 6-mile drive from Alma to the Bristlecone Pine Scenic Area on appropriately named Windy Ridge. From the parking area, you can stroll around the bristlecone pine forest on a flat shelf on the tundra.

The Bristlecone Pine Scenic Area was established by the Forest Service in 1964 to preserve these ancient, high-elevation trees—some of which are up to several thousand years old—from logging (see Trees of Treeline, p. 71).

Two other attractions lie along the way for history buffs. One is the old cemetery at Buckskin Joe. The turnoff for the cemetery is a little over 1 mile west of Alma in a meadow just before the old townsite of Buckskin Joe. Turn on the dirt road (suitable for cars) that goes north into the trees, or park and walk from the road. The forested cemetery is just a couple hundred yards off the main road. Old wooden fences and grave markers date from the mid–19th century, when the town was flourishing.

The other is an excellent example of an arrastra. This primitive device—a small, hollowed-out basin, several feet across, in the shape of a doughnut—was used for grinding gold ore. To see it, drive some 2.5 miles west from Alma to just below the huge abandoned Paris Mill, and park in the wide spot in the road. Walk back down the road about 100 yards to find the arrastra beside Buckskin Creek.

The arrastra for grinding ore beside Buckskin Creek.

An Unforgettable Ghost Town

Shrugging off my day-pack I sat down gratefully on a nearby rock. It was lunchtime and I burrowed in the pack and pulled out some cheese. Potato chips, a fruit pie, and a beer completed the repast. Not exactly the healthiest combination, perhaps, but I hoped that the rest of the hike—to the Hagerman Tunnel, then back to the jeep at the trailhead—would raise my metabolism enough to burn off the bad stuff.

My father and I, both railroad enthusiasts, were exploring the trail leading up the final stretch of railbed to the Hagerman Tunnel, west of Leadville. He was interested in the railroad and historical aspects of the area and lingered to study the railbed in more detail. I chose to hike ahead to the site of Douglass City, a construction camp for railroad crews that built the tunnel through the Continental Divide at the end of the trail.

I looked at the faint track through the grass in front of me that was once the main—and

The Hagerman Pass road passes the Busk-Ivanhoe Tunnel, visible in the center of the photo.

only—street of what impressively called itself a "city." Even though it was a sunny day, it was a bit eerie. Only a few half-collapsed log walls and timbers from the workmen's cabins were left scattered on the ground as a last tribute to the men who labored to complete this section of the railroad. Even though remote, it must have been a fairly lively little community. At one time, eight saloons and a dancehall rounded out the buildings of the town. Moreover, the Forest Service sign in front of me informed me that the innocent pleasures of these hardy men included "drinking, shooting, fighting, and knifing."

I finished lunch and, after poking around the town a little longer and enjoying the colorful wildflowers that had taken over the main street, I started back down to meet my father. We had agreed to meet by the site of a former trestle that figures prominently in early photographs of the railroad, so I cut back down to the main trail and started toward the trailhead.

As I reached the former railbed, a figure in gray was just vanishing into the trees along a loop of the railbed below me. That must be him, I said to myself. I hurried to catch up. I took a shortcut to the lower loop, thinking that I could still head him off and we could walk out to the jeep together. However, he wasn't there. The railbed stretched empty for a quarter mile in both directions. I thought that I must have been mistaken.

I never did find him, so I just figured that he was a faster walker than me and set out to follow him. When I reached the jeep at the trailhead, my father was sitting on a rock studying a map of the area.

"Aha, I thought I could catch up with you back up there," I said. "You move pretty fast for an old guy." He grinned, then gave me a puzzled look. "What do you mean, catch up with me? I've been sitting here for three-quarters of an hour." "You've been here for three-quarters of an hour," I repeated stupidly. "But I just saw you on the railbed."

It was his turn to stare at me. "No. Wasn't me."

I looked around the parking area. There were no other cars. "Have you seen anyone else here?" I asked. "No," he replied, giving me a peculiar look. Divining my thoughts, he added: "Nobody's been here. I've been here all by myself."

I didn't explain, but the thought has always nagged at me. Whom had I seen? Was it euphoria from the sight of Douglass City and the high altitude? Was it the beer for lunch? Or was it a ghost from the long-gone days of the railroad? I have often wondered, but I'll never know.

HAGERMAN PASS

LOCATION: About 10 miles west of Leadville.

HIGHLIGHTS: Follow part of the abandoned railbed of the Colorado Midland Railroad, and take an optional hike to see a 19th-century railroad feat, Hagerman Tunnel.

ACCESS: A potholed dirt road suitable for most vehicles leads to the trailhead for the Hagerman Tunnel; a 4WD is required to travel over the pass. Hagerman Pass crosses the mountains at 11,925 feet before descending to Ruedi Reservoir, the Roaring Fork River, and the town of Basalt on the other side.

LENGTH: From Leadville to the summit of the pass is about 16 miles. From the summit of the pass to Basalt is about 46 miles.

MAPS: San Isabel National Forest.

HOW TO GET THERE: Drive west on 6th Street in Leadville to Turquoise Lake Road and drive along the south side of the lake. About 3.5 miles past Sugarloaf Dam, the road splits; take the left fork onto FR 105, the Hagerman Pass road, and head up the hill to the southwest. You follow the abandoned railbed for about 4 miles to Carlton Tunnel, then continue up the road another 4 miles to the summit of the pass. From there, descend to a series of small settlements before passing Ruedi Reservoir and joining CO 82 at Basalt.

Lyle Lake is a beautiful hiking or backpacking destination.

Visitors en route to the Hagerman Tunnel and the tundra can drive or walk along the old railbed through subalpine meadows that put on spectacular displays of flowers in July. On the east side of the pass, stop and look at the closed-off entrance to the Busk-Ivanhoe Tunnel. On the west side, take the time to drive back eastward on FR 527, which joins FR 105 about 3 miles below the summit of the pass on the west side. This road leads for 1 mile to pretty Ivanhoe Lake, a liquid asset of the Fryingpan-Arkansas water-diversion project that supplies Front Range cities.

Perils of a High-Altitude Railroad

This pass was named for James J. Hagerman, a Michigan iron magnate who had retired to Colorado Springs to take the cure for consumption (tuberculosis). In 1883, Hagerman built the Colorado Midland Railway to link Colorado Springs to Grand Junction, with a side trip to haul silver ore from Aspen to the smelters at Leadville. The train would pick up coke at Glenwood Springs on the way west, then carry supplies back to Aspen on the return trip, passing underneath the Continental Divide each way through the Hagerman Tunnel (see Hagerman Tunnel hike, p. 162), completed in 1887. Hagerman Pass, above the tunnel, was originally a trail; however, it did not receive much use until it was upgraded to carry men and supplies between the two portals of the tunnel during railroad construction.

Rotary snowplows cleared the tracks on high passes after winter storms.

The problem for this railroad, and others like it, was the winter. Railroad tunnels through the mountains were built at or above treeline; hence they were exposed to storms, blizzards, snowslides, and drifts. In winter, rotary snowplows often ran continuously during storms to keep exposed sections of the tracks clear. A series of 13 wooden snowsheds were built over the highest sections of track and above the portals on each tunnel approach. Some snowsheds were several miles long, and some even had engine turntables and repair facilities inside.

The railroad inevitably incurred high expenses maintaining high-altitude tracks, trestles, and snowsheds. Disasters also occurred: On one occasion, a train loaded with cattle lay buried for 78 days, stalled in a severe snowstorm. Finally in 1893, the Colorado Midland Railway built the 9,394-foot-long Busk-Ivanhoe (later Carlton) Tunnel, 700 feet lower in elevation, connecting the railroad stations of Busk on the east side and Ivanhoe on the west side of the Continental Divide, and reducing the need for snowsheds.

After the rail route was abandoned completely in 1917, Carlton Tunnel functioned as a one-way road tunnel. Today, Carlton Tunnel has a third use: for diversion of water from Lake Ivanhoe, on the west side of Hagerman Pass, east to Turquoise Lake and the Fryingpan-Arkansas water project.

Turquoise Lake

to Leadville and (24)

Busk Creek

FR 105

Hagerman Lake

Busk Creek

Hagerman Pass
11,925 ft

Opal
Lake

Windsor
Lake

Douglas City
townsite

Continental Divide

Carlton Tunnel

Hagerman Tunnel
(no access)

FR 105

FR 527

Ivanhoe Lake

Lyle Creek

Lyle Lake

Lake

TR 1919

Ivanhoe Creek

to Basalt and (82)

N

MILES

0   1   2

Hagerman Tunnel

FEATURES: A walk along the old railroad bed to the ruins of one of the highest railroad tunnels in the nation, with a side option to see a historic railroad camp.

HOW TO GET THERE: On the east side of Hagerman Pass, go past the Carlton Tunnel portal and up the hill for about 1 mile to a large trailhead parking area on the right. Passenger cars can drive to this trailhead, but proceed with caution beyond the Carlton Tunnel; if in doubt, hike from Carlton Tunnel to the trailhead.

HIKE DIFFICULTY: EASY TO MODERATE: Hike along the railroad grade up to the tunnel.

LENGTH: From the trailhead to the Hagerman Tunnel is 3 miles.

The Hagerman Tunnel was 2,064-feet-long and provided passage for trains going through the Continental Divide. It was completed in 1887 but only operated for five years. Elevation at the tunnel is 11,528 feet. On the trail to the tunnel, stop to admire Hagerman Lake, which lies just to the right of the railbed. The east entrance to Hagerman Tunnel is open but filled with ice year-round and can be dangerous to enter. The west portal is blocked by a deep pool of water in the summer that turns to ice in the winter. On the way, stop at Douglass City (below), the construction camp for the railroad.

The Hagerman Tunnel.

Douglass City

FEATURES: Ruins of a historic townsite that border on meadows strewn with vibrant wildflowers in summer.

HOW TO GET THERE: Follow instructions above for the Hagerman Tunnel hike.

HIKE DIFFICULTY: EASY TO MODERATE: Essentially a flat initial hike on the railbed, then a steeper section to the old townsite.

LENGTH: From the trailhead parking to Douglass City is 1.5 miles.

Follow the railbed for about 1.5 miles to where the trail suddenly drops down a steep slope in front of you. This is where a large, curved, 1,084-foot-long trestle once stood. Don't go down the slope, but make a sharp right turn up the old wagon road to the site of once rip-roaring Douglass City, the construction camp for the tunnel. Enjoy the subalpine flowers here in summer. Either return to the railbed or follow the wagon road through Douglass City, past Opal Lake, and climb back up to the railbed at the Hagerman Tunnel.

Windsor Lake

FEATURES: This dramatic, 15-acre lake at 11,650 feet makes an interesting hike to treeline, not far from Hagerman Tunnel.

HOW TO GET THERE: The trail starts at the Carlton Tunnel on the east side of Hagerman Pass, by the creek at the east side of the parking area.

HIKE DIFFICULTY: EASY TO MODERATE: The trail has a steep section in the middle but flattens out in the last quarter mile to the lake.

LENGTH: The lake is 1 mile from the parking area at Carlton Tunnel.

The trail is a pleasant hike up a timbered slope, then on a flat shelf to the lake. Windsor is less visited than others in the area and can provide a solitary escape in its sheltered mountainous bowl.

Lyle Lake and Mormon Lake

FEATURES: Two beautiful lakes, respectively at and above treeline, await on easy hikes to tundra shelves.

HOW TO GET THERE: The trailhead is on the west side of Hagerman Pass, about 3.5 miles below the summit, just before the junction with FR 527.

HIKE DIFFICULTY: EASY TO MODERATE: Both lakes are easy hikes from the trailhead.

LENGTH: Lyle Lake is 1.5 miles from the trailhead; Mormon Lake is 3 miles.

TR 1919 is a gentle climb up a wooded valley for about 1.5 miles to Lyle Lake at 11,369 feet. The trail continues above treeline for 1.5 miles to Mormon Lake.

Parry primrose often grows close to water in tundra meadows.

WESTON PASS

The road on the east side travels through meadows and stands of aspen before climbing gently through pine forests to the exposed summit. Descending the west side from the top, the road crosses a large valley, then reenters the forest for the last stretch to US 24. The summit of the 11,900-foot pass is a lonely—and visually striking—place.

A fine hike from the summit starts south up an old jeep road to an L-shaped ridge for fine views of the upper Arkansas valley, the reservoirs at Twin Lakes, and the Collegiate Range behind them to the west. After about 1 mile, the jeep road drops down into a boggy drainage, then climbs back up to a ridge on the Mosquito Range at above 12,600

LOCATION: About 10 miles southeast of Leadville.

HIGHLIGHTS: This former wagon route still traverses the picturesque Mosquito Range backcountry.

ACCESS: Much of this gravel and graded-dirt road is suitable for passenger cars with high clearance, depending on road and recent weather conditions, but proceed with caution. A 4WD or pickup truck makes the trip easier. The final mile or so of the eastern approach to the summit is rocky and steep, requiring adequate vehicle clearance and power. On the west side, several sections require high clearance, and travel by passenger car is not advisable.

LENGTH: From US 285 on the east side to the summit is 16 miles; from the summit to US 24 on the west side is 11 miles.

MAPS: Pike National Forest on the east side; San Isabel National Forest on the west.

HOW TO GET THERE: About 5 miles south of Fairplay on US 285, go west onto CR 5, which leads to the summit of the pass. After about 7 miles, bear right at the junction with CR 22 to continue west, or you will end up back at US 285.

Colin Campbell #1 mine just below the summit of Weston Pass.

feet. Large herds of elk congregate on the tundra in this area in the summer, often just below the ridge on the west side. Depending on how far you wish to go, this hike can be several miles long. A short hike on the tundra is to the Colin Campbell #1, a mine at the end of a short spur road a few hundred yards just below the summit on the west side.

Like most of the other high-mountain crossings, this was originally an Indian trail that was upgraded into a wagon-and-stagecoach road. The pass is named for the Weston Ranch, which supplied beef to the nearby mining towns. In the 1860s, the pass was a major wagon route from South Park to the mines near present-day Leadville, and the road teemed with wagons, stagecoaches, and prospectors rushing to find their fortunes in the gold fields. Though Weston Pass was an easier, lower route than the Mosquito Pass crossing to the north, the latter soon received more use because it was shorter. With the 1880 arrival of the railroad in Leadville, the traffic on both passes subsided.

HIKES ALONG THE WAY **Ptarmigan Peak**

FEATURES: A strenuous hike up a 13,739-foot peak northeast of the pass.

HOW TO GET THERE: From the summit of Weston Pass, the hike leads northeast—believe it or not—up the steep slope in front of you.

HIKE DIFFICULTY: MODERATE TO STRENUOUS: The first stretch is a very steep climb to the ridgetop (1,400 feet elevation gain in 0.75 mile); from here, it's a relatively level walk to the top of Ptarmigan Peak.

LENGTH: From the summit parking area, the top of the peak is about 1.5 miles.

Serious hikers will appreciate this challenging thirteener climb by way of the high ridge northeast of Weston Pass. The first part is along a thin trail that may be hard to detect, and you may have to bushwhack up the slope. Once on the ridge, follow it north for about 1 mile to the summit of the peak for outstanding views of nearby ranges. Rocky Mountain bighorn sheep frequent these slopes.

HIKES ALONG THE WAY **Gold Basin**

FEATURES: A short hike or 4WD drive to an alpine basin and majestic peaks.

HOW TO GET THERE: The 4WD spur road up into Gold Basin is about 3 miles down the west side from the summit of Weston Pass, on the right (north) side.

HIKE DIFFICULTY: EASY TO MODERATE: About 700 feet elevation gain in the first mile—quite steep.

LENGTH: 1 mile to the end of the road; optional how far you go beyond that.

Either hike up this steep jeep road or drive it with a suitable vehicle. Watch the ridge and slopes above this basin for Rocky Mountain bighorn sheep from the Buffalo Peaks herd. Several branch roads continue from the parking area under a power line, passing old mining claims and ending on low peaks with nice views.

Weston Pass

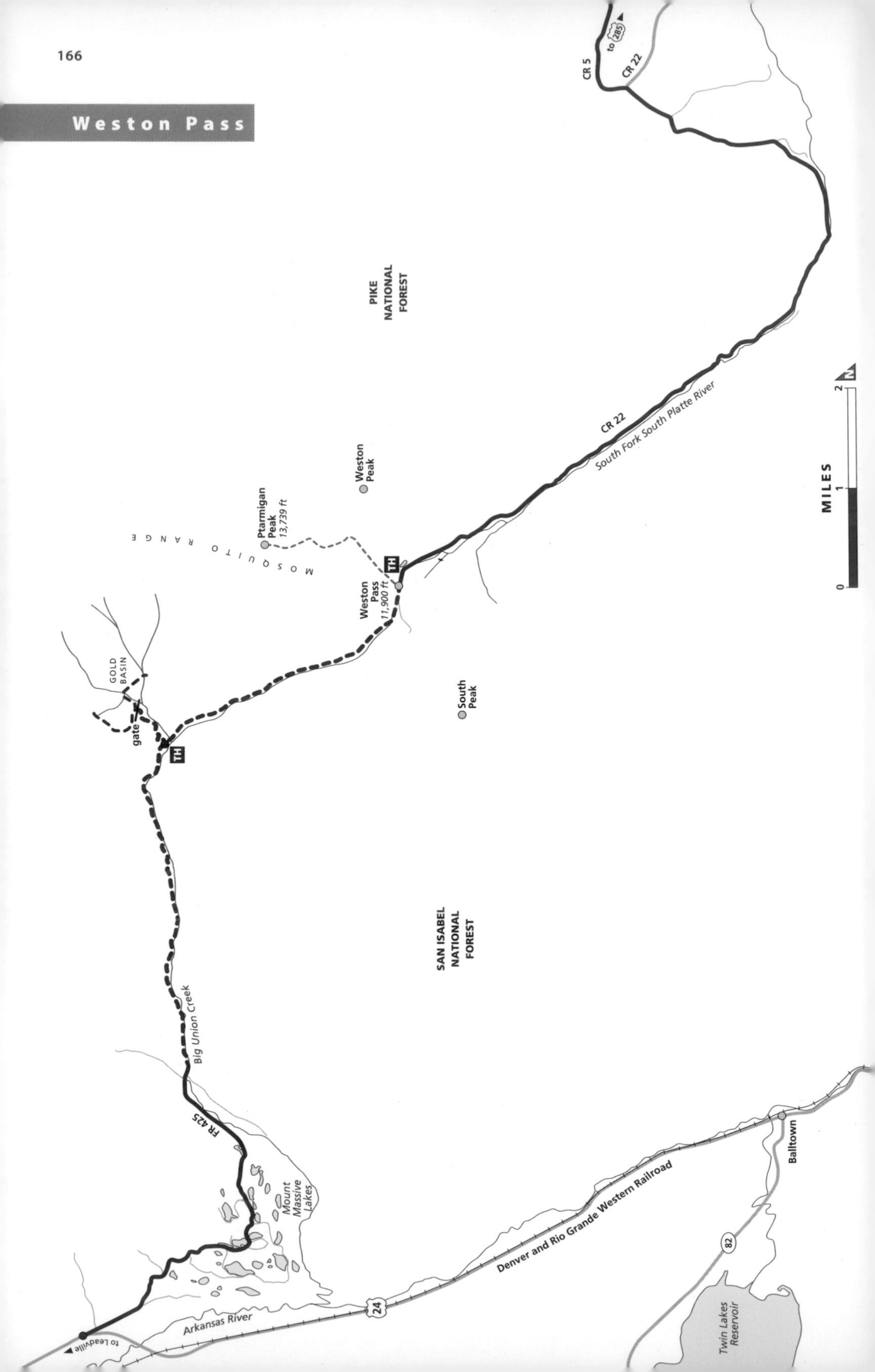

PIKE
NATIONAL
FOREST

CR 5

CR 22

to 285

CR 22

South Fork South Platte River

Weston
Peak

Ptarmigan
Peak
13,739 ft

MOSQUITO RANGE

Weston
Pass
11,900 ft

TH

GOLD
BASIN

gate

TH

South
Peak

SAN ISABEL
NATIONAL
FOREST

Big Union Creek

FR 425

Mount
Massive
Lakes

Denver and Rio Grande Western Railroad

Balltown

82

24

Arkansas River

to Leadville

Twin Lakes
Reservoir

MILES

0   1   2

N

The Life of the Tundra

Gazing toward the ground one day in June, occupied with my own thoughts, I was roaming absent-mindedly across the tundra when a rock at my feet unexpectedly sprouted wings and, with a whirring sound, half-flew, half-ran across the grass. At least, that was my first impression. When I regained my composure, I realized that what had really happened was that I had almost stepped on a ptarmigan, without ever seeing it there.

The ptarmigan is a bird, about the size of a small chicken, that lives around and above treeline all year. In summer, the bird's plumage is a mottled combination of brown, black, and tan that perfectly matches its surroundings. I stopped and scanned the ground around me. So perfect was this bird's plumage that I couldn't see it.

I sat down on a nearby rock and tried to collect my thoughts. Seen from the plains, the mountaintops look like cold, bare places that couldn't possibly harbor life. Yet I had—almost literally—run across a good example of the richness of life on the tundra.

It was about nine o'clock in the morning and already the sun was warming the thin air at 12,500 feet. I had started hiking a little after dawn wearing a down jacket and wool hat, but I was now too hot. I pulled my hooded sweatshirt over my head and stuffed it in my pack.

Out of the corner of my eye I saw movement. Cautious this time, I turned my head slowly. About 15 feet away from me were two more ptarmigan—a male and a female—that I hadn't noticed when I sat down. These two didn't seem afraid of me. I could hear soft clucking noises as they continued to

Bighorn sheep live mainly above treeline in valleys and high ridges.

putter around a nearby grassy spot between two rocks. They reminded me of an old married couple going grocery shopping. Look at this, look at that, peck at a bug here, at one there.

Apparently satisfied by whatever they had been doing, the female shook herself slightly, ruffled her feathers, and lay down. The male continued to walk around her with a stiff-legged gait, occasionally pecking in the grass when he saw something of interest.

Another movement caught my eye. From a rough pile of broken rock beyond the two ptarmigan, a little streak of brown scuttled from rock to rock, stopped and looked around, accelerated across another rock, stopped again, and jumped into a grassy area. The two ptarmigan paid no attention as the tiny ball of brown fur that was a pika raced past them and stopped abruptly in a patch of alpine avens. Here was another tundra resident. In a few moments the furry little animal, stalks and flowers dangling from the sides of its mouth, made a dash back to the rock pile that was apparently its home. Another pika, obviously emboldened by the first, zigzagged out of the rocks onto the same patch of grass. From somewhere in the distance I could hear the shrill whistle of a marmot.

On a previous trip up a nearby mountain, my wife and our two daughters had sat down behind some rocks for shelter from the wind while we ate our picnic lunch. Halfway through my sandwich, one of the girls tugged at my sleeve.

"Look, Dad," she whispered in awe, pointing ahead of us. About 50 feet away, two bighorn sheep ewes were staring at us from around the end of the rocks. One of them walked out and started to graze, apparently little concerned with this group of lunching humans invading its territory. The other one watched us for a few more moments, then joined its companion and began contentedly nibbling at the tundra grass.

As we watched, both slowly moved away out of sight again behind the rocks. With some patience—and a little luck—it is easy to observe and enjoy the life of the tundra.

MOUNT ANTERO

LOCATION: About 12 miles southwest of Buena Vista.

HIGHLIGHTS: Fourteener Mount Antero is one of the best gemstone areas in the United States.

ACCESS: Passenger cars can reach the turnoff at Alpine on FR 211; from this point, the rugged road requires a 4WD to climb Mount Antero.

LENGTH: From Alpine to the crossing of Baldwin Creek is 2.5 miles; it is another 4 miles to the summit of Mount Antero.

MAPS: San Isabel National Forest

HOW TO GET THERE: From Nathrop on US 285 south of Buena Vista, go west on paved, then dirt, CR 162/FR 211 for about 12 miles to the summer-home colony of Alpine. To reach Mount Antero, make a sharp left (south) onto the Baldwin Creek road (FR 277), opposite Alpine Reservoir. Follow FR 277 through forested slopes for about 2.5 miles to a fork in the road. Take the left fork (FR 278) to cross the creek; the road climbs up Baldwin Gulch and switchbacks up a shelf to a flat shoulder just south of the summit of Mount Antero. Hike from here to the summit.

For those who want to climb the summit but don't want to hike the jeep road, another option is to take the Little Browns Creek Trail (TR 1430) on the east side. To reach this trail, go 11.5 miles south of Buena Vista on US 285, turn right onto CR 270, which turns into CR 272, and drive about 5 miles total to the Browns Creek Trailhead; start hiking west, following signs for Little Browns Creek Trail. The hike to the summit is a hefty 7.5 miles one-way and about 5,300 feet of elevation gain.

The view back down the road near the summit of Mount Antero.

This picturesque 14,269-foot mountain has yielded its share of mineral wealth, including topaz, aquamarine, and clear and smoky quartz crystals. Commercial beryllium mining in the 1950s improved the road almost to the top of Mount Antero.

The route up Mount Antero involves short switchbacks along a narrow jeep road on the side of a very steep mountain. If a drive like this sounds appealing to you, you will enjoy it. You'll encounter many social roads from the final prospect holes, but basically just consider the final stretch to be a halfmile hike to the summit. On any weekend in the summer, you will might see gemstone collectors poking around the prospect holes on the top. Fish enthusiasts will appreciate a stop at the Chalk Cliff Fish Hatchery, 2.5 miles west of Nathrop on CR 162, for a look at how trout are raised.

Mining ruins above Baldwin Lake.

HIKES ALONG THE WAY   **Baldwin Lake**

FEATURES: A lovely 10-acre alpine lake in a vast valley beneath Mount Antero. Mining ruins can be found above the lake.

HOW TO GET THERE: Drive up the Baldwin Creek road (FR 277) about 2.5 miles to the road fork just before the Baldwin Creek crossing. The left fork goes to Mount Antero, but take the right fork instead to continue alongside the creek for another 2.5 miles to Baldwin Lake at the end of the valley.

HIKE DIFFICULTY: MODERATE: Instead of driving to Baldwin Lake, another option is to park at Alpine or the fork in FR 277 and hike up the road to the end of the valley.

LENGTH: From the fork in FR 277 to Baldwin Lake is 2.5 miles.

The jeep road follows Baldwin Creek up the valley, with a gradual gain of 1,200 feet up to the lake, at 12,100 feet. Don't be fooled by a series of large ponds before you reach Baldwin Lake, but keep going until you reach the road's end and the real lake. About 1.5 miles from the fork, a side road to the north leads about a half mile to some interesting mine ruins in the tundra basin about 500 feet higher up.

HIKES ALONG THE WAY Boulder Mountain

FEATURES: A drive or hike to another part of the neighboring tundra on a high peak for impressive views.

HOW TO GET THERE: A little more than a mile south of Alpine on FR 277, take an unmarked jeep trail (formerly FR 283) that cuts uphill to the right and switchbacks up Boulder Mountain to a mine near the top.

HIKE DIFFICULTY: MODERATE TO STRENUOUS: This is a steep rise of about 2,600 vertical feet in 5 miles.

LENGTH: From FR 277, the mine is about 5 miles; the summit of Boulder Mountain is another 0.5 mile.

Though this hike is on the bed of an old jeep road, it climbs rapidly up a series of tight switchbacks along the ridge to old mine works about 600 feet below the summit. To reach the summit of 13,528-foot Boulder Mountain, bushwhack southwest up the rocky slope from the mine.

Mount Antero

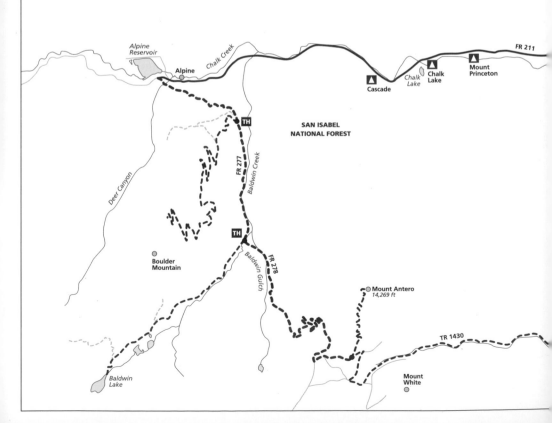

*The globeflower blooms
early in the summer in
wet, cold areas.*

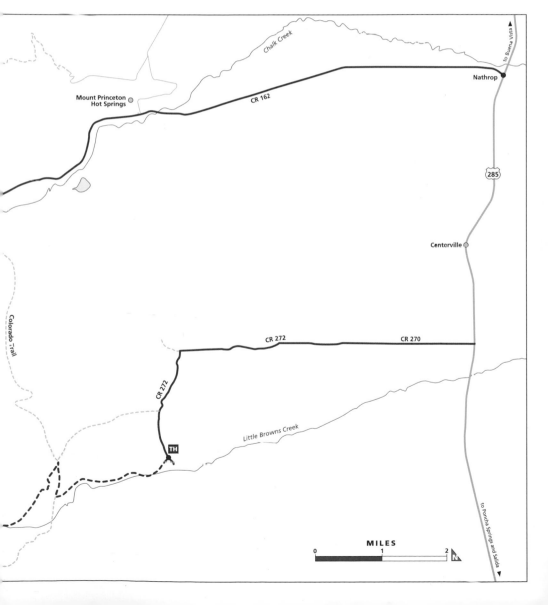

THE ALPINE TUNNEL

LOCATION: About 20 miles southwest of Buena Vista.

HIGHLIGHTS: This abandoned railroad tunnel, completed in 1881, extends 1,772 feet through the Continental Divide in a lovely tundra valley.

ACCESS: From the west, the old railbed road to the tunnel's west portal is suitable for passenger cars with high clearance, depending on road conditions, but proceed with caution. A 4WD or pickup truck makes the trip easier, and is required for the approach from the east over Hancock Pass.

LENGTH: The drive or hike from the trailhead at Hancock to the east portal is about 3 miles; from the west side parking area to the west portal is about 0.5 mile.

MAPS: San Isabel National Forest for the east side; Gunnison National Forest for the approach to the west portal and west side.

HOW TO GET THERE: To reach the Alpine Tunnel's east portal from US 285 at Nathrop, head west on CR 162/FR 211, which is paved for 9 miles, then dirt for 7 miles, toward the picturesque former mining town of St. Elmo. Just before town, angle to the left (south) onto FR 295, and drive 5 miles to the townsite of Hancock. Park, then hike on the railbed for about 3 miles to the east portal.

The easiest approach to the west portal is from US 50; turn off at Parlin, 12 miles east of Gunnison, and follow CR 76 northeast another 12 miles or so to Pitkin. From Pitkin, continue east for about 3 miles on FR 765, then turn sharply south onto FR 839 and drive up the railbed for another 10 miles to the west portal parking area. (You can also cross the Continental Divide between the east and west portals by hiking over Altman Pass or taking a 4WD across 12,140-foot Hancock Pass; see Hancock Pass–Tomichi Pass Loop, p. 175.)

The road is closed about 0.5 mile before the tunnel to protect the restored site of the previous railroad station. Park and walk to the exhibit area and the tunnel entrance farther on.

The railbed with the Alpine Tunnel entrance just visible in the distance.

The Alpine Tunnel's 11,496-foot east portal, which was called Atlantic, has long since caved in, and—beyond the striking high-country environs—there isn't much to see on that side. The 11,521-foot west portal, however, occupies a beautiful alpine basin and has much to offer for history and railroad buffs alike. Interpretive signs abound; the 1883 telegraph office, a station platform, and an outhouse have all been restored; and even a stretch of the original rails has been relaid. The ruins of the railroad station, workers' boarding-house, and stone engine house, the latter destroyed by fire in 1906, are also worth seeing.

The west portal is occasionally, if unofficially, opened by thrill-seekers, but note that entry is dangerous and not advisable. Rails and ties are still in the tunnel which heads north to a cave-in. Standing water and a dank atmosphere discourage further exploration.

The First Railroad Tunnel Under the Continental Divide

The Denver, South Park & Pacific Railroad, linking Denver to Gunnison, began construction in 1874. This narrow-gauge railroad traversed the tundra and bored under the Continental Divide at the Alpine Tunnel, at above 11,500 feet in elevation, southwest of Buena Vista. Construction of the tunnel began in mid-1880, but due to the site's high elevation, remote location, and severe winter conditions, the project wasn't completed until late 1881. It was the first tunnel built under the Divide. Builders resorted to using some 400,000 board feet of California redwood to brace it's fractured walls. Even so, the first partial cave-in occurred in 1895, and in 1910, the railroad abandoned the line.

HIKES ALONG THE WAY Williams Pass

FEATURES: A fairly gentle tundra hike over the Divide at 11,762-foot Williams Pass, a marshy former wagon road.

HOW TO GET THERE: From the parking area at the Hancock townsite, take the trail leading west toward the east portal to a gated fork at about 0.25 mile; bear left onto FR 298A (on the east side), the Williams Pass road, and climb up through the trees. On the west side, this route is TR 539 and accessible from FR 839, the Alpine Tunnel road.

HIKE DIFFICULTY: EASY TO MODERATE: The old jeep road climbs on both sides to a level, marshy area at the top of the pass.

LENGTH: From the Hancock townsite to the summit of Williams Pass is 2 miles; from the summit to the west portal via FR 839 is 2.5 miles.

Now a pleasant hiking and occasional jeep trail, the old Williams Pass road is opened by the Forest Service to vehicles only in August because of severe deterioration of the road, large rocks, and the alpine meadow at the summit, which is full of swampy patches. From the top, follow TR 539 along a winding descent to FR 839, the Alpine Tunnel road.

HIKES ALONG THE WAY Altman Pass

FEATURES: A hike across the top of the tunnel, with the option of an extended hike to the Tincup Pass road.

HOW TO GET THERE: From the west portal of the Alpine Tunnel, a trail leads steeply up the slope on the east side of the tunnel, summits 11,940-foot Altman Pass, and ends at the east portal.

HIKE DIFFICULTY: EASY TO MODERATE: A 1-mile hike that starts above tree-line and remains there for the duration of the hike.

LENGTH: It is about 0.5 mile to the summit of Altman Pass and 1 mile from the east portal to the west portal. The east portal and eastern access to the pass from the townsite of Hancock via FR 298 is 3 miles.

Altman Pass (11,940 feet), also called Alpine Pass, was used by workers traveling between the two portals of the tunnel during construction. From the pass summit, hikers can connect with the Continental Divide Trail and follow north 1 mile on a mostly level stretch to 10-acre Tunnel Lake, at 12,000 feet. This trail then continues some 3 miles to the north to a junction with the Tincup Pass road.

The Alpine Tunnel

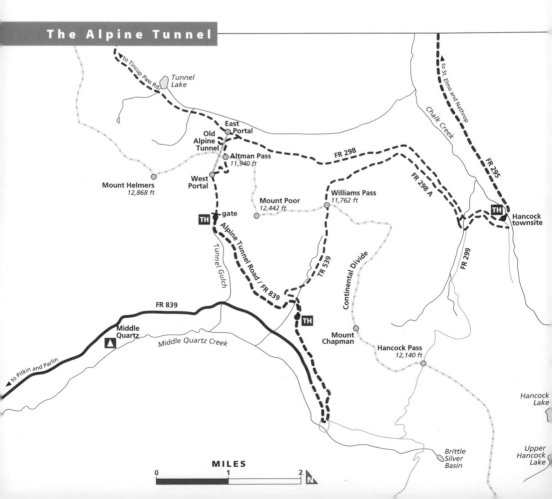

HANCOCK PASS–TOMICHI PASS

LOCATION: About 22 miles southwest of Buena Vista.

HIGHLIGHTS: Linked 4WD roads cross two spectacular alpine passes, just south of the Alpine Tunnel. You can drive them as a loop trip from Nathrop or as an out-and-back.

ACCESS: A gentle climb along an old railbed, the east side of Hancock Pass can be driven with care in passenger cars as far as the Hancock townsite. The road then climbs steeply to many high stretches of tundra before reaching the summit.

The west side of Hancock Pass is steep and narrow, descending in a series of switchbacks to the trees, where it joins FR 839 to Pitkin. Tomichi Pass is visible as a diagonal line angling straight up the side of the mountain to the south. As the road reaches the bottom of the valley in Brittle Silver Basin and the stream that flows through it, the jeep road to Tomichi Pass (FR 888) joins it from the left (east). Turn left and follow the road up to the summit of the pass.

LENGTH: From US 285 at Nathrop to the Hancock townsite is 21 miles; from the townsite to the Hancock Pass summit is 2 miles. It's 1 mile from there to the FR 888 junction, and another mile to the Tomichi Pass summit. From the summit south to Sargents on US 50 is 15 miles. The entire trip from Nathrop and back via Monarch Pass is east on US 50 to US 285 is about 87 miles.

MAPS: San Isabel National Forest on the east side of Hancock Pass; Gunnison National Forest for the west side of Hancock Pass and for Tomichi Pass.

HOW TO GET THERE: To approach the east side of Hancock Pass from Nathrop, go west on CR 162/FR 211, which is paved for 9 miles then gravel for 7 miles, toward the picturesque former mining town of St. Elmo. Just before town, angle to the left (south) onto FR 295 and drive 5 miles to the Hancock townsite, where the road branches. Heading south, the left fork will become TR 1422, which goes to Hancock Lake. The road straight ahead is FR 299 to Hancock Pass; on the west side it becomes FR 266, and south of Tomichi Pass it is FR 888.

The shelf road over Tomichi Pass. The white speck is a jeep that rolled off the road.

The shelf road up Tomichi Pass is steep, narrow, and exposed, with an extreme drop-off on the downhill side. As such, this pass should only be attempted in narrow-track vehicles by experienced drivers who are not affected by heights. Take note of flattened pieces of vehicles that have rolled off the side of the road into the valley below and evaluate your four-wheel driving skills accordingly. For those who choose to make the trip, the drive and views are spectacular. An alternative for those who are uncomfortable with this type of road is to hike from the junction of the road from Hancock Pass to the summit of Tomichi Pass and back.

At 11,979 feet, the Tomichi Pass route saw some use in the 1880s and 1890s by miners traveling to and from the settlements to the south, Tomichi and Whitepine. Devastated by an avalanche in 1899, Tomichi today is remembered only in a cemetery along FR 888, 2 miles north of Whitepine. At 12,140 feet, Hancock Pass shows little historical legacy and was not even officially named until 1962. Never very prosperous even in its mining days, this remote area contains between its two passes the stunning Brittle Silver Basin and headwaters of Quartz Creek.

STOPS NOT TO MISS Tomichi Cemetery

FEATURES: A treat for those who enjoy historic cemeteries.

HOW TO GET THERE: Descending on the south side of Tomichi Pass, about 3 miles south of the summit, watch for the old cemetery in the trees on the left side of the road. Stroll around and ponder the 19th-century gravesites.

Tomichi has completely disappeared but lives on in the name of the pass and creek that runs by it. In the 1880s, the settlement was reputed to have had 1,500 inhabitants, but a major snowslide in 1899 carried away most of the buildings and mine equipment. The town never recovered and what remains today is a picturesque cemetery with graves of pioneers and miners who once lived there.

Historic cemeteries are often the only reminders of old mining towns.

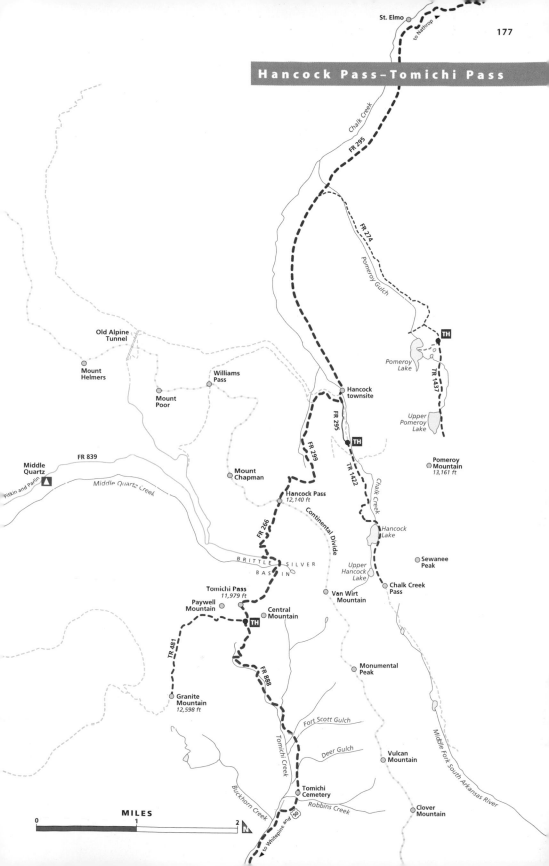

St. Elmo

to Nathrop

Chalk Creek

FR 295

FR 274

Pomeroy Gulch

TH

Pomeroy Lake

TR 1437

Upper Pomeroy Lake

Old Alpine Tunnel

Mount Helmers

Williams Pass

Mount Poor

Hancock townsite

FR 295

FR 299

TH

Pomeroy Mountain
13,161 ft

TR 1422

FR 839

Middle Quartz

Pitkin and Parlin

Middle Quartz Creek

Mount Chapman

Hancock Pass
12,140 ft

Continental Divide

FR 266

Chalk Creek

Hancock Lake

Sewanee Peak

BRITTLE SILVER BASIN

Upper Hancock Lake

Chalk Creek Pass

Tomichi Pass
11,979 ft

Paywell Mountain

Central Mountain

TH

Van Wirt Mountain

TR 481

FR 888

Granite Mountain
12,598 ft

Monumental Peak

Fort Scott Gulch

Deer Gulch

Vulcan Mountain

Tomichi Creek

Middle Fork South Arkansas River

Buckhorn Creek

Tomichi Cemetery

Robbins Creek

Clover Mountain

to Whitepine and 50

MILES

0   1   2

N

HIKES ALONG THE WAY Granite Mountain

FEATURES: Great views into the Quartz Creek and Tomichi Creek drainages.

HOW TO GET THERE: The trail starts at the summit of Tomichi Pass and leads along the ridge to the southwest.

HIKE DIFFICULTY: MODERATE: This is all above treeline as it follows along a high, rocky ridge.

LENGTH: From the top of the pass to Granite Mountain is 2 miles.

From the summit of Tomichi Pass, TR 481 goes to the top of 12,598-foot Granite Mountain. If you wish to hike farther, trails from the summit descend into various creek drainages on the west side of the Continental Divide.

OTHER NEARBY HIKES Pomeroy Lakes

FEATURES: Two 12-acre lakes in a huge, level tundra basin above 12,000 feet.

HOW TO GET THERE: About 2.5 miles before reaching the Hancock townsite from St. Elmo on FR 295, FR 274 leads south up Pomeroy Gulch. The road becomes TR 1437 at the lower lake and continues to Upper Pomeroy Lake.

HIKE DIFFICULTY: MODERATE: The steepest part is the hike up the valley to treeline and the lower lake; from there, the hike to the upper lake is almost level.

LENGTH: From the turnoff on FR 295 to Pomeroy Lake is 3 miles; Upper Pomeroy Lake is a little more than 1 mile beyond the lower lake.

This is a steadily climbing drive or hike through forested slopes into a beautiful alpine basin containing the two lakes. If you drive, the road is closed at the lower lake, requiring a hike to the upper lake. Pomeroy Mountain (13,161 feet) forms the majestic backdrop to Upper Pomeroy Lake.

OTHER NEARBY HIKES Hancock Lakes & Chalk Creek Pass

FEATURES: A high-altitude lake in a tundra basin at 11,660 feet.

HOW TO GET THERE: From the Hancock townsite, instead of starting the ascent of Hancock Pass, continue to the left (south) on FR 295 for 2 miles. Just north of the lake, the route becomes TR 1422. Alternatively, park at the road junction and enjoy the trip to the lakes as a hike or bicycle ride.

HIKE DIFFICULTY: EASY TO MODERATE: This is a gradual uphill hike along the road.

LENGTH: 2 miles from the road junction to Lower Hancock Lake; another 0.25 mile to Upper Hancock Lake; 2.5 miles from the road junction to Chalk Creek Pass.

The road climbs gradually uphill to 12-acre Lower Hancock Lake. There is a second smaller lake behind the first. Hikers who want more can follow the trail past the upper lake to the summit of Chalk Creek Pass, which is on a short, steep (360 feet in 0.25 mile) section of trail that leads to the ridge above.

THE ALPINE LOOP

LOCATION: West of Lake City, southeast of Ouray, and northeast of Silverton.

HIGHLIGHTS: Engineer Pass (12,800 feet) and Cinnamon Pass (12,620 feet) crown a spectacular byway across the San Juan Mountains tundra, with magnificent views, wildflowers, ghost towns, and historic structures along the way.

ACCESS: Much of the lower approach to Engineer Pass from Lake City is good for passenger cars with high clearance, depending on the road and weather conditions, but proceed with caution. A 4WD or pickup truck makes the trip much easier. The roads to Engineer Pass west of Capitol City and back over Cinnamon Pass are definitely 4WD.

LENGTH: It is 18 miles from Lake City to the top of Engineer Pass; from the summit of Engineer Pass to the summit of Cinnamon Pass is 7 miles; and from Cinnamon Pass back to Lake City is 24 miles. Linking 4WD roads from Ouray and Silverton to the byway bring its official distance to about 65 miles, but the Lake City–based loop described here is 49 miles and takes about eight hours to drive, including time to enjoy the sights.

MAPS: Uncompahgre National Forest.

HOW TO GET THERE: From the south end of Lake City, take the Henson Creek road (CR 20/BLM Road 3300) west. As far as Capitol City, the road is suitable for passenger cars, but the surface deteriorates as it goes up Engineer Pass and may have large potholes. The summit and west side of Engineer Pass, and the return over Cinnamon Pass, are only suitable for 4WD vehicles. From the top of Engineer Pass go south along CR 2/BLM 4500 toward the ghost town of Animas Forks. Just south of town, take CR 5/BLM 3306 east up the hill to Cinnamon Pass; CR 4 continues on the east side of the summit, and you'll rejoin smoother road along CR 30 east of Sherman to take you back to Lake City. Some do the loop drive in reverse.

Access to the Alpine Loop from the west is via two rugged spur roads of the scenic byway that start from Ouray and Silverton, respectively. Reach Engineer Pass from Ouray by driving about 3.5 miles south of town on US 550 to a marked turnoff to the east. Take 4WD FR 878 about 9 miles to Engineer Pass. From the pass, drive south on CR 2 toward Cinnamon Mountain, then east on CR 5 over Cinnamon Pass. Alternatively from Silverton, drive northeast on CO 110 (CR 2/BLM 4500/FR 586) through the ghost towns of Howardsville and Eureka. Just before the turn west to Animas Forks, bear right onto CR 5 to cross east over Cinnamon Pass.

On the Engineer Pass road in late June.

D riving these two passes offers a rewarding, easy way to take in some of the best tundra country in Colorado. The many side roads at the top are excellent for driving or hiking—once the snow melts, usually sometime in July. The 65-mile loop, which connects the historic towns Lake City, Ouray, and Silverton, is a designated national backcountry byway.

The road over Engineer Pass was built in 1877 as a stagecoach route connecting Lake City to Animas Forks and Mineral Point. Historic buildings and mines mark this route. Rose's Cabin, to name one, about 14.5 miles from Lake City on CR 20, was a 22-room hotel and eating establishment frequented by stagecoach travelers. The Cinnamon Pass road back to Lake City roughly parallels the Engineer Pass road several miles to the south. Named after the mountain, which was in turn named for its reddish hue, the pass was a former American Indian trail that became a supply route to remote towns in the Silverton-area mining district.

Lake San Cristobal, just south of Lake City on the way to Cinnamon Pass, was formed some 750 years ago when a massive mudslide dammed the Lake Fork of the Gunnison River. A later slide occurred about 300 years ago. Early settlers thought that the mudslide looked and smelled like a pungent, yellowish stew they made called slumgullion stew. We should perhaps be thankful that the lake today bears a mellifluous Spanish name, because the pass above the lake is still known as Slumgullion Pass.

STOPS NOT TO MISS   Animas Forks

FEATURES: A historic ghost town set in a valley at 11,584 feet.

HOW TO GET THERE: The town is to the west of CR 2/BLM Road 4500 between Engineer Pass and Cinnamon Pass. Stroll around and enjoy the old buildings.

Animas Forks was laid out in 1877. A mining boomtown then sprang up, with stores, hotels, a newspaper, and two smelting works. The town even survived the massive blizzard of 1884. A picturesque two-story wooden house with a bay window was supposedly owned by Thomas Walsh, the owner of the Camp Bird Mine. His daughter, Evalyn Walsh McLean, at one time owned the fabulous Hope Diamond. Animas Forks later became a railroad stop in 1906, but the town's fortunes rose and fell with the mines, and by 1917 the spur was retired. The town has been abandoned since the 1920s.

The Walsh House in Animas Forks.

The flowers of the Colorado blue columbine are a pale color at treeline.

STOPS NOT TO MISS American Flats

FEATURES: Large fields of wildflowers set in hundreds of acres of gently rolling meadow at around 12,500 feet.

HOW TO GET THERE: Just before reaching the summit of Engineer Pass, find an old, closed jeep trail to the north. Park and head right (north), following the old road for a few miles onto American Flats. Just enjoy the flowers from the car or stroll in the meadows.

This is a good walk for older individuals or those who cannot tolerate high-altitude walks yet still appreciate seeing the tundra wildflowers. The peak of the profuse blooms here typically occurs in July. Matterhorn and Wetterhorn Peaks make an ideal backdrop to the showy display. American Lake is about 3 miles from the start of the old jeep trail. Be aware of becoming disoriented in this large, open area, as there are few visual reference points to help you find your way back to your car.

HIKES ALONG THE WAY Carson

FEATURES: Historic interest in an alpine meadow at the head of Wager Gulch.

HOW TO GET THERE: The turnoff to Wager Gulch, which is CR 9/FR 568, is about 11.5 miles south of Lake City on the Cinnamon Pass road (CR 30).

HIKE DIFFICULTY: MODERATE: This rating is if you hike up the old road to the town from the Cinnamon Pass road. If you drive up the steep, rocky 4WD road, there is no hiking, just a stroll around the old buildings.

LENGTH: From the turnoff on the Cinnamon Pass road to the townsite is 3.5 miles; it is an additional 1.25 miles to the crest of the saddle behind the town on the Continental Divide.

Authorities do not agree on the location of the original townsite of Carson. Some place it just in the trees at 11,500 feet. Others claim that Carson was actually built in the saddle on the Divide at 12,360 feet, just below 13,393-foot Bent Peak to the west and 13,334-foot Coney to the east, and that the collection of cabins below was a different, later settlement. Whichever was the actual townsite, Carson reached a peak in the 1890s, when 400 to 500 men worked in the local mines.

At the Divide, the Wager Gulch Trail links with the Colorado Trail, which along this stretch merges with the Continental Divide Trail. Beware of summer storms here, because the saddle is underlaid by iron ore, which tends to attract lightning.

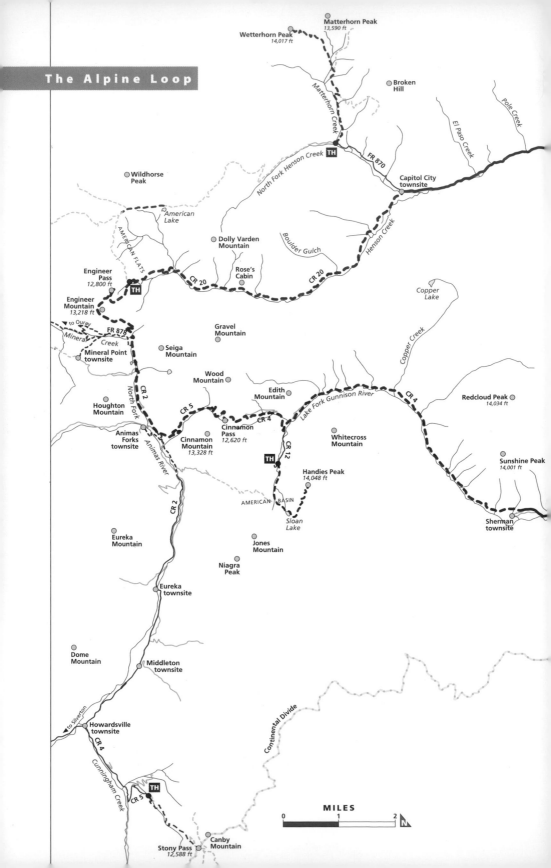

Matterhorn Peak
13,590 ft

Wetterhorn Peak
14,017 ft

Broken
Hill

Pole Creek

El Paso Creek

Matterhorn Creek

North Fork Henson Creek

Wildhorse
Peak

American Lake

TH

FR 870

Capitol City
townsite

Henson Creek

Copper
Lake

Dolly Varden
Mountain

Boulder Gulch

Rose's
Cabin

CR 20

CR 20

AMERICAN FLATS

Engineer
Pass
12,800 ft

TH

Engineer
Mountain
13,218 ft

Gravel
Mountain

Copper Creek

to Ouray

FR 878

Mineral Creek

Seiga
Mountain

Mineral Point
townsite

Wood
Mountain

Edith
Mountain

Lake Fork Gunnison River

CR 4

Redcloud Peak
14,034 ft

North Fork

CR 2

Houghton
Mountain

CR 5

CR 4

Animas
Forks
townsite

Cinnamon
Mountain
13,328 ft

Cinnamon
Pass
12,620 ft

CR 12

Whitecross
Mountain

Sunshine Peak
14,001 ft

TH

Animas River

Handies Peak
14,048 ft

AMERICAN BASIN

Sloan Lake

Sherman
townsite

Eureka
Mountain

CR 2

Jones
Mountain

Niagra
Peak

Eureka
townsite

Dome
Mountain

Middleton
townsite

Continental Divide

to Silverton

Howardsville
townsite

CR 4

Cunningham Creek

TH

CR 5

MILES

0   1   2

N

Stony Pass
12,588 ft

Canby
Mountain

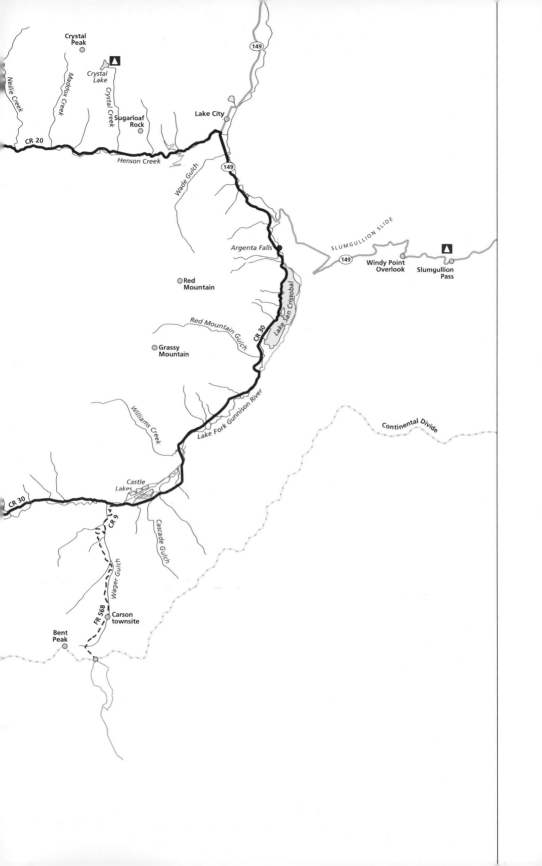

Subalpine valerian

HIKES ALONG THE WAY American Basin and Handies Peak

FEATURES: A fourteener at the head of a charming alpine basin.

HOW TO GET THERE: About 2 miles below the top of Cinnamon Pass on the east side, take CR 12 to the south and follow it about 0.25 mile into American Basin.

HIKE DIFFICULTY: MODERATE TO STRENUOUS: Though this hike is fairly short, it involves a 2,600-foot elevation gain at high altitude.

LENGTH: From the parking area in American Basin to the summit of Handies Peak is 2 miles.

Handies Peak is not considered by most mountaineers to be a challenging climb, but it is a very attractive one. Follow the trail alongside the creek that is the infant Lake Fork of the Gunnison River and hike south toward Sloan Lake high up below the ridge at the end of American Basin. The summit of Handies Peak will become visible as a bump on the horizon to the left (east). American Basin usually has robust wildflower displays in the summer.

OTHER NEARBY HIKES Wetterhorn Peak

FEATURES: Wetterhorn Peak (14, 017 feet) and nearby Matterhorn Peak (13,590 feet) in the Uncompahgre Wilderness (formerly Big Blue Wilderness) are justifiably popular with mountain climbers.

HOW TO GET THERE: From the south end of Lake City, take the Henson Creek road (CR 20/BLM 3300) 9 miles west up the Engineer Pass road to Capitol City. Turn off to the north onto FR 870 for 2 miles to the Wetterhorn trailhead.

HIKE DIFFICULTY: STRENUOUS: Challenging and not for the faint of heart because of the precipitous rocky slopes and ledges that lead to the final summit.

LENGTH: From Capitol City to the summit of Wetterhorn is 4 miles.

The starting point for this peak on the Engineer Pass road is Capitol City. This unassuming town was once promoted by local mill owner George S. Lee, who renamed the town from the less-grand Galena City and aspired to make it the state's capital, with himself as governor. He built a self-styled governor's mansion there, complete with bay windows and an orchestra hall. Unluckily for him, however, the population of Capitol City never reached higher than about 800.

The ascent of Wetterhorn is not considered particularly difficult by mountain climbers, but rope skills may be crucial for the final scramble to the summit in order to avoid a fall down the 600-foot southwest face. Matterhorn Peak is often used as a vantage point to photograph Wetterhorn Peak.

Alpine forget-me-not

OTHER NEARBY HIKES ## Stony Pass

FEATURES: A trip south to the Continental Divide with fine views to the south from atop a 12,588-foot pass.

HOW TO GET THERE: From Engineer Pass, travel south on CR 2 some 7.5 miles to the Howardsville townsite, then bear left (southeast) onto CR 4. After 2 miles, turn off onto CR 3 to the left (east) and go about 3 miles to the top of Stony Pass.

HIKE DIFFICULTY: EASY: No hike required, unless you wish to park in Howardsville and hike up the Stony Pass jeep road. The road climbs evenly for about 2,300 feet through the trees and rapidly emerges onto the tundra to provide panoramic views.

LENGTH: From the turnoff on CR 2 to the summit of the pass is 5 miles.

From a tundra standpoint, the west side of Stony Pass is more impressive than the east. Once atop the pass on the Continental Divide, enjoy the views of the Needles Range and Weminuche Wilderness to the south. The drive down the east side of Stony Pass, however, still has grandeur. The east side of the pass road is FR 520, which is a long, bumpy, unimproved road that passes Rio Grande Reservoir en route to CO 149 west of Creede. This route, via Spring Creek Pass on CO 149, is an alternative to Cinnamon Pass (if far longer) for returning to Lake City.

NEARBY STOPS ## Mineral Point

FEATURES: A short drive off the Alpine Loop leads to an abandoned townsite in an attractive alpine meadow at 11,720 feet.

HOW TO GET THERE: Descending the gulch from Engineer Pass toward Animas Forks, CR 2/BLM Road 4500 passes the turnoff to FR 878, the road to the west that descends to Ouray. Turn right (west) onto FR 878; after about 0.75 mile, watch for an unnumbered road to the left (south) that leads 1 mile to Mineral Point.

Mineral Point was first settled in 1873 and thrived until the late 1890s. The townsite lies on a 60-foot-wide outcropping of quartz, for which it was named, and which contains several valuable mineral veins. This silver-mining town had a sawmill, store, and hotel, along with restaurants, saloons, and log dwellings. All that remains today to mark the location of one of the largest 1870s-era mining camps in the vicinity are some stone foundations and crumbling logs.

IMOGENE PASS

LOCATION: This 13,114-foot pass lies southwest of Ouray and about 6.5 miles east of Telluride.

HIGHLIGHTS: This challenging and very popular 4WD route travels through sublime alpine country and past the famous Camp Bird and Tomboy Mines.

ACCESS: Skilled 4WD enthusiasts will encounter several challenging sections near the summit on the east side; the west side drops steeply down a magnificent valley to Telluride.

LENGTH: From Ouray to the Camp Bird Mill on the east side is about 5 miles; from the mill to the summit of the pass is 6 miles; and from the summit it is 1.5 miles down the west side to the town of Tomboy, then 5 more miles down to Telluride.

MAPS: Uncompahgre National Forest.

HOW TO GET THERE: From US 50 in Montrose, drive 26 miles south on US 550 to Ouray. Drive through town and take CO 361/FR 853 past Box Canyon Falls to the Camp Bird Mill on a graded gravel road alongside Canyon Creek. Just before the mill, angle right (north) and take FR 853.1B, which is the ledge road to Yankee Boy Basin. After 1.5 miles, just before the Sneffels townsite, FR 869 makes a hairpin turn back to the left and starts up through the timber to Imogene Pass. Drive 6 miles to the top of the pass. On the west side, the road drops steeply to the ruins of the mine town of Tomboy and then goes on down to Telluride in the valley below.

The barren summit of Imogene Pass.

Named, like the nearby basin, for the wife of a co-owner of Camp Bird Mine, Imogene Pass was originally built to carry ore from the Tomboy Mine to Ouray; the Camp Bird ruins lie alongside the pass road on the east side. As a key route in mining's heyday, the pass is among the most historically rich in the San Juan Mountains.

Atop the pass, look for the ruins of Fort Peabody, a curious, tiny militia outpost built during a period of intense labor strife in Telluride in 1903–1904.

The pass also hosted the first alternating-current, long-distance electrical transmission line in the United States. Electrical power was generated at a hydroelectric station at Ames, south of Telluride, and transmitted by wire to Camp Bird on the other side of the mountains. A company repairman was stationed permanently atop the pass to repair storm-damaged wires.

Because of lingering ice and snowdrifts, Imogene Pass can often only be driven between late July and mid-September. Be sure to stop at the summit to savor the spectacular views of the tundra and the Red Mountain mining district.

STOPS NOT TO MISS Tomboy

FEATURES: A superb example of an old mining community.

HOW TO GET THERE: Tomboy is located on the west side of the descent from Imogene Pass. Alternatively, if you are coming from Telluride, travel east on FR 869 toward Imogene Pass. This is a narrow, steep, 4WD road with shelf sections and should be attempted only by experienced drivers. Otherwise park and hike to the mines. High-clearance vehicles can sometimes reach Tomboy under good conditions. Enjoy a casual walk to see the ruins of buildings and mining artifacts.

Named after the Tomboy Gold Mines Company, Tomboy thrived from 1880 to 1927 with several hundred people, including families, living here year-round. Now all that remains are the scars of mining activity and former buildings. Marmots and pikas are common in rock piles around the old mining equipment.

HIKES ALONG THE WAY Governor Basin

FEATURES: Historic mining ruins perched in an alpine basin near the crest of the mountains, with summer wildflower fields en route.

HOW TO GET THERE: Take FR 853 south from Ouray, and just before the Camp Bird Mill, bear right onto FR 853.1B toward Yankee Boy Basin. About 0.5 mile west of the abandoned mining town of Sneffels, take a sharp turn to the left (south) onto FR 853.1C and drive up into Governor Basin.

HIKE DIFFICULTY: MODERATE: A moderate climb up the 4WD road.

LENGTH: From the turnoff onto FR 853.1C, it is 2 miles to the Humbolt Mine at the top of the basin.

The ruins of the Virginius Mine (opened in 1877), at 12,200 feet, and the Humbolt Mine, at 12,600 feet, are in Governor Basin. Experienced hikers should explore the old burro trail across Virginius Pass to Telluride, which climbs from above the Virginius Mine, passes around Mendoza Peak on St. Sophia Ridge, and drops to the Smuggler Mine in Marshall Basin on the other side for a distance of 1.5 miles.

Ouray

550

Uncompahgre River

Red Mountain Creek

Crystal Lake

Canyon Creek

FR 853

Thistledown

Canyon Creek

Weehawken Creek

Senator Gulch

Camp Bird townsite

Imogene Creek

FR 853.1B

FR 869

Upper Camp Bird townsite

Imogene Pass
13,114 ft

United States Mountain

Rock Lake

Chicago Peak

Potosi Peak

Sneffels Creek

Sneffels townsite

Tomboy townsite

Teakettle Mountain

Cirque Mountain

FR 853.1B

GOVERNOR BASIN

FR 853.1C

Virginius Mine

Humbolt Mine

Mendoza Peak

FR 869

Marshall Creek

Mount Sneffels
14,150 ft

Blue Lake Pass

YANKEE BOY BASIN

Stony Mountain

Gilpin Peak

Mount Emma

Greenback Mountain

Liberty Bell

Telluride

San Miguel River

145

MILES

HIKES ALONG THE WAY **Yankee Boy Basin**

FEATURES: This picturesque alpine basin, about 9 miles southwest of Ouray, blooms extravagantly with wildflowers in the summer.

HOW TO GET THERE: Angle right (west) just before the Camp Bird Mill, and take FR 853.1B on the thrilling section of ledge road under Hanging Rock to Yankee Boy Basin. A 4WD is required to reach the end of the road in the high alpine basin. Alternatively, you can park near Camp Bird Mill and hike 4 miles up the road into Yankee Boy Basin.

HIKE DIFFICULTY: EASY TO MODERATE: Frequent jeep traffic may detract from a hike up this 4WD road.

LENGTH: Yankee Boy Basin is about 4 miles from the Camp Bird Mill. Additional distance is optional, depending on your interests.

Picture-perfect Twin Falls, above the ghost town of Sneffels in Yankee Boy Basin, was at one time featured in beer advertisements. Stop and look around at the ghost town of Sneffels; both town and fourteener were named after the similar mountain in Jules Verne's *A Journey to the Center of the Earth*. The beautiful Blue Lakes sit at the far western end of the basin over Blue Lakes Pass in the Mount Sneffels Wilderness. A difficult trail through the basin is the most popular access to 14,150-foot Mount Sneffels.

Twin Falls in Yankee Boy Basin.

The Ghost in the Old Mill

I heard a mournful-sounding creak as one of the huge timbers high over my head groaned in response to some unseen force. Off to one side, somewhere in the darkness, there came an eerie flapping as the wind caught a loose piece of corrugated sheet metal, then snapped it back.

Did I believe in ghosts?

At that precise moment, I wasn't sure. Alone in the cavernous building that had once housed gold miners and workmen at the hundred-year-old Last Dollar Mill, I figured that this certainly could have been a place that they would hang around.

Complex machinery was used in the cavernous interior of this processing mill to extract the gold from raw ore.

My friend John, who was going to accompany me as I photographed the remains of the old mill, had cheerfully said that he'd never seen a ghost in all the years that he had owned the building. At the last minute, however, he was called to Denver for a business meeting, but he insisted that I go ahead with my plans.

As he gave me the key to the gate, he looked at me solemnly and said: "Don't let the Tommyknockers get you."

Tommyknockers? The impish little ghosts that inhabit the shafts and tunnels of old gold mines? Brought over by immigrant Cornish miners who worked in them? I should hope not!

But now, standing in the huge, darkened mill building with only a few shafts of light leaking in between the brown, weathered boards that had been warped by the high-altitude sun, and from the open door behind me, I felt eerily alone.

I picked my way carefully across the catwalk in front of the stamps—huge metal pile-drivers that were used to crush gold ore for further processing. In my mind I could almost hear the deafening roar that must have been present as the mill ran full-blast, twenty-four hours a day, to feed the owners' and stakeholders' cravings for gold.

I jumped involuntarily as my reverie was interrupted by a complaining squeal. Looking around, I saw a fat marmot sitting on the sill of a window that gaped open, its glass long gone. The animal's head was pointed accusingly at me.

Who are you, invading my territory? it seemed to be saying.

The timbers above me creaked again with a whispering sigh, and I was glad to go back out into the sunlight. As I walked out of the door, the marmot whistled and vanished from his perch on the windowsill.

Behind the mill, a line of towers with a heavy steel cable at the top stood like soldiers purposefully marching in single file down to the huge building. They were actually part of the tramway system that had once carried ore, in steel buckets suspended from the cable, from the mine high above me on a ridge down to the mill for processing.

Even though the mill stood at timberline, the mine was higher yet. In bad weather, which occurred frequently in winter at these altitudes, miners rode the swaying buckets up to the mine, because that was the only way of going to work. I shuddered at the thought.

I heard a squawk behind me. The marmot was back. He was glaring at me from under the step outside the door into the mill. Obviously that was his home, and I was in his territory. I took a few last photographs, apologized to the marmot, and left him to the undisturbed peace and quiet of the high mountains.

Marmots frequently live around and under old mining buildings.

CLASSIC HIKES

These hikes are all classics—among the best examples of Colorado's environment above treeline. Included here are hikes for all abilities, many of them accessed by a simple drive to a trailhead. In some cases, you may be able to travel farther along the access road with a high-clearance or four-wheel-drive (4WD) vehicle than with a typical passenger car. Instances such as these are identified in the text. Whichever way you get there, please enjoy the tundra with care!

CONTENTS

The summits of Buffalo Peaks look like the rounded head and shoulder of a buffalo.

Opposite: *Climbing fourteeners is a popular pastime, as on this fall afternoon on Grays Peak.*

MOHAWK LAKES

LOCATION: About 5 miles south of Breckenridge.

HIGHLIGHTS: Two fine treeline lakes at 11,830 and 12,100 feet lie near historic mining relics.

ACCESS: A passenger car can reach the first trailhead, but depending on weather conditions, a high-clearance vehicle may be needed to reach the second.

HIKE DIFFICULTY: EASY TO MODERATE: The hike to the lakes from the second trailhead is short, but steep.

LENGTH: From the second trailhead to Mayflower Lakes is 0.75 mile, and to Lower Mohawk Lake is 1.5 miles. Upper Mohawk Lake is another 0.5 mile beyond the lower lake.

MAPS: White River National Forest (though actually in Arapaho National Forest).

HOW TO GET THERE: Drive south from Breckenridge on CO 9 and turn onto Spruce Creek Road (CR 800), across the highway from Goose Pasture Tarn. Follow the road for a little less than 3 miles to the first trailhead. High-clearance and 4WD vehicles can continue about 0.5 mile farther on CR 800 to a second parking area or (if the road is dry) even another 0.25 mile to a water-diversion station.

T his relatively short hike makes a pleasant day outing from Front Range cities. These deep lakes in an alpine setting are surrounded by Western history. A short side-trail of a few hundred yards leads to Mayflower Lakes (11,300 feet), at treeline. This nice spot was the former site of the Mayflower Mill and its associated miners' cabins in the little settlement of Mayflower. The Mayflower Mine dates from

1887, and the Mayflower Mill was built to process ore from the mine. A small group of cabins called Mayflower, around Mayflower Lakes, housed area miners. Some nearby mines were operated by the Glen Mohawk Mining Company.

Another short side path, just above the Mayflower Lakes trail, goes to the bottom of

The top of the tramway station to the Mayflower Mill.

Continental Falls, just below Lower Mohawk Lake. Look for the remnants of a cable tramway station that used to transport ore to the Mayflower Mill down over the hill.

Opposite: *Early morning at Mohawk Lake.*

Mohawk Lakes

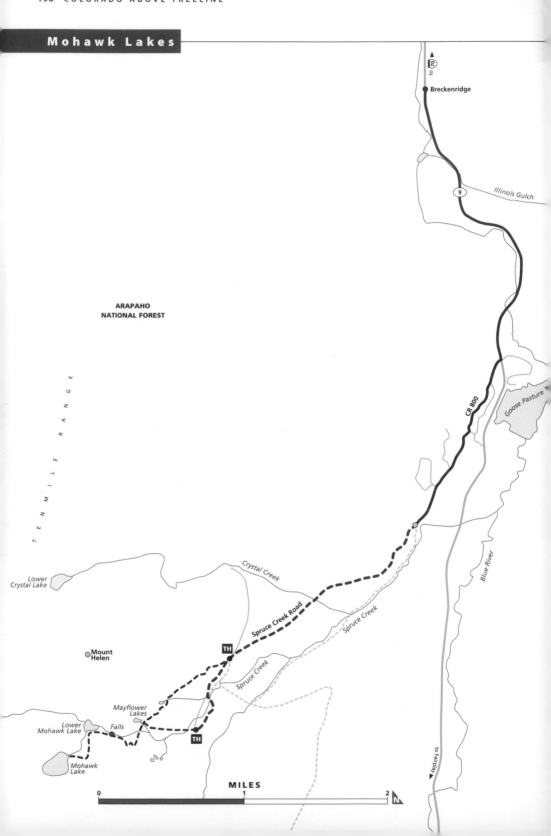

to 70

Breckenridge

9

Illinois Gulch

ARAPAHO
NATIONAL FOREST

T E N M I L E   R A N G E

CR 800

Goose Pasture

Blue River

Crystal Creek

Lower
Crystal Lake

Spruce Creek Road

Spruce Creek

TH

Mount
Helen

Spruce Creek

Mayflower
Lakes

TH

Lower
Mohawk Lake

Falls

Mohawk
Lake

to Fairplay

MILES

0   1   2

N

NOTCH MOUNTAIN

LOCATION: About 12 miles south of Avon on I-70.

HIGHLIGHTS: Access the closest and most spectacular view of Mount of the Holy Cross, a historically significant fourteener.

ACCESS: Graded dirt road to the trailhead.

HIKE DIFFICULTY: STRENUOUS: After a gentle grade along Fall Creek, the last part of the trail is a strenuous, steep climb up switchbacks at high altitude.

LENGTH: From the trailhead to the viewing point on the saddle on Notch Mountain is 5 miles.

MAPS: White River National Forest.

HOW TO GET THERE: From I-70 at Vail, head west for about 5 miles to Dowds Junction, then take US 24 south. Drive about 5 miles, through Minturn, to where US 24 starts to climb Battle Mountain. Turn right (southwest) onto FR 707/ CR 100, toward Tigiwon Campground. Follow the dirt road for 8 miles to the Half Moon trailhead. Take the Fall Creek Trail (TR 2001) south from the trailhead for about 2 miles, then turn off to the right onto TR 2000 for a very steep climb (2,000 feet in 3 miles!) that zigzags up switchbacks on Notch Mountain. An impressive view of Holy Cross awaits you. The stone Notch Mountain Shelter in the saddle at 13,060 feet was built in 1924 for pilgrims and visitors.

The Mount of the Holy Cross, as seen from Notch Mountain, provided inspiration for Christian pilgrimages and for migration to the West.

T he best time of year to see the cross is typically late July—when the snow has mostly melted off the mountain face but still lingers in the crevices. The cross is more distinct in some years than in others, depending on the winter snow-pack. The lake in the valley below Mount of the Holy Cross is named the Bowl of Tears. The cross is not visible from the nearby ghost town of Holy Cross City, but those unable or disinclined to make a strenuous hike can view it at a greater distance from a marked observation site on CR 16/FR 709, the Shrine Pass Road, between Vail Pass and Red Cliff, about 1.5 miles west of the summit of Shrine Pass.

A lesser-known yet equally curious snow formation appears each spring on 14,229-foot Mount Shavano. Snow trapped in crevices and gullies on the southeast face depicts a figure 800 feet tall with upraised arms, known as the Angel of Shavano. One legend says that this is the figure of an Indian princess who sacrificed herself to save her people from a severe drought. Her tears, in the form of melting snow, water the crops each year. The best time for viewing the angel is usually in late May and early June, before she melts away. The junction of US 50 and US 285 at Poncha Springs is the best place from which to see her.

Mount of the Holy Cross

Famous for the giant cross of snow that appears on its eastern face as the snow begins to melt in early summer, Mount of the Holy Cross (14,005 feet) has an unusual history. The cross, 750 feet wide and 1,500 feet high, is formed by snow that collects in winter in crevices on the mountain face. One legend recounts how two 18th-century Spanish priests passing through the area lost their way in a fierce blizzard. Just when they had run out of energy and lost all hope of survival, the clouds parted, and they saw the giant snowy cross gleaming from the mountainside in front of them. The sight gave them the renewed strength to find their way safely out of the mountains again.

The symbolic crucifix was considered mere fable until noted Western photographer William Henry Jackson took the first images of it in 1873. Since then, Mount of the Holy Cross and its snowy emblem have been the objects of many religious pilgrimages. In the 1870s, the mountain's renown was also furthered in the public's mind by a romantic Thomas Moran painting and a poem by Henry Wadsworth Longfellow. Although designated a national monument in 1929, Holy Cross lost the title was withdrawn in 1950 on account of low visitation and the relative inaccessibility the best vantage point, which is on top of Notch Mountain. Today, designation as the Holy Cross Wilderness protects the mountain and its vicinity. Controversy lingers as to whether the right arm of the cross has deteriorated or been damaged in recent decades or whether William Henry Jackson took his photographs during a year of superb snow conditions.

Notch Mountain

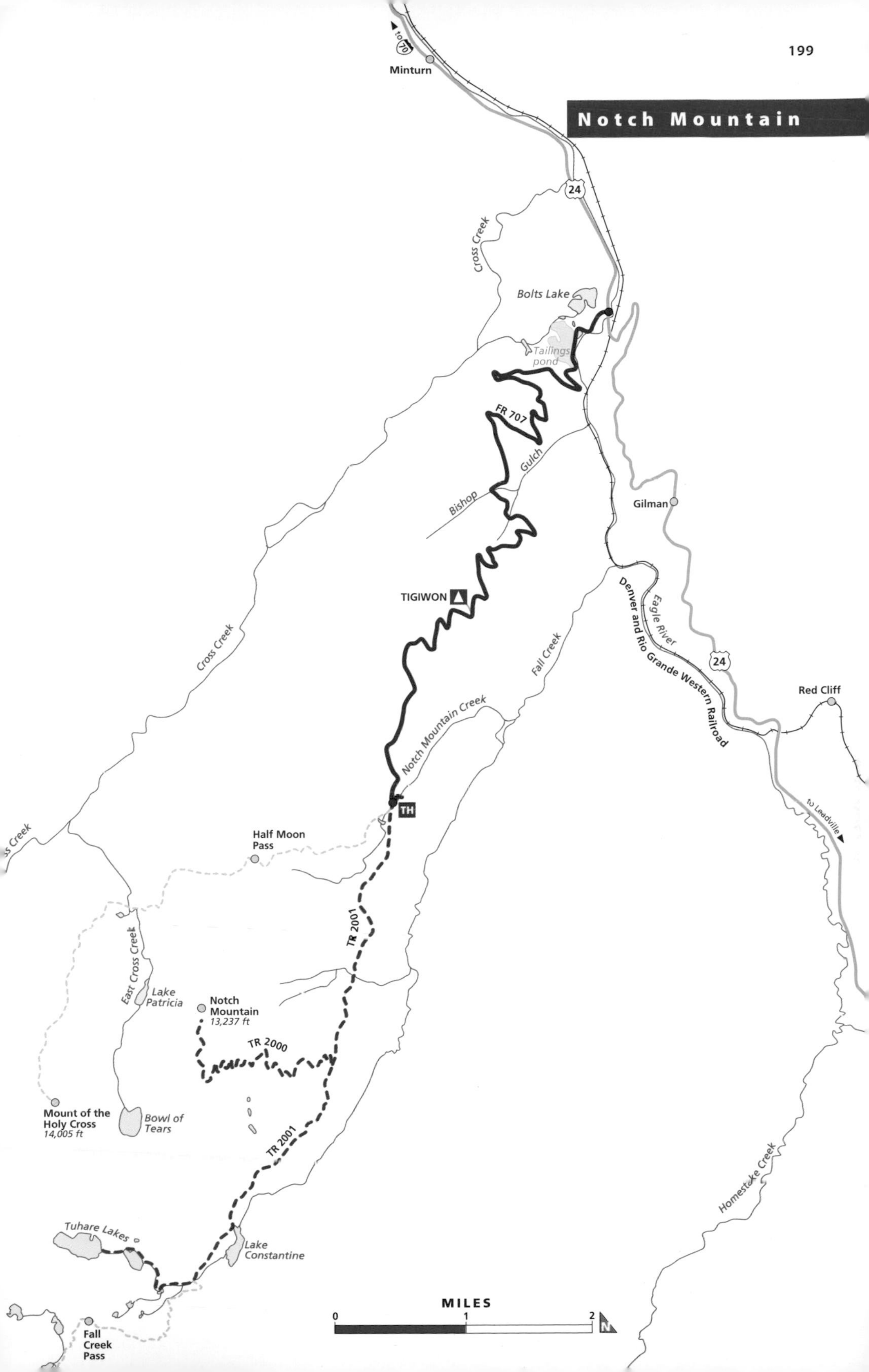

to I-70

Minturn

Cross Creek

24

Bolts Lake

Tailings pond

FR 707

Bishop Gulch

Gilman

TIGIWON

Fall Creek

Eagle River

Denver and Rio Grande Western Railroad

24

Red Cliff

Notch Mountain Creek

Cross Creek

to Leadville

TH

Half Moon Pass

East Cross Creek

Lake Patricia

TR 2001

Notch Mountain
13,237 ft

TR 2000

Cross Creek

Mount of the Holy Cross
14,005 ft

Bowl of Tears

TR 2001

Homestake Creek

Tuhare Lakes

Lake Constantine

Fall Creek Pass

MILES

0   1   2   N

OTHER NEARBY HIKES | Lake Constantine

FEATURES: A lovely 13-acre lake nestled among high peaks in an alpine valley.

HOW TO GET THERE: This trip starts at the Half Moon trailhead. Follow Fall Creek Trail (TR 2001) toward Notch Mountain. After 2 miles, at the junction with TR 2000, continue ahead on TR 2001 for another 2 miles to Lake Constantine.

HIKE DIFFICULTY: EASY TO MODERATE: The trail follows a modest climb alongside Fall Creek to the lake.

LENGTH: From the trailhead to the lake is 4 miles.

Those wanting a longer hike can continue on TR 2001 for another 1.5 miles up a rough, steep trail to Upper Tuhare Lake (12,365 feet) and Lower Tuhare Lake (12,090 feet) above treeline.

Lake Constantine is still surrounded by snow in mid-July.

The Revenge of Boreas

Did you tighten the tent stakes?" came a bleary voice out of the darkness. I rolled over and grunted as I felt something flapping against the bottom of my sleeping bag.

"Was that a yes or a no?" came another question. "Doesn't really matter," my friend added philosophically. "It's your turn now."

I unzipped my sleeping bag and groped around for my hiking boots. I slipped them on, not bothering to tie the laces, and crawled out through the door of the collapsing tent.

Outside, the wind that had started shortly after dark was gusting ceaselessly on the tundra, buffeting our nylon home—just as it had been doing all night long. Our mountaineering tent was an older style, with poles at each end and nylon cords to guy up the poles and sides of the tent. This would be our fourth attempt to reset the poles and guy lines, to try to keep the tent up in the wind.

I was sure that if there really were a Boreas, the ancient god of the north wind, he was probably laughing at us right now. Each time that one of us had carefully tightened the guy lines, rechecked the tent stakes, and reset the poles, the wind had blown part of the tent back down again. With malicious humor, Boreas had waited until we had both drifted back off to sleep, then reached out with clawlike fingers of wind to work the tent stakes out of the ground until the fabric again collapsed on top of us.

The evening before, as we were setting up the tent for the night on the only flat spot on the hillside, a group of young people carrying something had come stumbling unevenly down the steep trail from the ridge above us, which was the final approach to Notch Mountain. As they drew closer, I saw that the "something" was a stretcher holding a young woman with an inflatable splint on her leg.

"Trouble?" I asked. "Need any help?"

"We're fine," said a blond young man who looked to be the leader of the group. He nodded cheerfully at the stretcher. "Broke her leg as we were coming up the other side of the ridge."

I looked at him in surprise. "Wouldn't it have been easier to go back down the valley and out to Minturn?" I asked, sure that it would have been a shorter route toward help, rather than climbing up one side of the ridge and down the other.

"Nah," he said. "We were coming this way anyway. Our van is going to meet us at the trailhead." With that he gave a cheery wave, and the strange procession lurched off out of sight around the hill toward the Half Moon Trailhead.

Standing there now in the late night sky, with the wind whistling up the sleeves of my T-shirt, I wondered briefly if they had made it out or if they had been forced to stop for the night on the trail. I beat the tent stakes back into place with a rock, reset the tent poles, tightened up the nylon guy lines, and crawled back into my sleeping bag.

I had just drifted off to sleep again when, true to form, the tent collapsed on top of us for the fifth time.

"To hell with it," came a muffled grunt from the sleeping bag next to me. "I'm not going out again."

I agreed.

That decision made, I turned over and went back to sleep. Freed now from the worry of the tent blowing down again, we both slept soundly in our cocoon of nylon for the rest of the night.

MISSOURI LAKES AND FANCY LAKE LOOP

LOCATION: About 15 miles northwest of Leadville.

HIGHLIGHTS: A series of beautiful treeline lakes, two scenic passes, and an alpine basin with mining remnants make for a fine loop hike.

ACCESS: Reach the trailhead via a graded dirt road.

HIKE DIFFICULTY: STRENUOUS: Though not particularly strenuous, this hike is long and has several steep sections traversing two passes at the far end.

LENGTH: From the Fancy Pass trailhead to the summit of Fancy Pass is 2.5 miles. Then it's 1 mile across the tundra to Missouri Pass, and from there south and east back to the Missouri Pass trailhead is 4 miles. Add 0.5 mile along the road to return to the Fancy Pass trailhead for a total 8-mile loop.

MAPS: White River National Forest.

HOW TO GET THERE: Follow US 24 about 20 miles north of Leadville or 13 miles south of Dowds Junction (on I-70) to FR 703, the road to Homestake Reservoir. Drive southwest on FR 703 for 8 miles to the junction near Gold Park with FR 704, turn right, then drive 2.5 more miles to the Missouri Lakes trailhead. You can also continue, turning sharply northward, about 0.5 mile farther to the Fancy Pass trailhead, depending the direction in which you want to make the loop or which lakes are your destination.

One of the smaller Missouri Lakes.

The trail over Fancy Pass is an old wagon road once used to haul mining supplies over the pass to the Treasure Vault Mill—which was only in operation for three weeks. Watch for an interesting short, steep section of the trail just below the pass summit on the south side, where wagons were hauled up the final rocky section with ropes.

Most of the hiking in this area is through the beautiful Holy Cross Wilderness. You can choose to hike to Missouri Pass (11,986 feet) and back, hike to Fancy Pass (12,380 feet) and back, or hike both as a loop. This circuit can be done in either direction, though many hikers prefer the counterclockwise loop to Fancy Lake first. The hiking route (TR 2006) climbs steeply up an old jeep trail then turns into a foot trail to Fancy Lake (11,540 feet). Go past the lake and over the pass to Treasure Vault Lake, then head back over Missouri Pass (TR 2003).

Early morning at Mohawk Lake.

OTHER NEARBY HIKES Holy Cross City

FEATURES: A ghost town at 11,335 feet makes for a great hike—or one of the roughest 4WD trips in Colorado.

HOW TO GET THERE: As you would to reach Missouri Lakes, turn west from US 24 onto the road to Homestake Reservoir (FR 703). Drive southwest for 7.5 miles to the summer homes at Gold Park (0.5 mile beyond the Gold Park Campground) and watch for FR 759, a narrow jeep trail that goes steeply uphill to the right (north) alongside French Creek. Follow FR 759 to Holy Cross City.

HIKE DIFFICULTY: MODERATE: The first part of the drive or hike is steep and rough, then flattens out as it follows French Creek up the final part of the valley to the ruins of Holy Cross City.

LENGTH: From Gold Park to Holy Cross City is 3.5 miles.

In the early 1880s, the Holy Cross City mining district was booming. However, it was only to last for a few years. By 1884, many of the miners had left. The road to the townsite is one of the worst 4WD roads in Colorado—in fact, it is maintained by a Denver 4WD club to provide a challenging ride. Ruts, bogs, potholes, and boulders will test the frame, tires, and suspension of any vehicle. You may prefer to enjoy it as a hike. Hunky Dory, Fancy, and Cleveland Lakes, all picturesque tundra destinations, lie at the end of various short spur roads and trails at distances of 0.5 mile to 2 miles or so from the townsite.

Tenth Mountain Division Hut System

Hikers in the triangle defined by Leadville, Vail, and Aspen, which covers a famously picturesque section of the Continental Divide, may be curious about a series of modern wooden buildings in the area dotting scenic backcountry ridges between 9,700 feet and 11,700 feet. This is the Tenth Mountain Division Hut System, founded in 1980 by a group of backcountry enthusiasts to house backcountry skiers, snowshoers, mountain bikers, and backpackers. It was named for the U.S. Army division that trained on skis for deployment in Italy during World War II. Today, visitors bring their own sleeping bags, use woodstoves for heating, melt snow in winter for water, and eat and sleep in a communal setting. The system comprises 29 huts and some 350 miles of routes and is perhaps the most famous hut system in Colorado.

Missouri Lakes and Fancy Lake Loop

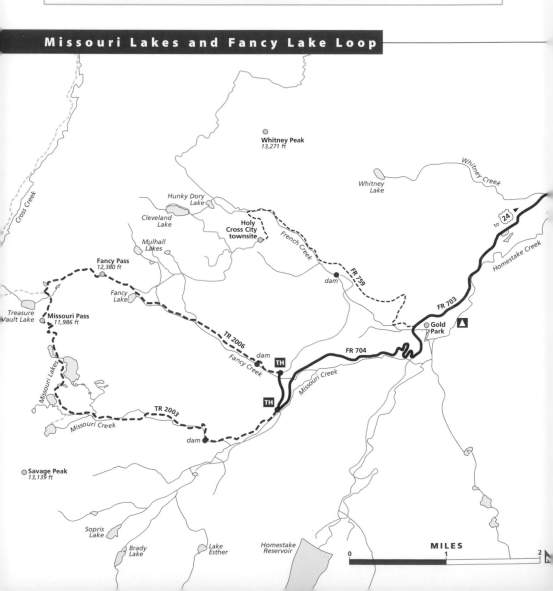

MOUNT ELBERT

LOCATION: About 12 miles southwest of Leadville.

HIGHLIGHTS: The route up to the 14,433-foot summit, Colorado's highest, boasts a rocky finale with panoramic views.

ACCESS: Reach the south trailhead via a paved road; the north trailhead via a graded dirt road.

HIKE DIFFICULTY: STRENUOUS: Though many mountaineers consider this easy, the trail involves a considerable elevation gain and hiking at high altitude.

LENGTH: From the paved parking lot at the end of the blacktop up the south trail to the summit is 6 miles; the hike from the northern trailhead at the end of the jeep road to the summit is 4 miles.

MAPS: San Isabel National Forest.

HOW TO GET THERE: From the junction of US 24 at CO 82, turn west onto the Independence Pass road. After 4 miles, just before the hydroelectric power plant on the left, on the north shore of Twin Lakes Reservoir, bear right onto a paved road up the hill. Go 1.25 miles, past Lake View Campground, and park at the trail-head on the left. High-clearance or 4WD vehicles can continue about 2 miles to the end of the jeep road that forms the first stretch of the trail, TR 1481.

An alternative trail (the old Main Range Trail) starts from the north. To access it, drive 4 miles south of Leadville on US 24 to Malta, then head west on CO 300 for 0.75 mile to a left on FR 110. Drive 6.5 miles and look for TR 1776, which starts 1.5 miles west of Halfmoon Campground at the Massive/Elbert trailhead. Just north of the Herrington Creek crossing, the trail forks; bear right off TR 1776 onto an old jeep road that continues south and west to meet TR 1481 at treeline to continue west to the summit. From FR 110 to the summit is 6.5 miles.

A third, steeper trail, popular with climbers, is TR 1484, which leaves TR 1776 about a half mile south of the Massive/Elbert trailhead and heads directly south-west up the ridge to the summit.

Twin Lakes and an early morning haze, viewed from the Mount Elbert trail.

The highest mountain in Colorado, 14,433-foot Mount Elbert stands about 12 miles southwest of Leadville, in the Sawatch Range. Mount Elbert was named after Samuel Elbert, territorial governor in 1873 and 1874. This is the second highest mountain in the continental United States, exceeded only by 14,495-foot Mount Whitney in California's Sierra Nevada.

Formerly, 4WD vehicles could drive to within a few hundred feet of the top of Mount Elbert, and a jeep is said to have made it to the summit in 1949 as part of a promotion to build a road to the top. In any case, the old road is now closed to all motorized vehicles and forms part of the hiking routes.

The South Mount Elbert Trail, TR 1481, is popular with hikers and peak climbers. The first stretch follows a fairly level 4WD road through a lovely aspen forest. At the end of the road, a footpath continues and passes several water-diversion streams and ponds. After about 0.25 mile, TR 1481 to the summit turns sharply west in a scenic aspen grove and climbs steeply to treeline. Just before leaving the trees, the hiking trail joins a faint former jeep trail from the Halfmoon Campground trailhead and continues upward across the tundra to the summit along a broad, sloping ridge. Note the fellfields on the tundra, and from the top, enjoy fine views of the Continental Divide to the west and Leadville, Twin Lakes, and the Upper Arkansas valley to the east.

Mount Elbert, the highest fourteener in Colorado at 14,433 feet, is a popular hike.

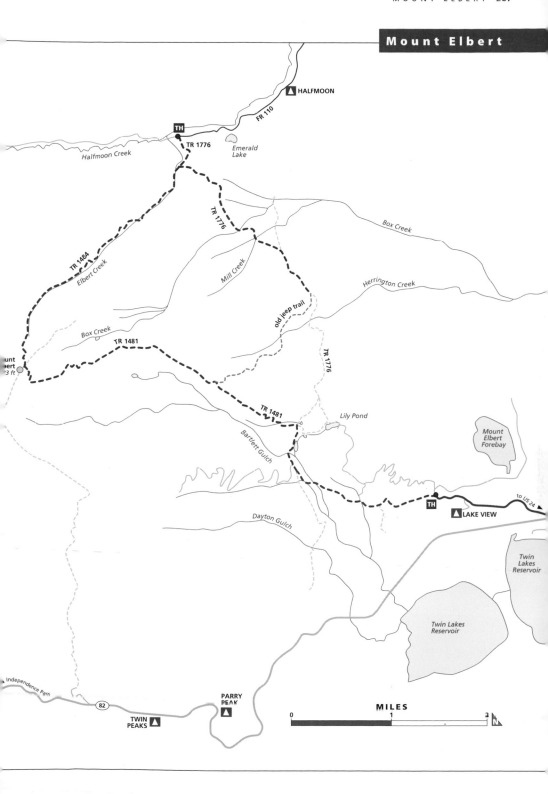

Mount Elbert

HALFMOON

FR 110

TH

TR 1776

Emerald Lake

Halfmoon Creek

TR 1776

Box Creek

TR 1424

Elbert Creek

Mill Creek

Herrington Creek

old jeep trail

TR 1776

Box Creek

TR 1481

Mount Elbert 3 ft

TR 1481

Lily Pond

Bartlett Gulch

Mount Elbert Forebay

TH

LAKE VIEW

to US 24

Dayton Gulch

Twin Lakes Reservoir

Twin Lakes Reservoir

Independence Pass

82

PARRY PEAK

TWIN PEAKS

MILES

0   1   2

LAKE ANN

LOCATION: About 15 miles west of US 24 between Buena Vista and Leadville.

HIGHLIGHTS: Wildflowers and an impressive view of the Three Apostles en route to a glacial lake in the Collegiate Peaks Wilderness.

ACCESS: The drive from US 24 to the trailhead is 12 miles of dirt road to Winfield, then 2 more miles to the trailhead, along a road that may be better suited to high-clearance or 4WD vehicles, depending on road conditions.

HIKE DIFFICULTY: MODERATE: Fairly gentle trail until the last mile or so, which goes steeply uphill to the final tundra shelf that holds the lake.

LENGTH: The hike from the trailhead to the lake is about 3 miles. If you park at Winfield, add 2 miles.

MAPS: San Isabel National Forest.

HOW TO GET THERE: From US 24, about 15 miles north of Buena Vista, turn west onto Clear Creek Canyon Road (FR 390), on the north side of Clear Creek Reservoir. Drive 12 miles to Winfield on a graded dirt road. Passenger cars may wish to park here, depending on road conditions. 4WD or high-clearance vehicles can continue south along the valley bottom for another 2 miles to the trailhead.

Greenish blue tinge of Lake Ann is a result of suspended particles in the water.

The trail to Lake Ann and Huron Peak from Winfield was once part of a gold and silver mining district. The ruins of several mines from the 1880s lie hidden in the trees nearby, and the trail passes through the abandoned site of the mining town of Hamilton. Reportedly, gold was initially found by some prospectors who had lost their mules. When they located the animals again, they also struck gold. The Banker Mine, which lies at the end of the 4WD road that forms the first part of the trail, was a major silver mine. Today, Winfield consists primarily of summer cabins.

The first part of the hike to Lake Ann is along the forested valley floor on an old jeep road (FR 390). The three jagged mountain peaks directly to the south are the Three Apostles. After about

The Three Apostles stand out behind the Lake Ann Trail.

1 mile of hiking, start watching for a faint trail (TR 1462) that veers off to the right through the willow bushes just before the jeep road starts to climb uphill through the trees. The trail becomes very thin as it climbs up the valley and across the tundra to Lake Ann, which sits in a steep-sided cirque at 11,805 feet. Look for a good example of a rock glacier on the south side of the lake. Lake Ann is on the Continental Divide Trail and Colorado Trail.

OTHER NEARBY HIKES **Huron Peak**

FEATURES: This short, energetic hike off the Lake Ann trail offers another chance to climb a fourteener.

HOW TO GET THERE: Drive to Winfield and follow the directions for Lake Ann. About 3 miles south on the old jeep road from Winfield, the Huron Peak trail goes southeast.

HIKE DIFFICULTY: STRENUOUS: Hard, steep climb up the mountainside.

LENGTH: From Winfield to the summit is 4.5 miles; from the trailhead to the summit is 2.5 miles.

Though the hike itself is not great, the view from the summit is one of the most scenic in the Collegiate Range. An alternative trail to climb Huron starts just south of Winfield and climbs to the ridge between Middle Mountain and Browns Peak en route to Huron Peak. This trail is about 5 miles long and remains high above treeline for a greater distance, which may or may not be desirable, depending on the weather conditions. The two trails can be combined for a 7.5-mile loop hike.

Lake Ann

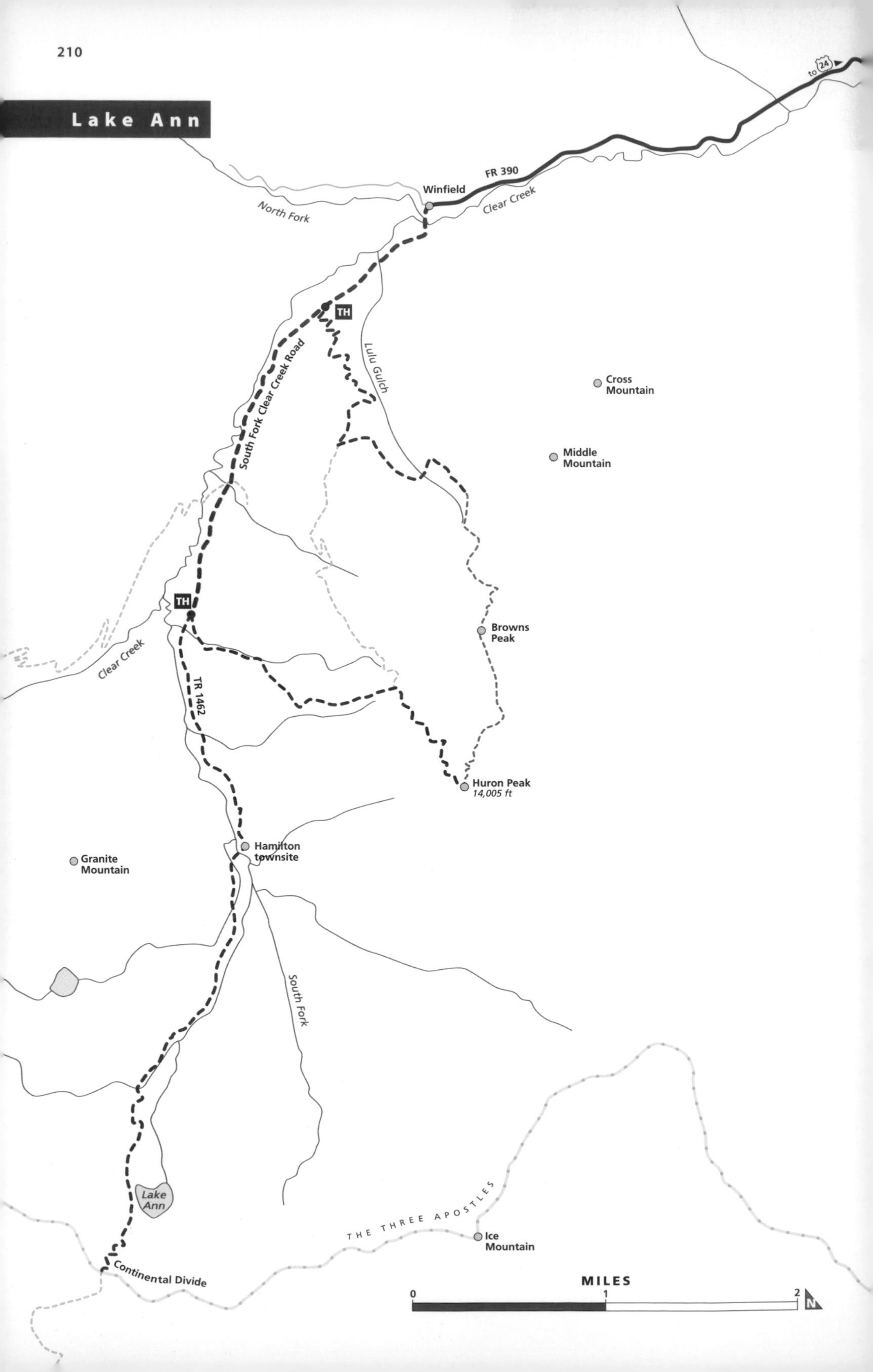

Winfield

FR 390

North Fork

Clear Creek

TH

Lulu Gulch

South Fork Clear Creek Road

Cross Mountain

Middle Mountain

TH

Clear Creek

TR 1462

Browns Peak

Huron Peak
14,005 ft

Granite Mountain

Hamilton townsite

South Fork

Lake Ann

THE THREE APOSTLES

Ice Mountain

Continental Divide

MILES

0   1   2

N

to 24

SNOWMASS LAKE

LOCATION: About 14 miles southwest of Aspen.

HIGHLIGHTS: Tucked into the Maroon Bells–Snowmass Wilderness, this is one of the finest treeline lakes in Colorado.

ACCESS: CR 11 is paved at first, then becomes graded gravel to the trailhead.

HIKE DIFFICULTY: EASY TO MODERATE: The first part of this hike is fairly flat as it follows Snowmass Creek to a series of beaver ponds; beyond this point, the trail climbs steeply for most of the rest of the way to the lake.

LENGTH: The hike from the trailhead to the lake is 8 miles.

MAPS: White River National Forest.

HOW TO GET THERE: From the old town of Snowmass (not the newer Snowmass Village) on CO 82, 4 miles south of Basalt, drive south on CR 11 for about 11 miles to the trailhead.

Snowmass Lake is one of the prettiest lakes in the Maroon Bells–Snowmass Wilderness.

The Maroon Bells–Snowmass Wilderness was one of the first wilderness areas in Colorado to be protected by the 1964 Wilderness Act, and it was expanded in 1980. This famous alpine region is a magnet for hikers and backpackers.

TR 1975 follows magnificent Snowmass Creek. The first part of the trail is fairly flat through meadows and woodlands. After about 6 miles, you will pass a series of beaver ponds, then climb steeply for the final 2 miles through thickly wooded slopes to the lake. The view coming out of the timber at the lake is spectacular, with the lake framed by the trees and the backdrop of Hagerman Peak behind the lake. This is a deep lake, surrounded by rugged, glaciated mountains. The elevation is 10,980 feet. Snowmass Lake is one of the most popular hikes in the area and camping spots close to the lake may be hard to find during peak times in the summer. To prevent overcrowding, camping is restricted close to the shore of the lake; however, this should not deter hikers or backpackers as it is one of the prettiest of all the timberline lakes in Colorado and is well worth the effort and extra company. At 84 acres, it is also the largest lake in the Maroon Bells–Snowmass Wilderness.

Beaver ponds on the trail to Snowmass Lake.

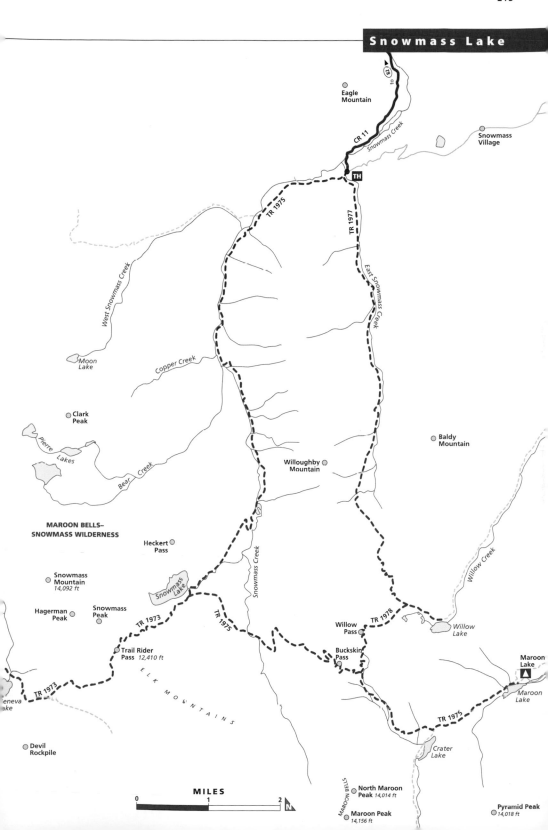

Snowmass Lake

Eagle
Mountain

Snowmass
Village

CR 11

Snowmass Creek

TH

TR 1975

TR 1977

West Snowmass Creek

East Snowmass Creek

Moon
Lake

Copper Creek

Clark
Peak

Baldy
Mountain

Pierre
Lakes

Bear Creek

Willoughby
Mountain

MAROON BELLS–
SNOWMASS WILDERNESS

Heckert
Pass

Snowmass Creek

Snowmass
Lake

Willow Creek

Snowmass
Mountain
14,092 ft

Snowmass
Lake

Hagerman
Peak

Snowmass
Peak

TR 1973

TR 1975

Willow
Pass

TR 1978

Willow
Lake

Maroon
Lake

Trail Rider
Pass 12,410 ft

Buckskin
Pass

TR 1973

E L K   M O U N T A I N S

Maroon
Lake

eneva
ake

TR 1975

Devil
Rockpile

Crater
Lake

MILES

0   1   2   N

MAROON BELLS

North Maroon
Peak 14,014 ft

Maroon Peak
14,156 ft

Pyramid Peak
14,018 ft

Birds on the tundra make their nests on the ground.

OTHER NEARBY HIKES **Trail Rider Pass and Geneva Lake**

FEATURES: A fine extended hike for backpackers who wish to continue past Snowmass Lake.

HOW TO GET THERE: At Snowmass Lake, hike on TR 1973 southwest to the pass and the lake.

HIKE DIFFICULTY: EASY TO MODERATE: An elevation gain and loss of about 1,700 feet over just 4 miles.

LENGTH: From Snowmass Lake to Geneva Lake is 4 miles.

TR 1973, which starts at a junction with TR 1975 at the outlet to the creek, continues around the south side of the lake and climbs steeply above treeline for about 2 miles to 12,410-foot Trail Rider Pass on the ridge behind. From the summit, the trail descends steeply for about 2 miles to Geneva Lake.

OTHER NEARBY HIKES **Buckskin Pass**

FEATURES: From Snowmass Lake, another pass-hike option to the east to reach various picturesque lake destinations.

HOW TO GET THERE: From Snowmass Lake, TR 1975 continues eastward to the top of the pass.

HIKE DIFFICULTY: MODERATE TO STRENUOUS: The hike climbs 1,600 feet in the last 3 miles to the 12,461-foot summit of the pass.

LENGTH: From Snowmass Lake to the top of the pass is a little over 3 miles; east of the pass, further hiking distance depends upon destination.

Named for a recalcitrant buckskin horse, Buckskin Pass boasts outstanding views from its summit. Fourteeners Snowmass Mountain and Capitol Peak dominate the skyline. Bighorn sheep often range just below the pass on both sides.

From the top of the pass, you have several options. One is to continue on TR 1975 for 4 miles to Maroon Lake and drive out from there, with an appropriate shuttle left at the lake. A second option is to join TR 1978 just below the top of the pass and descend 2.5 miles to Willow Lake, then backtrack on the same trail to Snowmass Lake. A third option for backpackers is to continue past Willow Lake and hike back to the Snowmass Lake trailhead along TR 1977 down East Snowmass Creek, for a total loop hike of 25 miles.

OTHER NEARBY HIKES **Willow Lake**

FEATURES: A beautiful alpine lake in an immense scenic bowl on the tundra, often covered in ice and snow until late July.

HOW TO GET THERE: From the Snowmass Lake trailhead on CR 11, take TR 1977 due south up East Snowmass Creek for about 8 miles to Willow Lake.

HIKE DIFFICULTY: STRENUOUS: A long if gentle hike, with a climb over a small saddle about a mile before reaching the lake.

LENGTH: From the trailhead to the lake is 8 miles.

An alternative way to reach Willow Lake, this hike is relatively gentle alongside East Snowmass Creek and can be done as a long day hike. As described under Buckskin Pass, see opposite page, backpackers can link various trails in this wilderness.

Ice on Willow Lake doesn't melt until late June or July.

NEARBY STOPS **Maroon Peak and North Maroon Peak**

FEATURES: An iconic Colorado view of these two peaks, famously known as the Maroon Bells, across Maroon Lake. Though not a tundra destination, a side trip to see these two fourteeners is a must.

HOW TO GET THERE: About 0.5 mile north of Aspen on CO 82, CR 13/FR 125 heads southwest up Maroon Creek to Maroon Bells. To protect this very popular and congested location, the Forest Service operates a shuttle bus from Aspen during the summer season. Check in Aspen for the details. Take a leg-stretcher around the lake if time allows.

About 10 miles southwest of Aspen at the edge of the Maroon Bells–Snowmass Wilderness, 14,156-foot Maroon Peak and 14,014-foot North Maroon Peak are among the most-photographed mountains in Colorado. Collectively known as the Maroon Bells, they are also among the most difficult of Colorado's fourteeners to climb with safety. The view of the pair across Maroon Lake, with blue sky above and golden aspen trees in front, have graced countless calendars, books, and souvenirs. But the Bells put experienced climbers to the test, because the grandeur at a distance is a hazard close-up: The peaks' loose, crumbling sedimentary rock surfaces make for poor anchor placement and worse footholds. Climbers face frequent bad weather on the summits, falling rock, and risky routes, and several climbing fatalities have earned these peaks a more dubious nickname, "The Deadly Bells."

FRAVERT BASIN AND HASLEY BASIN

LOCATION: About 15 miles northwest of Crested Butte.

HIGHLIGHTS: Spectacular views of the west side of the Maroon Bells and one of the best summer displays of alpine and subalpine wildflowers in Colorado.

ACCESS: The trailhead to this series of hikes starts on a good gravel road out of Crested Butte, which deteriorates to the point that 4WD is preferable for the final stretch over Schofield Pass.

HIKE DIFFICULTY: EASY TO STRENUOUS: Several hikes are accessible from this trailhead; the length and difficulty depend on your interests.

LENGTH: Variable, depending on your interests.

MAPS: Gunnison National Forest (though technically White River National Forest).

HOW TO GET THERE: From US 50 in Gunnison, drive northwest on CO 135, through Crested Butte, and take the graded gravel Gothic Road (FR 317) to the town of Gothic. Beyond Gothic, the road becomes steeper and rougher, though it's still navigable for most passenger cars for several miles. Finally, a high-clearance or 4WD vehicle is required for the last stretch over Schofield Pass.

Stop and park at one of the pullouts when you become uncomfortable with the road and proceed on foot north over Schofield Pass, continuing about 0.75 mile north of the summit to the trailhead, which lies to the right in the open expanse of Schofield Park.

Seasoned 4WD drivers may opt to approach the trailhead from the north; however, the final stretch of the north side of Schofield Pass is dangerous (25% grade, slide rock, off-camber) and should only be attempted by *expert* drivers in narrow, 4WD vehicles with a short wheel base.

Head out on TR 1970 and start enjoying the flowers and views. The peak of the flower display is usually in late June and July, though the trailhead is not accessible by car in some years until sometime in July, depending on winter snowpack. After about 2 miles, the trail splits. To the left is Hasley Basin. About 0.75 mile farther is TR 1974, which turns off to Fravert Basin via Frigid Air Pass. The two trails connect down in the valley, making a loop hike possible. The many intersecting trails in this area make a good map essential for hikers planning to do more than enjoy the tundra portions of the hike. Enthusiastic hikers who have arranged for a vehicle shuttle can continue on TR 1970 over West

Alpine clover

Maroon Pass and end up at Maroon Lake, on the front side of the Maroon Bells.

Unfortunately these hikes are only accessible in the height of the summer. Ten to fifteen feet of snow fall every winter in these mountains, and snowbanks sometimes linger until late during the succeeding summer.

Schofield Park

In the second half of the 19th century, the Colorado high country attracted swarms of miners frantically searching to find their fortunes—preferably before everyone else! Schofield Park was no exception. In the 1880s, the broad valley that is the starting point for these hikes housed 200 to 300 miners working a series of well-developed claims and living in 50 or so ramshackle cabins. The town of Schofield was so important at the time that there was daily stage and mail service from Crested Butte. After only ten years or so, however, the area entered a decline as did so many others like it, and miners left to follow their fortunes elsewhere. Harsh winters also contributed to the decline; one winter the town was reportedly buried in a 40-foot drift.

Wildflowers on the trail to Hasley Basin.

Fravert Basin and Hasley Basin

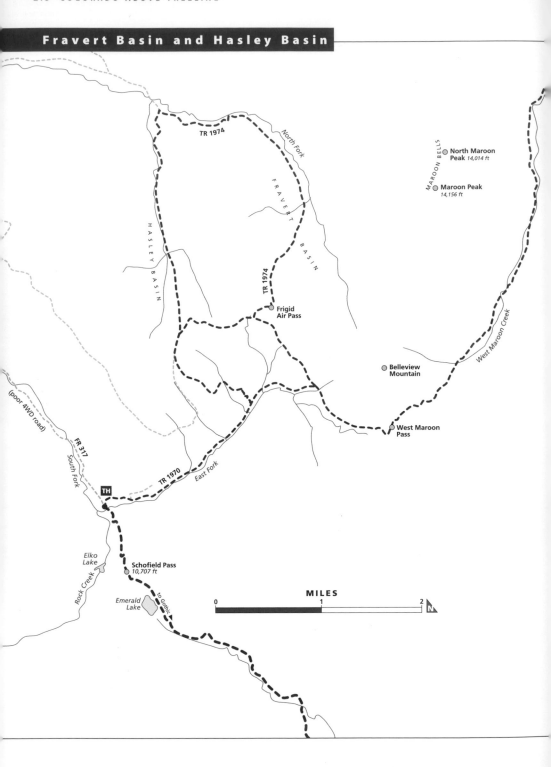

A Day on the Bighorn Survey

"The Mosquito Range has loads of sheep," the Division of Wildlife biologist had assured me as the two of us studied the topo map laid out on the hood of my car. He pointed with the end of a pencil. "Follow the trail along the stream here, and then climb up this draw to the south. There's a natural salt deposit just above timberline, and they come in to lick it.

"Can't miss 'em," he added confidently, with a grin.

I was thinking of these words as I struggled up the hill toward the bare ridge that was still several hundred feet above me. I had been hiking this particular valley for over three hours now and hadn't seen hide nor hair of a sheep yet.

I was burdened with a spotting scope, camera, binoculars, various lenses, a tripod, and the usual assortment of layered clothing, water, first-

Bighorn sheep ewes band together on wintering grounds at lower elevations.

aid kit, survival supplies, and all the other gear that seemed to have been attracted like a magnet to my pack to make it insufferably heavy while climbing almost straight up a mountain in the hopes of spotting some elusive Rocky Mountain bighorn sheep. I was participating in one of the periodic surveys of bighorn sheep populations in the mountains of central Colorado, but I was also hoping to get a few good photographs to round out the day.

I stopped to regain my breath and, since it felt so good, I shrugged off my pack, sat down, and lifted my binoculars to my eyes to scan the slopes above and around me. All I could see was broken, rocky hillsides covered with large, brown boulders about the size of bighorn sheep. At this time of day, some of them might even be bighorn sheep. I had started at sunup, when the sheep were most likely to be moving around, which makes their stocky bodies most visible in the tundra. Now it was almost nine o'clock, and I knew that most of the sheep would be lying down, contentedly digesting what they had breakfasted on earlier. In this almost-motionless position, they are hard to spot from a distance. On previous surveys, I had several times seen what initially appeared to be a large boulder on a distant hillside suddenly get up and walk around. Not today, though.

Wherever the sheep were, they were not on the route I had been assigned to hike. I knew they were there somewhere, because I saw fresh droppings and could detect their musky scent in flattened grass where they had bedded down for the night.

By mid-afternoon, I reluctantly realized that this was not my day, and I returned to my Jeep to drive back to the ranger station where we were to report what we had seen or, in my case, not seen. I had parked at the end of a forest road that wound up the mountain to just above timberline at a small lake surrounded by willow bushes. Now, as I plodded wearily toward the parking area, with my oversized pack buffeted by the bushes on either side of the narrow track, I thought only of the cold beer that was sitting in my cooler. I pushed my way through the last willow thicket and stopped in amazement.

There, right in front of me, they were.

At the sound of my approach through the bushes, twelve sheep faces turned toward me. With bland expressions of total innocence, they stood around my Jeep and looked at me, as if saying, Here we are. Why did you bother to climb that slope? We were waiting here all this time. Having satisfactorily conveyed those thoughts, they turned as a group and vanished into the bushes behind them. I took out my topo map and marked the location for the survey. At least I wouldn't go back empty-handed.

BUFFALO PEAKS

LOCATION: About 10 miles north of Buena Vista.

HIGHLIGHTS: A lengthy hike to an isolated tundra destination that is home to a small herd of Rocky Mountain bighorn.

ACCESS: The north trailhead to the peaks is on the Weston Pass road, which is a good graded gravel road to the trailhead. The south trailhead starts as a graded gravel road, but turns into a 4WD road for the last mile or so before the trailhead.

HIKE DIFFICULTY: MODERATE TO STRENUOUS: A strenuous trip because it involves a steep uphill climb to the summits after a hike to treeline at the base of the mountain. The north approach is longer but more scenic.

LENGTH: The hike is 10 miles one-way from the north. From the south is 5 miles one-way—or longer if you park before reaching the trailhead described.

MAPS: San Isabel National Forest shows the approaches with the best detail.

HOW TO GET THERE: Several trails access this area. The two most popular are from the north side and the south side. The north approach is from the Weston Pass road. Approximately 10 miles from US 285, 6 miles before the summit of Weston Pass on the east side, start at the Rich Creek–Buffalo Meadows Trailhead.

From the south, take CR 371 north from Buena Vista; after about 3 miles, veer right onto CR 375/FR 375, the Fourmile road. Follow this road north to the Four Mile Creek–Buffalo Meadows trailhead (TR 617). A high-clearance or 4WD vehicle is needed for the last mile of the steep, rough climb to the trailhead. If in a passenger car, park lower down when you feel uncomfortable with the road conditions.

The South Park area near Buffalo Peaks has a long history of ranching and cattle operations, which continue today. Buffalo Peaks Wilderness was declared a wilderness area in 1993.

Two connected, rounded peaks, standing in isolation above treeline, were named after their resemblance to the profile of a buffalo. West Buffalo Peak (13,327 feet) and East Buffalo Peak (13,301 feet) sit on the dividing line between Pike National Forest on the east side and San Isabel National Forest on the west side, anchoring the 43,410-acre Buffalo Peaks Wilderness.

From the north, start at the Rich Creek–Buffalo Meadows trailhead. Follow this trail (TR 616) for about 6 miles to Buffalo Meadows to a trail junction, then continue south on the Four Mile Creek–Buffalo Meadows trail (TR 617) to an unnamed pass in the saddle just below West Buffalo Peak. From here the summit of West Buffalo is an uphill scramble of about 2 miles.

From the south trailhead, follow the Fourmile Creek–Buffalo Meadows Trail (TR 617) north to the same unnamed pass west of West Buffalo Peak. Scramble directly east uphill from here the summit. From West Buffalo Peak, follow the highest part of the ridge southeast to the summit of East Buffalo Peak.

Opposite: *The Buffalo Peaks Wilderness is a compact but diverse area that isn't commonly visited.*

Buffalo Peaks

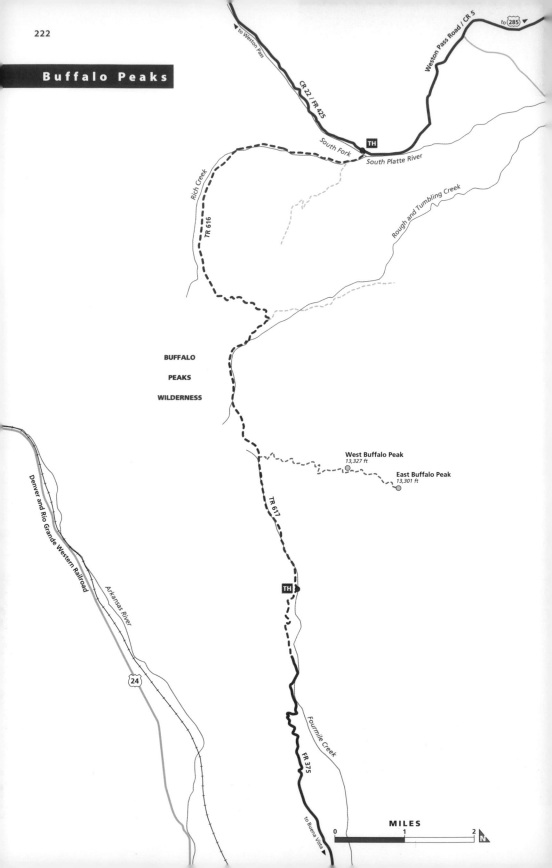

to Weston Pass

Weston Pass Road / CR 5

to 285

CR 22 / FR 425

South Fork

TH

South Platte River

Rich Creek

TR 616

Rough and Tumbling Creek

BUFFALO

PEAKS

WILDERNESS

West Buffalo Peak
13,327 ft

East Buffalo Peak
13,301 ft

TR 617

Denver and Rio Grande Western Railroad

Arkansas River

TH

24

Fourmile Creek

FR 375

to Buena Vista

MILES

0   1   2

N

MOUNT PRINCETON

LOCATION: About 9 miles southwest of Buena Vista.

HIGHLIGHTS: Take your pick of a long hike, or a 4WD trip with a short hike, up a fourteener with fine views.

ACCESS: Passenger cars can drive to the first trailhead. Parking farther along the road/trail requires first a high-clearance vehicle, and later a 4WD, to reach the end of the road.

HIKE DIFFICULTY: MODERATE TO STRENUOUS: Hiking from the main trailhead is strenuous; however, hikers with high-clearance or 4WD vehicles can opt for a shorter climb if they wish.

LENGTH: From the main Mount Princeton trailhead west to the footpath above treeline is about 5 miles, and the final stretch on the footpath to the summit is 2 miles, so the hike distance varies between 2 and 7 miles each way, depending on where you park.

MAPS: San Isabel National Forest.

HOW TO GET THERE: From Nathrop on US 285, head west on CR 162 for 4.5 miles to Mount Princeton Hot Springs. Directly opposite the hot springs, take a right (north) onto CR 321 and drive for a little over a mile to CR 322 (do not take the first road signed CR 322, which appears after only about 250 yards and dead-ends in private property). CR 322 will veer sharply left off of CR 321, toward looming Mount Princeton. Go west on CR/FR 322, the access road/trail that climbs to treeline. After a little over another mile you will come to the signed trailhead (be courteous—this is on private property). From the turnoff at Nathrop on US 285 to the trailhead parking area is a little over 7 miles. If you are in a passenger car, park here.

The first leg of Mount Princeton Trail continues along the access road, CR 322, which becomes FR 322 within San Isabel National Forest. From here, the road becomes progressively rougher as it switchbacks west up the mountainside to a final parking area at treeline. High-clearance vehicles can continue and park by a communications tower complex about 3 miles up the road. Beyond this point, the road becomes much rougher and requires 4WD for the next 2 miles or so to the final parking and turnaround on top of the ridge, in an area called Bristlecone Park.

A rocky trail leads up to the summit of Mount Princeton.

Southernmost of the fourteeners in the Collegiate Range, Mount Princeton forms an impressive and abrupt backdrop in the symmetrical arrangement of three peaks behind Buena Vista. Surveyors originally called this peak Chalk Mountain, in reference to the white cliffs of modified quartz, resembling chalk, that lie at its southern base and are still known as the Chalk Cliffs. The mountain was later renamed, along with others along the Collegiate Range, in homage to the schools of the Ivy League. These cliffs are supposedly a site of lost Spanish treasure which, if it ever existed, still remains elusive. More tangible riches came from the Hortense Mine on the southern sub-peak, which was one of the area's first rich silver producers.

This journey offers various degrees of challenge from relatively easy to quite difficult, depending on your desires. This can be a long hike, a shorter hike combined with a drive, or just a part-way drive. The easiest way to hike is to combine a 5-mile 4WD trip to treeline and then a 2-mile hike west to the summit for panoramic views. Hiking enthusiasts can park at the first trailhead and go by foot all 7 miles to the summit.

Those who don't prefer to hike the road but want to tackle a climb up a steep slope can follow an old trail that branches off near the start of the road and climbs alongside Merriam Creek to join the main trail again higher up (4 miles). This way involves an initial scramble of about 3,000 feet of elevation in a little over 2 miles!

Those ascending the shelf road via 4WD will especially enjoy the last half mile. The view from there is outstanding, including a sweeping view of Buena Vista far below, with the Front Range and Pikes Peak in the distance. The final 2-mile footpath to the summit starts just as the road emerges from treeline onto the tundra. With no place to stop, turn around, or park at this junction, just drive another half mile to the turnaround at the road's end and walk back down to the trail. Be sure to visit the dwarf forest of bristlecone pines that surrounds you on the ridge.

Whether you drive or climb this mountain, keep a close eye on the clouds, and be off the summit and final ridges before a storm moves in. The exposed summit is prone to lightning storms. Hikers can be struck by lightning on the mountain when they do not take the simple precaution of dropping below treeline in sufficient time to escape.

After hiking, it is pleasant to stop and soak weary muscles in the hot springs at the base of Mount Princeton on the way back home.

Mount Princeton

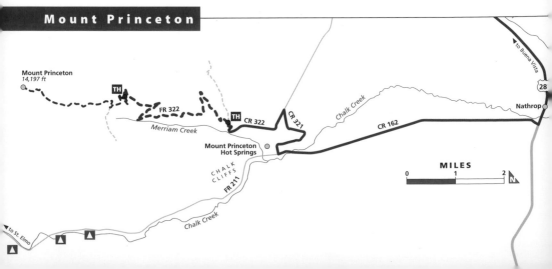

COMANCHE-VENABLE LOOP

LOCATION: About 30 miles southwest of Cañon City and southeast of Salida.

HIGHLIGHTS: Beautiful tundra lakes, a waterfall, and spectacular views of the San Luis Valley along a remote hike.

ACCESS: Paved road leaving Westcliffe, then a short stretch of graded, gravel all-weather road to the Alvarado campground and trailhead.

HIKE DIFFICULTY: STRENUOUS: The hike is steep, uphill, and long.

LENGTH: The entire loop is 12 miles. Distance to either Comanche Lake or Venable Lake is about 4 miles, and the connecting trail across the bench is about 4 miles.

MAPS: San Isabel National Forest.

HOW TO GET THERE: Take US 50 west from Cañon City toward Salida. After about 26 miles, turn left (south) at Texas Creek onto CO 69. Drive 25 miles to Westcliffe, then continue south on CO 69 about 2.5 miles to Schoolfield Road (CR 140) and turn right (west). Go about 6.5 miles toward Alvarado Campground, then follow the sign just before the campground to park at the Comanche-Venable trailhead.

The narrow shelf trail across the Phantom Terrace.

ecause of their remote location, Comanche and Venable Passes never became wagon, car, or train routes; they've only ever been horseback and foot trails. Venable Pass was named for Jack Venable, a homesteader in the Wet Mountain valley to the east, which has traditionally been cattle and hay ranchland. The high, isolated Sangre de Cristo Mountains, where this hike is located, were named Blood of Christ by early Spanish explorers after the effect of the setting sun, which often paints the bare summits with a brilliant reddish glow.

Beware of initially becoming disoriented on side trails around the parking area and trailhead that lead to other destinations. Once you're on the correct trail, this lovely loop on TR 1345 (Comanche Lake) and TR 1347 (Venable Lake) can be hiked in either direction, or out-and-back treks to either lake makes for a shorter excursion. About halfway between the trailhead and Venable Lake, stop at Venable Falls to see it cascade through a narrow gorge. The connecting section of trail along the alpine bench on the crest is called The Phantom Terrace. It is well named, because for hikers looking up from underneath—or even walking along it—the trail across the steep slope of the bowl at the head of the valley is virtually invisible. Pikas are common in the talus slopes on this stretch, as evidenced by their frequent piles of white nitrogenous waste all along the trail.

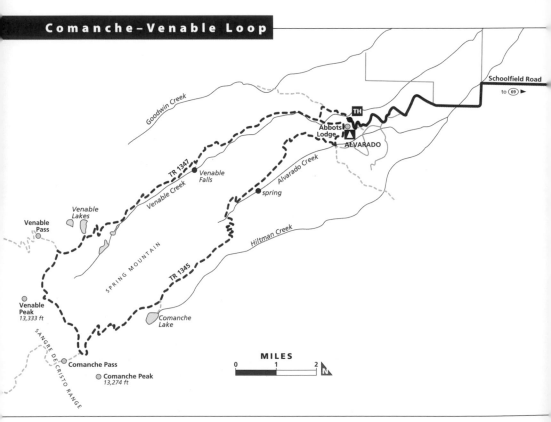

Comanche–Venable Loop

A Storm in the Sangres

I'm getting wet," observed my companion morosely. I turned my head slowly and looked at his face, which was only about 8 inches away from mine. Water was dripping from his nose, and I noted with interest that his skin had taken on a definite orange hue from the dreary light filtering through the plastic rain poncho that was thrown over our heads and shoulders.

"I don't think that this was made for two of us," I said, stating the obvious.

"I think—" he started, but he didn't complete his thought. A brilliant flash of lightning, accompanied almost simultaneously by a violent crash of thunder, drowned out whatever he had intended to say.

About three hours earlier, we had parked his jeep at the Alvarado Campground, about 2,500 feet below us, and started on the trail to Venable Pass in the Sangre de Cristo Mountains. We had planned to have a pleasant hike in the sunshine and to eat lunch at the summit. Then we would enjoy the magnificent view from the pass in both directions, take some photographs, and be back at the car by mid-afternoon to find a nice camping spot.

Storms can quickly form on summer afternoons above treeline.

In fact, a few minutes previously, dark storm clouds had suddenly started to scud rapidly across the sky from the west, quickly obscuring the sun. We were in a quandary. We were closer to the pass than to the shelter of the timber below. We were about 700 feet above treeline on an open hillside, with what we guessed to be less than half a mile of trail left to reach the summit of the pass. Eyeing the sky, we convinced each other that the clouds would blow through and that it was too early in the day for a storm. We could easily make it to the top of the pass and be back down in the timber before the storm came. Nyaaak! Wrong! Sound the game-show buzzer!

Our first clue was the hail. The hillside around us suddenly came alive with small white pellets flinging themselves into the air like errant grasshoppers. A first rumble of thunder echoed somewhere above us.

I scanned the hillside. "Quick, over there!" I pointed to a shallow, washed-out area just below the trail ahead of us.

We hurriedly slid down the wet slope to the bottom of the shallow cut. I dug frantically in my pack for my poncho and quickly pulled it over my head. I crouched down low so that I wasn't the highest object on the landscape, and I balanced on the balls of my feet to minimize my contact with the ground in case of a nearby lightning strike. When I was settled as comfortably as I could be, under the circumstances, I looked up to see my friend, who was regarding me silently.

"I didn't bring a poncho," he said, melting hail starting to run down his face from the brim of his ballcap.

"This could cost you a beer," I said, lifting the edge of the poncho to let him in.

We were lucky. We weren't hit by lightning. The storm was fast-moving, so we only had to spend about ten minutes squatting uncomfortably in the ditch. Though the sky remained dark and leaden, the hail stopped, and a shaft of sunlight even broke through the sullen clouds, moving rapidly across a landscape glistening white from the recent hailstorm. Though we were lucky and survived this lightning storm at high altitude, we were reminded of how quickly dangerous storms can blow up in the mountains—and how unforgiving nature can be.

APPENDIX A Glossary of Tundra Terms

Acclimatization: Adaptive changes in the body that take place to compensate for lower levels of oxygen at high altitude.

Acute mountain sickness: See *Altitude sickness.*

Alpine zone: The ecosystem above timberline or, in Colorado, above about 11,500 feet.

Altitude sickness: A collection of symptoms caused by a decrease in oxygen at high altitude; also called acute mountain sickness.

Annual plant: A plant that lives for only a single season and has to produce seeds to propagate the next year; there is only one species of annual on the Colorado tundra.

Anthocyanin: A pigment that produces red, blue, and purple colors in tundra plants; helps absorb UV radiation; attracts insects; and assists in sugar production.

Arrastra: A primitive ore-crushing device used to help separate gold from waste rock.

Banner trees: See *Flagged trees.*

Biome: Specific vegetation and the related animals in a region with a particular climate and other physical factors.

Tarns are fed by snowmelt and often have a vivid green or blue color due to glacial flour.

Colored snow: See *Pink snow.*

Continental Divide: An imaginary line that goes generally north/south down the North American Continent to define the watershed between the Atlantic and Pacific Oceans.

Cushion plant: A series of perennial plants, found commonly in fellfields, that grow in a low, matted, cushionlike form.

Ecosystem: An area containing characteristic plant life and animal life that interact as a single entity, and which is defined by localized soil conditions and by exposure to sunlight, moisture, and wind.

Ecotone: The transition between ecosystems.

Elfin timber: See *Krummholz.*

Erosion: The transportation of material from a higher elevation to a lower one.

Esker: A geological term for piles of gravel left by a glacier, but also used to describe the meandering core of dirt left from pocket gophers tunnels when the snow melts.

Fellfield: Areas of the tundra that consist of broken rock with small patches of soil between.

Flagged trees: Trees at timberline that have been shaped by the weather so that their branches grow straight out on the diamond side of the tree trunk only, looking like a flag flying in the wind; also called banner trees.

Forb: Generic term used to describe a broad-leaved, nonwoody, flowering plant that is not a grass or a sedge.

Fourteener: Mountain peak that is over 14,000 feet in elevation.

Frost heaving: Motion of rocks in the ground due to cycles of freeze and thaw in the soil.

Frost wedging: Gradual expansion of a crack in a rock by the influx and freezing of water.

Gopher garden: An area of soil disturbed by gopher digging that is covered with showy, colorful flowers.

Habitat: The environment an animal lives in.

Hanging valley: A small valley, carved by ice, perched above a main glacial valley below.

Hard-rock mining: Gold ore that is under the ground and has to be dug or blasted out and brought to the surface.

Hibernation: State of total inactivity in which some animals survive the winter.

Krummholz: The dwarf, crooked trees that are shaped by the elements at timberline; also called elfin timber.

Life zone: See *Ecosystem.*

Lode gold: Gold occurring in veins in rock, as opposed to placer gold.

Meltwater bogs: Areas of the tundra where the snowmelt is so great that the water cannot soak into the ground, thus creating boggy conditions.

Merriam life zones: A definition of ecosystems that was proposed by C. Hart Merriam, a 19th-century naturalist.

Pass: A low place in a mountain range that separates two watersheds.

Patterned ground: Pieces of rock formed into patterns as they are pushed to the surface of the tundra by frost action.

Perennial plant: Plant that goes dormant during winter, but revives and grows again the next summer.

Permafrost: Frozen soil that does not thaw in the summer.

Photosynthesis: The process by which green plants use sunlight, water, and carbon dioxide to create carbohydrates.

Pink snow: Snow-stained pink or magenta by the presence of a one-celled alga; may smell faintly of watermelons; also called *colored snow* or *watermelon snow.*

Placer gold: Flakes of gold in sand or gravel, deposited into a stream from lodes higher up.

Rhizome: An underground stem that spreads from a parent plant and surfaces to produce a new plant through vegetative reproduction.

Rock glacier: River of rock that moves slowly downhill, similar to an ice glacier.

Scree: Small rock debris, down to the size of gravel.

Scree slope: Mass of rock debris angled up against the bottom of a cliff.

Sedge: Plants that look like grasses, but are distinguished by their triangular stems.

Snow banner: A long plume of snow blown into the air from a ridge by the wind.

Snow mold: A fungus that creates a brown, crusty material on timberline trees.

Solifluction: The downhill slump of frozen soil when it thaws in the spring.

Stamp mill: Machinery used to crush gold ore for extraction of the gold.

Stolon: A runner that grows from a parent plant along the top of the soil and roots itself, producing a new plant through vegetative reproduction.

Stomata: Tiny pores on the underside of leaves through which excess water is released back to the environment.

Subalpine zone: The ecosystem just below timberline; below the alpine zone.

Talus: Rock debris, larger than a fist, that often occurs at the base of a mountain or rock face where it accumulates due to weathering.

Tarn: A deep lake that fills a glacial cirque after the glacier has melted.

Tramway: A series of buckets on a cable, used to transport ore from a mine on a mountain-side to a mill at a lower elevation.

Transpiration: The process by which excess water is released back to the environment through tiny pores on the underside of leaves, called stomata.

Treeline: The line around a mountain above which trees do not grow; also called timberline and tree limit.

Tundra: Treeless area above timberline that consists of the open meadows and rocky slopes that are the tops of the mountains.

Walking trees: Trees that appear to "walk" downwind over a period of years, as the upwind side is killed annually by the weather, but the downwind side continues to grow.

Watermelon snow: See *Pink snow.*

Weathering: The action of the elements, such as wind, rain, and running water, on mountains.

APPENDIX B Hikes with Difficulty Ratings

The ratings for these hikes, subjectively assigned by the author, take into consideration the length, overall altitude, and elevation change of the hike. Hikers may judge differently what is easy, moderate, and strenuous, depending on their particular physical conditioning and experience. For destinations in this book in which no hiking is required, such as Animas Forks, no listing appears.

SCENIC DRIVES

Trail Ridge Road
Ute Trail to Timberline Pass .. **Easy–Moderate**
Longs Peak . . . . **Strenuous**

Berthoud Pass
Vasquez Pass and Vasquez Peak . . . . **Moderate**
Jones Pass . . . . **Moderate**

Loveland Pass
Mount Sniktau . . . . **Moderate to Strenuous**

Mount Evans
Mount Goliath Natural Area . . . . **Easy**
Chicago Lakes . . . . **Moderate**
Lincoln Lake and
    Beartrack Lakes . . . . . **Moderate to Strenuous**

Guanella Pass
Silver Dollar Lake . . . . **Easy to Moderate**
Abyss Lake . . . . **Strenuous**
Square Top Lakes . . . . **Easy to Moderate**

Boreas Pass
Dyersville . . . . **Easy to Moderate**
Mount Silverheels . . . . . **Moderate to Strenuous**

Independence Pass
Linkins Lake and the
    Lost Man Loop . . . . . **Moderate to Strenuous**
Mountain Boy Gulch . . . . **Moderate**
Independence . . . . **Easy**
Grizzly Lake . . . . **Moderate to Strenuous**
Petroleum Lake . . . . **Moderate to Strenuous**

Cottonwood Pass
Browns Pass . . . . **Moderate**
Mount Yale . . . . **Moderate to Strenuous**
Ptarmigan Lake and
    Jones Mountain . . . . **Moderate**

Pikes Peak
Devils Playground . . . . **Moderate**
Barr Trail . . . . **Strenuous**
Crags Campground Trail . . . . **Strenuous**
Elk Park Trail . . . . **Easy to Moderate**

Greenhorn Mountain
Greenhorn Summit . . . . **Moderate**
Greenhorn Trail . . . . **Strenuous**

The Colorado Trail has frequent access points and is a great way to see Colorado's high country.

4 W D   T R I P S

Rollins Pass
Corona Lake . . . . Easy to Moderate
Corona Trail and Devils
   Thumb Pass . . . . Moderate
Rogers Pass . . . . Moderate to Strenuous

Waldorf
Argentine Pass . . . . Moderate
McClellan Mountain. . . . . Moderate
Grays Peak and
   Torreys Peak . . . . Moderate to Strenuous

Mosquito Pass
Oliver Twist Lake and
   Cooney Lake . . . . Easy to Moderate
Mosquito Peak . . . . Easy to Moderate
Mount Lincoln . . . . Moderate
Kite Lake and Mount
   Democrat . . . . Moderate to Strenuous

Hagerman Pass
Hagerman Tunnel . . . . Easy to Moderate
Douglass City . . . . Easy to Moderate
Windsor Lake . . . . Easy to Moderate
Lyle Lake and
   Mormon Lake . . . . Easy to Moderate

Weston Pass
Ptarmigan Peak . . . . Moderate to Strenuous
Gold Basin . . . . Easy to Moderate

Mount Antero
Baldwin Lake . . . . Moderate
Boulder Mountain . . . . Moderate to Strenuous

The Alpine Tunnel
Williams Pass . . . . Easy to Moderate
Altman Pass. . . . . Easy to Moderate

Hancock Pass–Tomichi Pass
Granite Mountain . . . . Moderate
Pomeroy Lakes. . . . . Moderate
Hancock Lakes and
   Chalk Creek Pass . . . . Easy to Moderate

The Alpine Loop
American Basin and
   Handies Peak . . . . Moderate to Strenuous
Carson . . . . Moderate
Wetterhorn Peak and
   Matterhorn Peak . . . . Strenuous
Stony Pass . . . . Easy

Imogene Pass
Governor Basin . . . . Moderate
Yankee Boy Basin . . . . Easy to Moderate

C L A S S I C   H I K E S

Mohawk Lakes . . . . Easy to Moderate

Notch Mountain . . . . Strenuous
Lake Constantine . . . . Easy to Moderate

Missouri Lakes and
Fancy Lake Loop . . . . Strenuous
Holy Cross City . . . . Moderate

Mount Elbert . . . . Strenuous

Lake Ann . . . . Moderate
Huron Peak . . . . Strenuous

Snowmass Lake . . . . . Moderate to Strenuous
Trail Rider Pass and Geneva Lake . . Strenuous
Buckskin Pass . . . . Moderate to Strenuous
Willow Lake . . . . Strenuous

Fravert Basin and
Hasley Basin . . . . Easy to Strenuous

Buffalo Peaks . . . . Moderate to Strenuous

Mount Princeton . . . . Moderate to Strenuous

Comanche-Venable Loop . . . . . . Strenuous

APPENDIX C Recommended Reading

General

Colorado Trail Foundation. *The Colorado Trail: The Official Guidebook*. Golden, CO: The Colorado Mountain Club Press, 2002.

Gellhorn, Joyce G. *Song of the Alpine*. Boulder, CO: Johnson Books, 2002.

Jones, Tom Lorang, and John Fielder. *Colorado's Continental Divide Trail: The Official Guide*. 2nd ed. Englewood, CO: Westcliffe Publishers, 2004.

Mutel, Cornelia Fleisher, and John C. Emerick. *From Grassland to Glacier*. Boulder, CO: Johnson Books, 1992.

Pearson, Mark, and John Fielder. *The Complete Guide to Colorado's Wilderness Areas*. 2nd ed. Englewood, CO: Westcliffe Publishers, 2004.

Smith, Dwight. *Above Timberline*. New York: Alfred A. Knopf, 1981.

Zwinger, Ann H., and Beatrice E. Willard. *Land Above the Trees*. Boulder, CO: Johnson Books, 1996.

Animals

Fisher, Chris, Don Pattie, and Tamara Hartson. *Mammals of the Rocky Mountains*. Renton, WA: Lone Pine Publishing, 2000.

Fitzgerald, James P., Carron A. Meaney, and David M. Armstrong. *Mammals of Colorado*. Niwot, CO: University Press of Colorado, 1994.

Geist, Valerius. *Mountain Sheep*. Chicago, IL: University of Chicago Press, 1971.

Rennicke, Jeff. *Colorado Wildlife*. Helena, MT: Falcon Press, 1996.

Winnie, John, Jr. *High Life: Animals of the Alpine World*. Flagstaff, AZ: Northland Publishing, 1996.

Fourteeners

Bourneman, Walter R., and Lyndon J. Lampert. *A Climbing Guide to Colorado's Fourteeners*. Boulder, CO: Pruett Publishing Co., 1988.

Crouter, George. *Colorado's Highest*. Silverton, CO: Sundance Publications, 1977.

Eberhart, Perry, and Philip Schmuck. *The Fourteeners*. Chicago, IL: Sage Books, 1970.

Roach, Gerry. *Colorado's Fourteeners: From Hikes to Climbs*. 2nd ed. Golden, CO: Fulcrum Publishing, 1999.

Geology

Baars, Donald L. *The American Alps*. Albuquerque, NM: University of New Mexico Press, 1992.

Chronic, Halka. *Roadside Geology of Colorado*. Missoula, MT: Mountain Press Publishing Co., 1980.

Chronic, John, and Halka Chronic. *Prairie, Peak, and Plateau*. Denver, CO: Colorado Geological Survey, 1972.

Ghost Towns

Brown, Robert L. *Colorado Ghost Towns*. Caldwell, Idaho: Caxton Printers Ltd., 1981.

———. *An Empire of Silver*. Caldwell, Idaho: Caxton Printers Ltd., 1968.

———. *Ghost Towns of the Colorado Rockies*. Caldwell, Idaho: Caxton Printers Ltd., 1969.

———. *Jeep Trails to Colorado Ghost Towns*. Caldwell, Idaho: Caxton Printers Ltd., 1966.

Eberhart, Perry. *Guide to the Colorado Ghost Towns and Mining Camps*. Athens, Ohio: Swallow Press, 1981.

Mining

Sagstetter, Beth, and Bill Sagstetter. *The Mining Camps Speak*. Denver, CO: Benchmark Publishing of Colorado, 1998.

Smith, Duane A. *Colorado Mining*. Albuquerque, NM: University of New Mexico Press, 1977.

———. *Rocky Mountain Mining Camps*. University of Nebraska Press, Lincoln, NE: 1974.

Passes

Edmondson, Clyde, and Chloe Edmondson. *Mountain Passes*. Longmont, CO: Clyde and Chloe Edmondson, 1970.

Helmuth, Ed, and Gloria Helmuth. *The Passes of Colorado*. Boulder, CO: Pruett Publishing Co., 1994.

Koch, Don. *The Colorado Pass Book: A Guide to Colorado's Backroad Mountain Passes*. 3rd ed. Boulder, CO: Pruett Publishing Co., 2000.

Plants

Beidleman, Linda H., Richard G. Beidleman, and Bettie E. Willard. *Plants of Rocky Mountain National Park*. Estes Park, CO: Rocky Mountain Nature Association, 2000.

Duft, Joseph F., and Robert K. Moseley. *Alpine Wildflowers of the Rocky Mountains*. Missoula, MT: Mountain Press Publishing Co., 1989.

Guennel, G. K. *Guide to Colorado Wildflowers*. 2 vols. 2nd ed. Englewood, CO: Westcliffe Publishers, Inc., 2004.

Nelson, Ruth Ashton. *Handbook of Rocky Mountain Plants*. Niwot, CO: Roberts Rinehart Publishers, 1992.

Strickler, Dee. *Alpine Wildflowers*. Helena, MT: Falcon Press, 1990.

Willard, Bettie E., and Chester O. Harris. *Alpine Wildflowers of Rocky Mountain National Park*. Estes Park, CO: Rocky Mountain Nature Association, 1970.

Railroads

Abbott, Dan. *Colorado Midland Railway*. Denver, CO: Sundance Publications, Ltd., 1989.

Chappell, Gordon, Robert W. Richardson, and Cornelius W. Hauck. *The South Park Line*. Golden, CO: Colorado Railroad Museum, 1974.

Griswold, Phelps R. *The Denver and Salt Lake Railroad*. Denver, CO: Rocky Mountain Railroad Club, 1996.

Helmers, Dow. *Historic Alpine Tunnel*. Colorado Springs, CO: Century One Press, 1971.

McFarland, Edward M. *The Midland Route*. Boulder, CO: Pruett Publishing Co., 1980.

Trees

Arno, Stephen F. *Timberline: Mountain and Arctic Forest Frontiers*. Seattle, WA: The Mountaineers, 1984.

Kelly, George W. *A Guide to the Woody Plants of Colorado*. Boulder, CO: Pruett Publishing Co., 1970.

Index

Note: Citations followed by the letter "p" denote photos; citations followed by the letter "m" denote maps.